ELEPHANT MAN

The great ivory hunters of days past

Jason Swemmer

Cover illustration: Water Hazard *by Sir John Seerey-Lester (1945-2020), original oil on panel, 16" x 20", with full permission.*

World-renowned artist, the late John Seerey-Lester and award-winning painter Suzie Seerey-Lester are both distinguished wildlife and landscape artists whose works depict large mammals, birds of prey, magnificent underwater creatures and environmentally sensitive tableaus. www.seerey-lester.com

Dedications

Dedicated to the memory of the ivory hunters: some of the bravest, craziest, most non-conformist and most extreme sportsmen in history;

and

To the memory of my mother, Shirley Louise Swemmer, who despite an early life fraught with hardship and adversity, as well as a lifetime marked by hard work and self-sacrifice, still reminded her sons to dream…

Acknowledgements

To Tony Sánchez-Ariño, a living legend and probably the last of a fabled breed, for writing the foreword and sharing some of his experiences, which are vast and unequaled; many grateful thanks. I am truly humbled and honoured.

To hunters everywhere, who harbour the warrior spirit in their chests, who have felt the excitement coursing through their veins and who have tasted the strange, coppery taste of fear when hunting dangerous game; no further words are required, you understand.

To Suzie Seerey-Lester, for permission to use another of the late John Seerey-Lester's incredible works for the cover image. John's works hang in many valuable collections, including that of the White House. Again, I am extremely honoured.

To the team at Angel Key Publications, for their guidance and patience.

Lastly but by no means least, to my family, who has had to put up with my wildlife talk, even when it's an overdose for them; thank you for indulging me.

Contents

Foreword

Tony Sanchez-Ariño with his first elephant in 1952, when he was 22 years old, shot in the rain forest of Equatorial Africa. - Tony with his last elephant shot when he was 83 years old, N° 1317 -

To Jason Swemmer with best personal wishes,

Tony.

February 2021 -

Pictures courtesy of Tony Sánchez-Ariño

Before I commence with these notes, I would like to explain that I am not a naturalist, nor an expert in zoology. I have merely been a professional hunter in Africa over sixty-two consecutive and full years, with my main focus always being the 'Ivory Trail' and lion hunting.

I must confess to never paying too much attention to any so-called 'Big Game' animals aside from Africa's dangerous Big Five: Elephant, Lion, Buffalo, Leopard and Black Rhino, with the notable exception of those rare trophies, the Bongo and the Lord Derby Eland, but only for the difficulty in hunting them; which was great and hard sport if they were hunted in the proper way: tracking them for endless hours and days, and not with the help of dogs, so popular today and in my personal opinion, the most miserable way to kill any Big Game animal, except perhaps for bird shooting…

My friend Jason Swemmer has granted me the honour of writing the foreword to his most interesting book "Elephant Man", something I have done based on my own experience in the field, not from any scientific standpoint; I feel that Jason has covered that magnificently in the chapter "Nature's great masterpiece", to which I would add not a thing.

It is evident that Jason has been very interested in elephants from a young age and throughout his life, harbouring a deep knowledge of them; this book provides ample proof of that. Together with the elephant itself, just as evident is his interest in the ivory trade and the professional hunters who devoted their lives to hunt this magnificent animal, many of them losing those lives to their mighty opponent on that ivory trail.

This book is the result of many years' work and research on the matter, and rightly considers the elephant to be the masterpiece of nature; I fully concur without any doubt. As I write these notes, I have just celebrated my ninety-first birthday; I have fond recollections of my friendships with some of the great old elephant hunters of the past, such as George Rushby and Harry Manners; each is featured in his own chapter here.

Looking back to the happy old days, when we were able to traverse the entire continent of Africa south of the Sahara Desert, the horizon our only limit, I bemoan the current situation: super-controlling governments hiring 'hunting concessions' out to safari companies, normally at an extremely high tax and featuring private game ranches…at the end it seems to have lost all the romance and become mere plastic safaris to me, a survivor of the old school.

As Jason mentions, elephants have been hunted for their ivory – the 'white gold' – since time immemorial, and this activity has continued until the present day. During Colonial times, elephant hunting was controlled without any problem. Since the independence of the African states around the 1960s, however, that control was replaced by a distinct lack thereof in most places, resulting in the most concerted and ruthless elephant poaching on record. There was a marked and sustained increase around the end of the year 1970, which has largely continued until the present day.

It has been proven that many of the poachers were actually working for corrupt senior officials in many of these countries, including several presidents, such as Bokassa in the Central African Republic, the so-called 'Mama Nguina', wife of president Jomo Kenyatta in Kenya, Idi Amin in Uganda and Mobuto in the old Belgian Congo (now the Democratic Republic of the Congo), where some close relatives managed and oversaw all the poaching in the country.

That is to mention but a few, all of whom made fortunes off the wholesale slaughter of the elephants; this disaster continues unabated to the present day, with little hope of change: such are the sky-high levels of corruption in African countries.

In this book, thanks to Jason, the reader will enter into the fantastic world of the ivory trade which started thousands of years ago, of the elephant and of the men who devoted their lives to hunt them; men of legend who wrote some of the best pages of African hunting history, always alone in the middle of nowhere and facing a hard existence day after day, because elephant hunting was no bed of roses!

When I started my adventures on the ivory trail in those now-distant days of 1952, most of the hunting was conducted on foot; endless walking with the sparsest of camping equipment to stave off the worst discomfort, eating poorly and sleeping worse, in particular during the many years I hunted the rain forests of Equatorial Africa. But it was a fantastic life, a life made possible with only the help of my rifle and the grace of the Almighty!

In this book the reader will sense some of the glorious hunting days, unfortunately now lost to the winds and never to return; but thanks to this book and Jason's work, the memory of that fascinating era will be kept alive for the present and future generations of hunters and adventurers. We should be grateful for this interesting book and its many memories. I have always felt that elephant hunting was the most exciting and rewarding, their tusks the finest trophy one could ever wish for.

I have spent the greatest part of my life on 'the elephant trail', having shot my last jumbo at the age of 83 years (number 1,317). If it was within my power to reverse time, I would merely start the same adventure from the beginning, with my .416 Rigby rifle in my hands. Dear Jason, many thanks again for your book; yours,

Tony Sánchez-Ariño

Professional Hunter

Valencia, Spain

February 2021

Introduction

With the possible exception of the whale, no other animal evokes as much emotion as the elephant, certainly when the subject of hunting them is brought up. But, as is so often the case when human emotions are used instead of common sense, the truth isn't quite so black and white. In the modern age, people are generally safe from any physical harm by whales. In the days of the old whaling barques, sailors regularly paid with their lives when pursuing, harpooning and gathering whales, so hunting them was no one-sided slaughter. Good, I hear the students that attend the school of Disney shout; serves them right! But if we can get off the soft an' fluffy for just a second: people don't willingly go out to die a horrible death. Back in those days, a whale was merely a commodity; just like the elephant has been for eons. The elephant, however, has described a very different path through history, much of which has run alongside that of that other intelligent mammal, the primate.

As terrestrial contemporaries, it was inevitable that our paths would cross often and not always peacefully. On our human journey to the current and supposedly-advanced state in which we now find ourselves, we investigated just about every species we happened upon from a culinary perspective, once we figured out how. Otherwise, how would we know what was good to eat? It was by this trial-and-error method that we discovered the sheer deliciousness of most ungulates, plus the odd feathered snack. We also discovered that fellow predators – and yes, dear Disneyite, we were and still are predators – taste pretty poor and besides, are most unco-operative stock animals. They keep trying to escape and devour their keepers. The pachyderms – literally "thick skin" – obviously don't fit into either group (ungulate or carnivore) but provided a different angle. Due to their sheer size, these animals brought about a real windfall for the entire community when one was brought down, in skins, tools from bone and of course, in meat.

Today the term pachyderm is almost universally used to refer to the elephant but by definition it also covers the five species of rhinoceros as well as the two species of hippopotamus. In our earliest times of societal development, people in our undeveloped state started to piece together traps and collective methods of bringing down animals larger than ourselves. Back in those days of giant mammals, that meant most everything. As man thrived and our population expanded, we became able to utilise the biggest animals, which would have included mammoths, mastodons and other early forms of elephant. To an extent this has continued right up to the present day, with a real zenith from the early eighteenth century up until the early decades of the twentieth century. This was the time of the great ivory hunters, when ivory was an extremely valuable commodity, weapon technology was advancing and vast herds still roamed the continent of Africa.

Modern times are very different; ivory trading is largely banned (no international trade is permitted by CITES member-countries, the Convention on International Trade in Endangered Species of Wild Fauna and Flora), although the trade still continues illegally from within those member countries, largely fuelled by demand from the Far East. The biggest threat to elephants over the past century has been the exploding human population. This means habitat loss, and has resulted in the age-old animal migratory routes becoming inaccessible. Most elephants now survive in nature reserves but this in itself is unnatural as the old routes are cut off, and the situation has created two major problems. One, elephants are a force of nature, and after man have the ability to alter their environment more than any other land-animal. They decimate an enclosed area, turning forest to grassland, and with their old migratory paths cut off, the devastated area has no time to recover in their temporary absence. The second problem is equally serious and much more visible. Elephants are large, intelligent and powerful enough to leave their enclosed areas, by force if necessary, to access the crops of people in or just outside the reserves.

These conflicts result in death for either or both parties with monotonous regularity. Most rural African families can have their entire year's harvest consumed by a single elephant in just one night. For subsistence farmers, this cannot be tolerated and people often confront crop-raiding elephants, with disastrous consequences. These elephants fit into the first sub-category that game departments cluster as problem animals: crop raiders, stock raiders, and man-eaters. Animals that develop these habits need to be controlled, and for the latter two sub-categories, that means shot. For crop raiders, attempts are initially made to drive the animals back into the reserve, but if that doesn't work, those animals too are shot if relocation isn't an option.

Many people have said to me - and not at all in jest - that people should be moved out / shot / forced back into cities only (take your pick) so that the animals can have the run of things that they used to enjoy before we started to overpopulate the planet. I get the frustration, but good luck with that. The realities of life in the twenty-first century are such: well over seven billion people now populate planet earth and with advances in modern medicine, don't expect that trend to change. It's easy in a first-world country, or a first-world city, to castigate people in sheer disbelief at the mere suggestion of shooting an elephant. You'll never see one, save for the passive zoo dweller, through a documentary television screen or perhaps on safari in an African (or south east Asian) reserve.

But go and live among the rural inhabitants of Africa, where elephants make nightly raids on crops, destroying your livelihood at a single sitting. Run up to a herd clanging your pots to scare them off, feel the paralysing terror as you smell and hear the massive beast that grows impossibly big in the torchlight the closer you get, hear the infuriated scream as the world's biggest land animal spins about, unbelievably fast, and sets off after you in a race you immediately know is lost. Try to apply your Dumbo philosophies then.

Yeah, I didn't think you could either.

We are faced in the world of elephant conservation with the following inescapable reality: the animals must be in reserves to prevent their large-scale decimation by poachers. The animals in reserves, however, outgrow their area as sure as night follows day. This leaves the ranger with two options, to relocate and/or to cull. Culling was a common default policy in South Africa's Kruger National Park, one of the very best-run game reserves in all the world. Harsh though it may seem, one vital learning from the process of culling - which eventually and at least to some extent is inevitable - was to eradicate an entire family group, the babies included. This was learned over time as the surviving babies became lethal people-killers in later years. Remember that old adage, an elephant never forgets? Turns out it was spot-on. The procedure has thus been adjusted but relocation – itself costly and risky – is much more common nowadays due to the public outcry over the practice of culling.

Relocation isn't as easy as first thought, though. When rangers started the practice, they found that the young bulls that were the equivalent of teenaged humans became quite unmanageable and spent a great deal of their time killing other animals, particularly rhinos. These myopic behemoths, which escape from a bullying elephant with far more difficulty from a sheer speed perspective than would a kudu, for example, often tried to push back. The outcome was almost always a dead rhino, with giant tusk stab-wounds in its neck. The phenomenon was most starkly played out in the Hluhluwe-Umfolozi game reserve, in South Africa's KwaZulu-Natal Province. During the 1990s, 36 rhinos were killed there by adolescent elephants. Over time it transpired that mature bulls (30 to 40-year-olds) had to be brought in from Kruger to rectify the social structure and bring the youngsters back into line. This was duly done but each reserve in Africa can only take so many elephant. Culling is eventually inevitable.

Throughout Africa, when an elephant is shot, be that as a problem animal, on a hunting safari or from a culling program, the entire animal is utilised. In contrast, ivory poachers only want the tusks, and most often the entire multi-ton beast is left in a rotting heap for the sake of two tusks that are most often hacked out due to time constraints (leaving the carcase to decompose for 2 or 3 days allows them to be drawn out intact), with occasional removal of feet and some skin. Nothing under the sun appeals to rural Africans more than meat, so it stands to reason that the sudden demise of an animal sporting several tons of meat would be a popular event. Throw in the truly massive herds of elephant that roamed Africa two or three hundred years ago, the development of the colonial economies and the resulting ivory trade, and the scene was inexorably set for one of the most unique and exciting times in the history of man.

A similar time could have been the giant herds of bison that European settlers encountered in modernising the continent of North America, but those animals ran away when harassed and fired upon. They are also far smaller and far less intelligent than elephants, and they usually frequented wide, open plains. Most of the American cowboys (and the indigenous tribes that lived off the bison herds, admittedly far less destructively) were mounted on horses. Hunting the African elephant involved many long miles of traipsing on foot, through areas where horses could not survive due to tropical diseases, often in brush so thick as to offer low-to-no visibility, surrounded by grass so tall as to hide even elephants in close proximity, and - when conflict was inevitable - faced with a very different prospect to that confronting the people that hunted the bison. Elephants have incredible senses, particularly hearing and smell, and often as not will come looking for the hunter when a shot is fired.

Zambia's Luangwa River Valley features the Luangwa Integrated Resource Development Project, established by hunting concessions in conjunction with the area's tribal chieftains and ruling councils. The income from the concessions' controlled harvesting established economic infrastructure which directly resulted in one of Africa's highest rural standards of living. By 1991 – four years into the initiative – the loss of elephants to poaching was a mere 120 animals in total, where before 1987, the *annual* toll was 3,600. The herd recovered at the rate of 500 animals a year. The local human population took pride protecting their resources and resisted poaching attempts, and is a glowing working example of the concession idea when it is properly run. Contrary to popular documentaries, controlled hunting is actually the most effective mechanism of animal conservation. Kenya banned commercial hunting in 1973 and the poaching of elephants leapt to previously unheard-of levels. This is because commercial hunting is actually the most viable form of conservation, as clearly shown above.

Botswana has the largest wild elephant herds in Africa, and manages its wildlife better than just about any other African country. In recent years, this was thanks in no small part to the wise visionary approach to conservation of Lieutenant-General Ian Khama, President between 2008 and 2018. Parts of the country are still remote and Botswana hasn't been nearly as commercialised as Kenya and Tanzania, all of which helps conserve the wildlife, but the use of hunting concessions greatly assisted the conservation process. Botswana has several large and renowned game reserves but the hunting concessions covered probably four times as much space as did the reserves. Land preservation is the main pillar in the process of saving the megafauna and other endangered animals.

Botswana announced however in late 2013 that commencing in 2014, large-scale commercial hunting would cease. I was surprised and felt that perhaps too many of the preservationist fringe had President Khama's ear…fortunately, sanity prevailed in early 2019: the current President (Masisi) announced a lifting of the ban early in that year. Wise move; controlled, ethical hunting successfully conserves habitat and wildlife as does no other system. That is an irrefutable and proven economic fact.

It is the active management of wildlife, head over heart, which will save the magnificent beasts that define Africa. The modern world sadly dictates that wild creatures have to be attributed a value to justify their existence, in the face of rampant human population expansion. But given the human expansion, that value is imperative to save the planet's animals. This book will also, however, tell of another time, of an age that seems surreal by modern standards, and of the legendary figures that carved those legends out of the savage wilderness that was the old Africa. A time when men were men and – just occasionally – elephants were nervous, if I might borrow a phrase. It will tell of the ivory hunters.

Jason Swemmer, Brisbane, Australia, 2022.

1. Nature's great masterpiece

The African elephant; so much has been written about this animal that has played a considerable role in life alongside humankind, and indeed, in the human psyche. The elephant today is represented by two genera, *Loxodonta* (the African) and *Elephas* (the Asian). African elephants are represented by two extant species, the African bush elephant (*Loxodonta Africana*), which is the largest living terrestrial animal, and the African forest elephant (*Loxodonta Cyclotis*). Large bulls of the bush species can reach 4 metres tall (13ft) at the shoulder, and 7 tons (15,000lb) in weight. The forest elephant is much smaller, male shoulder heights reaching 8 feet (2.4m) and when explorers first saw them, they were astounded, especially those that had prior exposure to the massive bush species. The Asian elephant consists of three distinct sub-species: the Sri Lankan Asian (which has a more pronounced forehead and is the largest of the Asian sub-species), the mainland Asian, and the Sumatran Asian, the smallest.

John Donne famously wrote the following immortal phrase: "*Nature's great masterpiece, an elephant; the only harmless great thing.*" There is however a small problem; the first half of his statement is undisputed, the second bit, well…not so much. Elephants are anything but harmless. Their ability to wreak destruction on their habitat is unequalled in the animal kingdom and they kill people at an alarming rate, every year. The pressure placed on them by people in various ways is well-known, but the fact remains, harmless they are most definitely not. As for being nature's great masterpiece, very few people would doubt that for a second. George Rushby, a phenomenally successful hunter and the man that eliminated the prolific Njombe pride of man-eating lions in the late 1940s (in Tanganyika, now Tanzania) recalled being fixated when encountering his first elephants in Portuguese East Africa, now Mozambique. His reaction to their habits, their movements and their vocalisations was almost one of being hypnotised.

To an extent, the wildlife on different continents has evolved at a similar rate from slightly different bases. It's a fascinating phenomenon; take Africa and the Indian peninsula, for instance. Both have rhinos; both have leopards; both have buffalo. Africa retained lions as the large apex feline, India has tigers. A few lions survive in India. These cats are that similar under the skin that it takes an expert to differentiate between the two. Incidentally, there is fossil evidence that tigers may have actually lived in Africa long ago, and likely fell afoul of the collective front posed by lions and hyenas. Scientists have long contended that a tiger – being slightly larger – would likely defeat a lion in single combat, but the fact that lions formed groups would eventually result in them driving tigers out of any given common area. This fossil evidence suggests that this happened, and that they are correct. But I digress; both continents have vultures, hyenas, civets, porcupines, monkeys, honey-badgers, jackals; and both have elephants.

That however is where the similarities end. Although the Asian elephant is an impressive animal and has been much more closely associated with people for centuries, the African elephant is bigger, stronger, more magnificent and defiant in every way and will form the basis for this work. This not being a nature journal or biological textbook, I don't want to flog the horse to death but some pointers on taxonomy bear mentioning. The African elephant has a very differently-shaped skull to the Asian, sporting a convex forehead (rounded outward, doesn't dip inward) with no compression and no bulges; that head carries ears that are far more massive and unlike the Asian's, exceed the height of the neck. The trunk is two-lobed at the tip, where an Asian elephant's has a single finger-like lobe. The Asian elephant's back is convex (rounded) or level while the African's is concave. Usually, the African bush elephant has four or five toenails on each front foot and three, four or five on each hind foot, while the Asian (and the African forest elephant – go figure) have five on each front foot, and four or five on each hind one. This isn't a hard-and-fast rule though, with more or less seen on all these species.

The two most spectacular megafauna on the African continent are lions and elephants. It's what the tourists come to see, what the hunters go to hunt, what adorn a thousand different products from pinafores to paintings, statuettes to fluffy toys. But the real scale-tipper is the elephant. The elephant is what defines African wildlife. Compare the North American continent to Africa, for instance. National Geographic recently aired an interesting program whereby an American "Big 5" was chosen. The Big 5, for those who must have been living under a rock for the past while, are not the largest 5 animals. They are the 5 considered the greatest challenge and the most dangerous to hunt by the old explorers, hunters, settlers and adventurers in Africa from the eighteenth century onward: elephant, lion, leopard, buffalo and black rhinoceros. As mentioned in my first book, *No Covenant*, the leopard was long-considered to not even constitute dangerous game until the advent of the hunting bodies and their ethical hunting standards.

Once these were put into place, and the animal has to be hunted under conditions where it has a sporting chance, let's just say that the leopard warrants inclusion! The North American selection was as follows: grizzly bear, grey wolf, cougar, bison and moose. The moose, the largest deer, is a huge and potentially dangerous animal, and the bison is a real behemoth. Both compare favourably with Africa's buffalo and at a push, even the black rhino. The cougar (puma, mountain lion) compares to the leopard, although any hunter will tell you that it competes based on size and prey size only; a leopard is an infinitely more dangerous animal. Regardless, they can broadly be compared. As an apex predator the North Americans have Africa at least matched: grizzly bears compare favourably with lions, no question. But there is nothing whatsoever on the North American continent that can hold a candle to the elephant.

There is much wonderment in an elephant; it is a miracle of evolution, an engineering masterpiece. But its trump card – as if one were needed in the world's largest animal – is a fantastic 5kg (11lb) brain that is perhaps only surpassed in the animal kingdom by the great apes and is thought to be at least the equal of the dolphin / killer whale pair. Elephants have been known to exhibit grief, mimicry, art and play. They have shown a sense of humour and capacity for learning. They have also demonstrated the use of tools, compassion, co-operation, self-awareness and even language.

An elephant has always been thought to have a superior memory and indeed it does. Rangers throughout Africa and throughout the past two centuries have many stories to verify this. There was Rocky, a large male Kruger elephant that over a great deal of time allowed a ranger to hand-feed him oranges. When the ranger returned to the area Rocky most frequented, the man would stand at a certain place on a small hillock and call out his name into the wilderness. On schedule, Rocky - likely named for the pleasing rocking motion that elephants use when ambling purposefully along - would come when called and sample the fruity delights the ranger brought. Understandably, there appeared over time to be a relationship of sorts that developed between the two.

That ranger was assigned elsewhere and when he returned many years later, he doubtfully but hopefully went to the same hill, armed with fruit, and called Rocky's name out over the bush. Sure as eggs, the giant bull came when called as if the man had never been away, and was as happy to see the puny human as the ranger was at the elephant's astounding memory. Sure, the cynics will say the fruit fuelled these actions, but that's unlikely to have been the sole reason; it reflects considerable memory regardless. This story had a sad end though, and even that illustrates the relationship man has had with these creatures for ages. An unscrupulous person noted the elephant's habit and the huge creature's impressive dentures didn't escape his attention either. One day in the ranger's absence he called the elephant and when the magnificent male dutifully ambled into view, he was shot and the tusks were hacked from his head.

An elephant is an amazing creature from tip to toe, and there's a lot that fills that area between the two points! Its giant feet leave a reasonably circular front print, and oval rear prints. Just incidentally, there is a size-correlation between an elephant's front foot and its shoulder height, which holds for both genera. The circumference of the front foot doubled gives the approximate shoulder height, with very little margin of error. Initially, that sounds strongly unlikely but it's true. An elephant's foot-circumference is far larger than one might think. So, a large-footed jumbo would indeed be a large animal, but there is no correlation between foot size and tusk size. Reasonably small elephants have packed some staggering ivory and massive ones have carried modest tusks, which look even smaller against the animal's great bulk. Life being what it is, nothing is ever certain however, and wild animals have a knack of proving to be the exception to the rule; as may be appreciated, in a good season of plenty, the foot may fatten out a bit, likewise shrinking in times of drought. A cow feeding a calf can often lose condition; but these changes aren't marked ones, and the foot-circumference-doubled rule largely holds true.

The huge feet have a giant elastic tendon at the sole, which allows the animal to walk soundlessly should they choose. Many hunters, explorers and adventurers have commented on an elephant's ability to quietly disappear while pursued, and this foot structure is the key to this ability. The sole fits around an object, such as a rock or branch on the ground. Technically, an elephant could stand on a person's head and not do them any damage, if they chose. The massive sturdy legs cart that huge bulk about their entire lives, so they have to be strong and hard-wearing, while also capable of great and rapid mobility. Although an elephant cannot jump, it can cover ground at an astonishing rate and sustain that pace for many miles. 40-50km/h (25-31mph) can be attained which outstrips the fastest human comfortably, and the fastest human runs on a tartan-coated athletics track, not though the uneven, boulder-strewn bush. People also need to dodge around small bushes and shrubs. Elephants don't bother, snapping small trees like twigs in their rush. Bottom line: you can't outrun an elephant. No-one can.

An elephant's tail is large (up to four feet long) and features long black hair at the point, which tends to thin as the animal ages. Elephant hair bracelets are common in Africa, and the black cords are thick and plastic-like. It's difficult to believe that they are hair. The large tail has occasionally been taken by poachers for decoration or mementoes. In the days of the old ivory hunters, the carcass was claimed by lopping off the tail. There are a few stories of elephants that were stunned but not killed, and when the hunters returned to the "carcase", having removed the tail at the time of shooting, the animal is nowhere to be found, having recovered and made off. This situation would do nothing for the subsequent safety of people encountered by such an elephant; a cut-off tail would smart something frightful. An elephant's skin is a thing of great character; the lines and patterns of the creases and cracks are the subject of countless photographs, and lend themselves well to black-and-white or sepia imagery.

The skin has purpose like everything in nature, first and foremost of which is to hold the entire beastie together. It is thus understandably thick and reasonably loose-fitting, although moving it like a puppy's to illustrate this may prove difficult! The way it folds when the animal moves supports the statement. It ranges from over an inch thick (2.5-3cm) on the back and head to extremely thin on the ears and around the eye, perhaps even paper-thin. The ears are huge, and if placed on the horizontal plane like a table top, eight people could sit around each in comfort. They are covered in a network of capillaries and are as large as they are, principally to regulate temperature. Blood circulates through the giant ears, and these are flapped in the air to cool the blood, which then re-enters the rest of the animal at a reduced temperature. Flapping them also waves insects away and helps gather sound from different directions, in much the same fashion as would an antelope or carnivore that swivels its ears. Elephants hear amazingly well at low frequencies, 1 kHz being their most sensitive level.

The trunk is what defines an elephant more than any other organ and it is truly a wonder. It contains around 150 thousand individual muscles, and can be so gentle as to pick up a single peanut and break the shell without harming the seed, or so savage as to brain a lion. It is a combination between the nose and upper lip and gives the elephant an advantage not found elsewhere in nature, certainly nasally. The trunk is used to lift things, carry things, to pull down branches and crop clumps of grass. It can provide comfort to a baby elephant, spray gallons of water over the animal's back to cool it or down its throat to drink. It is used as a snorkel in deep water, and is used to trumpet loudly. As a nose its scenting ability is legendary. The trunk contains no bone and very little fat.

An elephant's mouth is designed to suckle milk for the first five or six years of its life, but from the age of three years and onward, they start to sample the staggering array of shrubbery and woodland that make up the diet of a good, average bush elephant. A large bull can consume anything approaching 550lb (250kg) of vegetation and 300 litres (80 gallons) of water on a daily basis. Grasses, shrubs, entire trees, pods, fruits, bark and more disappear into the great inside of the creature, and soil and soft rocks will be chewed and swallowed too if a certain mineral is sought. For instance, at the Mount Elgon National Park in Kenya, elephants have actually enlarged the Kitum cave over time in their search for salt. They gouge chunks out of the wall with their tusks and put the pieces into their mouths. Buffalo, hyena and bushbuck have been seen to consume chunks left by the elephants.

Elephants have four huge molars in use at any one time, each weighing some 5kg (11lb) and measuring 30cm (12in) in length. Another set lies just behind these. The front set is principally used and when those break or wear out, the back set shift forward to replace them. This – the replacement - will happen five times over the animal's life and after that – somewhere between the ages of 40 and 60 years – the animal will basically die of starvation. Occasionally elephants have more than this over their lifetime, but their life's allocation is usually 24 teeth. Asian elephants, incidentally, have far more compound plates on each molar than do African elephants, whose loops are more lozenge-shaped. But it is the tusks that have shaped much of the history shared by man and elephants. Tusks are fixed teeth, the animals' second set of incisors. They typically range from 50-99lb (23-45kg), with lengths of 5-8ft (1.5-2.4m). In the days of the ivory hunting boom, the sought-after "hundred pounder" meant tusks of 100lb (45kg) each side. The record tusks in the British Museum are truly gigantic, and came from a huge bull shot on the slopes of Mt Kilimanjaro in what is now Tanzania. They were acquired in Zanzibar in 1898 and the elephant had been shot by an Arab hunter, Senoussi, who worked for the notorious Kavirondo-born, Muslim-convert, slave-trading warlord Shundi (and not the notorious Tippu Tib, as is often claimed). They weighed 237 and 226 pounds respectively (108 and 103kg) when fresh, and now weigh 226 and 214 pounds (103 and 97kg), after losing moisture over time as does any natural substance. Both are just over ten feet long (3m) and are as awe-inspiring as one would expect them to be.

A pair of tusks from the same elephant is seldom if ever similar in size; this is because elephants, like people, are left- or right-handed, or rather, left- or right-tusked. As most people are right-handed, so most elephants are right tusked, with that tusk favoured for digging up roots and shrubs and as a result, most elephants carry shorter, thicker tusks on that side. Tusks are relatively soft and many break off, in part or completely, leaving elephants with a single tusk, or occasionally with none (African elephant males and females normally carry tusks; in Asian elephants only the bulls have them). This naturally limits the animal's ability to defend itself and gather food effectively, and tuskless animals are often aggressive. Another contributing factor to this aggression could be that breakages might result in nerve damage. An elephant-sized toothache must be wholly unpleasant.

Old hunters often wrote of the twig that grows inside an elephant's head; there is indeed such a thing but it isn't a twig. Elephants have a gland situated more-or-less on the temple, which visibly leaks liquid. When bulls are in musth, or in season, their testosterone levels soar and the glands literally pour liquid. As the animal brushes past branches and shrubs, a build-up of dust and even small particles of bark is inevitable. Much like ear-wax in people – and remember, elephants can't take an ear bud to their gland orifices on a weekly basis – the eventual build-up over time equates to a lengthy twig-like mass. An elephant's head can weigh over 300kg (660lb) and the skull is understandably large. Parts of it are immensely thick and dense, while others are honeycombed to save weight; otherwise, the animal would be unable to lift its head. The inside of an elephant is no less amazing than the outside. Elephants often traverse great distances away from water and thus take provisions with them. They have a huge internal water-stomach in which many gallons can be kept. For a human, accessing this water - which is relatively clean if a bit warm - can mean life or death in the remote places. Many a hunter or explorer that was dying of thirst has been saved by a dead elephant in this way. An elephant's digestive system is not the most efficient though, with only around 40% of consumed food being digested (compare a lion, which digests 80%). This means elephants have to spend much of their time eating, and because of the sheer quantities involved, it doesn't require wizardry to understand the destructive capability of a large herd. I have many times seen the path made by a feeding elephant herd, as have many people that have spent time in Africa's game reserves. The carnage has to be seen to be believed. This poor digestive ability is reflected in an elephant's dung; I have often marvelled at how unprocessed the plant matter appears once it's traversed an elephant's insides.

The elephant suffers from a similar perception problem on the part of most human beings, and certainly those in first-world countries, as does the hippopotamus. In popular culture, hippos are often portrayed as ballet tutu-wearing, round happy bouncy funny fatties with rounded or blunted teeth. The reality is in stark, awful contrast: hippos kill a considerable number of people every year in Africa, probably 300-350. A full-grown bull hippo can literally bite a crocodile in half, and it has been recorded and verified. Anything able to snap a thirteen-foot (4m) croc in two is not to be underestimated. When I was in Kenya's Maasai Mara reserve in 2005, we photographed lions at near-touching distance and were fortunate to escape a very real elephant charge. Our driver turned off the engine and was subsequently fired after a bull called off his attack, swinging away and past us by literally a metre. But by far the most dangerous time we experienced was at the Mara River, where we were permitted to alight from the vehicles, provided we were accompanied by an armed ranger. The tension in the air was palpable, electric; and it was because of the presence of hippo. We were far from them but despite that, one could absolutely feel the danger in the air.

Elephants are similar; I remember as a child when watching the old Tarzan films that featured Johnny Weissmuller and other similar old hunting fare, being absolutely terrified out of my wits when the elephant herd crossed the road and threateningly spread their ears, trumpeting, at the people. I just as clearly remember my utter disbelief when other people weren't perturbed, or not as much as I was. What the hell were they missing? Can you not see how large the animal is? Can you not hear the sheer rage in its screams of anger? Don't you think the creature could cause hideous damage if it were that way inclined? As I got older, I felt better about my innate terror of an angry elephant: many things happened to prove that my fear was justified. For one, I outgrew the portrayal of elephants by Walt Disney.

After I left school, two friends and I spent several weeks in South Africa's Kruger National Park, doing it tougher by camping, not staying in the luxury chalets and *rondavels* (round huts). We were close to several elephant on several occasions, which made one of my friends extremely jumpy. One day we edged up behind and to the side of a large bull, who watched us the entire time, my nervous friend getting more and more apprehensive with each passing second that ticked by. The vehicle we were in – a small sedan – was not exactly new, like most teenage rides. It exhibited a particular reluctance to quickly and smoothly engage reverse gear. In a game reserve like Kruger, this is hardly a plus-point.

Heeding our colleague's apprehension at length, my other friend – who was driving – stopped trailing the bull, bringing the car to a standstill beside a large bush, while the bull walked slowly on. Suddenly, we heard a loud crack on the other side of the bush we'd stopped against. Another bull, unseen, had just pulled a branch off a tree perhaps two metres from us. Then commenced a botty-clenching period of note while the driver tried to engage the reluctant reverse gear, which eventually occurred and we made our rapid escape. By this time, my apprehensive friend was nearly beside himself. When he'd recovered, he told us the reason for his general fear of anything elephantine. Some two or three years before - in the mid-1980s - he and his family were in the same game reserve, Kruger. For no obviously apparent reason, an elephant had suddenly charged their car. He then placed his front feet on the bonnet and pushed the entire front end of the car flat into the tarmac, engine included.

By this time the family – parents, my friend and his small sister – were understandably upset and much shouting, screaming and fear was the order of the day. This may have further annoyed the elephant, but it certainly didn't discourage him. He started to hammer the car roof in with his trunk, a task at which he succeeded with aplomb. My friend's mother panicked, as some people do in life-and-death situations, and decided she'd run for it, attempting to open her door. Luckily her husband saw this and grabbed her so she couldn't get out. Within a few seconds the damage rendered by the elephant's seismic attentions to the car roof rendered her incapable of opening the door in any case, but for a short while there she was inches away from making the last mistake of her life. After a while the bull decided their car had been suitably modified and made off, leaving the gibbering family to wait until salvation arrived in the shape of a vehicle filled with rangers, summoned by another passing Park visitor. Understandably, my friend and close proximity to elephants weren't two subjects that happily go together quite like cheese and wine.

Anyone who fails to be moved by Dumbo has no heart; Walt Disney's most famous baby elephant is adorably cute and the sequence where his captive mother cradles him in her trunk through the bars of her box car is a real tear-jerker. Problem is, as can be seen above, it just ain't true. Or rather, a great deal of it isn't. Elephants are indeed extremely intelligent and are capable of the most advanced emotions, but sweet, rounded and cuddly, they aren't. And the problem I have come to realise that such films have left as their legacy is an irrational "nurture and protect" mindset, again principally in first-world nations. For the people that share space with wild elephants every day, conflict is as regular as it is inevitable. The outcome isn't tough to imagine, and this invokes my "I told you so" node that nestles deep in my brain. Surely one should be afraid of anything that is so obviously *capable* of causing so much damage, based on the principle that it *can* if it wants to? I am aware that dozens of people have had wonderful, peaceful close encounters with jumbos; I dispute that not at all. I'm just stressing: they can rub you out if they so wish, and it has happened often.

One school of thought would say yes, but this is just added incentive not to annoy such a creature, ever. Theoretically, that makes sense. In practice, dear Westerner, life is very different for millions of people in both Africa and Asia that live in the elephantine firing line on a daily basis. On thousands of smallholding farm plots, elephants raid the farmers' crops as a matter of course. Over the course of a single night, one elephant regularly consumes a family's entire livelihood. The same school of thought that refuses to annoy elephants then reasons that the animals were here first, so they mosey about like they owned the place because…well, because to the elephant, they do. Again, being detached from the challenges faced daily by millions of Africans (and Asians) blurs the lines of reality. The large human population is only going to increase. People are here to stay and quite frankly, a human life is indeed worth more than an animal's.

Yes, they have been coerced into this due to humans encroaching on their space; yes, they have been hunted. But this is a real human problem, now, today. I am in no way proposing killing the animals like a salivating murder-drunk psychotic; I believe for their own protection as well as that of people, that the Big 5 game animals (and a few other large creatures besides) should be inside well-managed fenced areas, be these game reserves or hunting concessions. These spaces should naturally be as large as is possible to finance and manage. The loss of habitat is the greatest danger to the world's megafauna. In addition, people should if at all possible be moved out of these same areas. If we don't, death-by-elephant – a wholly unpleasant way to die – will be the lot of many more people, and countless elephants will likewise die as a result. Elephants kill an estimated 500 people each year, 400 of these in Africa. By contrast, lions are thought to kill around 200 a year. I actually think the lion tally is closer to 500 annually, as lions usually kill people to consume them. This means that more horror accompanies deaths by lion, but also means that evidence is removed by the very act of consumption, so 200 is very conservative.

Regardless, the bottom line is that elephants kill at least as many people each year as what lions do, and possibly even twice as many. Read that again; still think they're kindly and infallible? Sorry, John Donne, but the only harmless great thing? I'm not buying. Call it human pressure, call it tormenting elephants, hunting them, call it what you like. The truth is that elephants kill people. Regularly. So how many elephants are poached each year? Recent estimates (2011-12) range between 20 thousand and 25 thousand. Bet THAT got your attention. At the risk of actually canvassing support from the green fringe, that is an absurd figure. Driven by an insatiable demand from the Far East (70% of the illegal ivory gathered goes to China), poaching is an extensive reality. We need to stop that loss. Mere preservation does not work. Active wildlife management is required or people and elephants will suffer many more avoidable casualties. The massive fees generated by sport hunting do more to protect the species by preserving habitat and preventing poaching than does any other method.

But why this mass slaughter, which for centuries was unbelievably perilous? How could anything be worth the dangers, the risks, the huge chance of failure, the likely death by horrendous means, the solitude? What could be so valuable?

2. The ivory trade

The mere mention of the ivory trade invokes memories of wild adventure, slaughter, danger, far-off places, of wild times long ago where guns ruled, and men were larger than life. But what are the origins of this fixation, this drive to gather a substance from one of the most dangerous creatures on the planet, and to traverse enormous distances, braving all manner of perils in order to do so? Don't for a second think that the activity isn't dangerous; it is unquestionably one of the most dangerous pursuits on this fair planet. I have not hunted elephant before, but you need your head examined if you doubt the danger; either that or you aren't aware of what it actually entails.

If you hail from Africa and have thus been exposed to elephants, real wild African ones in large reserves, you will know the danger they present even if you've never picked up a rifle. In the past, elephant hunting would have been far more dangerous. Firearms were unwieldy and unreliable, ammunition even more so. Medicinal knowledge was sketchy at best when it was even available. Transport beyond walking and rarely, mounted on horses, was non-existent. So, getting anywhere was tough; if something happened, getting you to hospital…well, yeah…you get the idea.

*   *   *

The gored man lay on his back in the sun. Large blue-green flies competed for the choicest bits in and around the massive trauma which dominated the scene, a huge open hole right in the middle of his torso. There was another similarly-sized hole through his right bicep and his face and head had half the skin rubbed raw by the flailing trunk. Incredibly, his lungs had been missed when the infuriated cow elephant drove a tusk straight through his chest. He staggered upright, somehow alive and now ambulatory. That he looked a fearful fright was roundly evidenced when his men rushed over to him; in a time and a profession where squeamishness hardly existed, and certainly not among these men, lead gunbearer Squareface literally burst into tears! When they could mentally process that this medical anomaly was indeed still alive, despite what their eyes were telling their brains, the men helped Arthur Neumann back to his tent and started the process of putting the torn hunter back together.

If in modern times one happened to be that one-in-a-thousand and actually survived being gored through the chest by an adult elephant, surviving the subsequent trip by helicopter to a hospital sufficiently advanced to at least all but eliminate such niceties as dying of infection would be pushing your luck. Now imagine that there is no hospital. At all; *nada*. For thousands of miles. And even if there were, there was no way whatsoever to reach it. Philosophically, Arthur Neumann mentions the extreme discomfort and pain as well as the inconvenience of the subsequent months. Convalescing in these conditions was almost like driving the point home. Elephant hunting is an extremely hazardous occupation. There is a large chance of getting dead, in some of the most creative ways to boot. But the late 1800s added so many other potential pitfalls by modern standards that it beggars belief how anyone could survive at all for any length of time, much less flourish.

Today, despite the constant presence of Murphy (of Murphy's Law fame, as Peter Capstick often wrote), a modern elephant hunt involves a decent stalk on foot, an approach to a point where the professional hunter deems it still safe for his well-heeled client (the client has to be well-heeled; elephant licenses are not cheap, and those that are available are much sought-after), a good heart or lung shot from the client's expensive and reliable .460 Weatherby magnum rifle, a follow-up walk before jumbo's adrenalin spurt succumbs to the fatal wound, and that is that. Back then, as well-evidenced by this exact occasion that befell Neumann, myriad things could and did go wrong almost as a matter of course. As the irate cow elephant charged, Neumann pulled the trigger and the dull click that sounded will have put a mental full-stop to his life, at least in his mind's eye. When at last he had to turn and run, Neumann still performed a minor miracle by reloading and cocking the errant weapon on the run. With the cow nearer than his shadow, he half-swung about and managed to fire, but again the rifle – or the ammunition – wasn't interested. Neumann flung the gun aside and dived off the path, hoping against hope that the elephant would continue on by. She didn't.

Over time – lots of time – Neumann's right arm actually closed and commenced healing but then he managed to prick his hand on a thorn. Whether the thorn was poisonous is not known; it was doubtless anything other than sterile and sanitary, any number of bacteria-carrying animals or people possibly having touched or brushed against it. Perhaps his just-healed arm still harboured some volatile bacteria. It was likely a combination of all of these, because in short order Arthur Neumann's right arm swelled to twice its normal size, and agony was his lot for the next few weeks. At length and almost apoplectic, Neumann had his men cut the arm to drain it. This was exceptionally painful and worse, seemed not to help. That infection ran rampant was obvious; when at long last the arm started discharging great gobs of matter and the pain started to ease, it continued to do so until the remnants of the arm and hand were half the size of the normal one, with great holes visible right through the flesh of the fingers.

After this ordeal, and the tragedies that befell the safari later, one could be forgiven for assuming that Neumann would conduct this three-year bout of ivory hunting only, and never return, while many of his contemporaries returned several times and for far longer periods. Truth be told, many of his contemporaries suffered similarly on their hunts, and Neumann returned later on for similar spells! So, what drove men to these levels of extreme danger, risk and discomfort? Can anything be worth all that? Apparently; ivory, the white gold, the challenge to obtain it and the reward to be gleaned from it, was sufficiently tempting. In addition - and this is the part that appeals to most men with adventurous spirits, especially today with modern life's trappings and rat race, and fuelled by these ivory hunters' books and writings - the life of the ivory hunter was the ultimate expression of being answerable to no-one. The hunter determined where he went, for how long, with whom, what he ate and drank, how much he took with him, what time he returned and many other little measurable and immeasurable decisions that imprison the modern human being in the form of constraints. It was the purest form of freedom.

As can however be gleaned from the above few paragraphs, this was a dubious freedom. To risk such dangers and many more besides, the commodity would have to be rather sought-after, one would think. The first records of actual trade in ivory come from the Phoenicians, who provided it to the first consumer market, that of Ancient Egypt, some 1,500 years ago. There is however evidence from rock paintings that the ancient Egyptians were consumers of the local product as far back as 4,000 BC, and that a lively trade flourished down the economic thoroughfare that was the Nile. Indeed, the very word ivory has its stem in the Ancient Egyptian âb (from âbu – elephant), via the Latin ebor or ebur. The Phoenicians were renowned ivory carvers and counted among their clients King Solomon, who lined his fabled temple with their ornaments. History tells us that Solomon reigned over what is now Israel between 970 and 931 BC. When the Phoenicians founded Carthage in the ninth century BC, they were able to access the elephant in the Atlas Mountains, and during the three Punic wars with Rome (between

264 and 146 BC) they even tamed elephants for use as war machines, effectively the first tanks.

Next up, the Greek and Roman civilisations churned out prodigious quantities of highly-valuable artworks using ivory. As a result, and in much the same way that the Barbary lion was all but eliminated from North Africa by the Roman habit of gathering them for the games, the elephant populations in Syria and North Africa were reduced to near-extinction. The Romans then turned for their consumption to Axum in what is now Ethiopia, as well as to Eritrea. There, large herds roamed until as recently as the sixth century AD, but by then the North African elephants had finally disappeared. As the Roman Empire collapsed, a ready substitute consumer was already well-established: China. As far back as the first century BC, the Chinese started commercially exporting Asian ivory along the Silk Route to the western nations. By the tenth century AD, both they and India were major consumers. In that regard, not much has changed; during the catastrophic 2011 year, in which 25 thousand African elephants were killed for their ivory, India swallowed up 15,000 pounds (nearly 7 tons) of that which was recorded, while the Chinese took the lion's share: over 90 thousand pounds found its way there (more than 40 tons).

The avenues to provide the East with African ivory developed before the tenth century AD, and stretched from Somalia down to Mozambique. Arab and Indian merchants established trading posts over this area, the economic expansion of which accompanied the spread of Islam. Zanzibar became the trade hub for the entire East Africa region as the slave trade blossomed along with the others. The mixed cultures – Arabic, African and Indian – developed a type of *lingua franca*, a working language or catch-all, which came to be known as Swahili, the forerunner of today's version. Things changed in the year 1498; Vasco da Gama took control of Zanzibar as Portugal decided to establish itself along Africa's east coast. Armed expeditions took control of the trading ports, while forts and bases were established all the way up and down the coast. By 1698 however, the combination of pressure from the Dutch, who had established themselves in the Cape (which was to become South Africa), and their other global colonising, stretched Portugal's resources and the Arabs overthrew them along the Swahili Coast with the support of the Sultan of Muscat (now Oman).

As for the Dutch, their foothold at the southern tip of the continent meant that in ivory terms, a regular supply – thought to be around 20 tons (44 thousand pounds) – was dispatched to Europe each year. The Portuguese still controlled ports to the south of what would become East Africa however, especially in what was to become Mozambique, but sometime in the 18th century their habit of heavily taxing anyone making use of their ports resulted in the ivory trade collapsing there. The Arab and Indian traders moved north to what became Tanzania and Kenya, where the trades – both ivory and slaves – still flourished through the focal point of Zanzibar. These two have been inexorably linked. The "black gold" was used to cart the "white gold" to the ports, where both would be sold. The thriving East African economy was in stark contrast with Delagoa Bay (now Maputo Bay); by the late 18th century elephants were all but gone from Southern Africa and the ivory trade to the port ceased. During the early 19th century, the slave trade intensified as the French established plantations on Mauritius and Réunion, around the same time that the Sultan of Oman established plantations on Zanzibar.

The Portuguese hadn't been idle on the west coast of Africa either; even before da Gama overthrew the Arabs in Zanzibar, they had established a series of trade ports much as they did down the east coast. There, the commodities became renowned in the names given the different coasts. The Gold Coast (now Ghana) featured a gold trade, the Ivory Coast was used to dispatch tusks and the Slave Coast (now largely Nigeria and Benin) was the main area where slaves were taken, to be swallowed by the demand for labour in the southern USA, the Caribbean and Brazil. By the early 16th century, the Portuguese had also opened the Kongo kingdom (later Congo) to the ivory trade and from Guinea in particular, the flow of tusks was considerable. Meanwhile, the Dutch and English were competing hammer-and-tongs against one another in Sierra Leone which accelerated the slaughter of elephants there. Over the 16th and 17th centuries, it is estimated that the world market had some 200 tons of ivory dumped into it in total, although, inefficient trade channels by modern standards notwithstanding, this seems too paltry a figure.

The demand for ivory accelerated at the end of the 18th and the start of the 19th centuries, especially in Europe and the American continents. Naturally, this drove the price up. One of the biggest contributors to this demand was billiard balls, mainly because these had to be cut from the tusk centre. If not, they wouldn't roll properly; the net result was that only four or five could be cut from any decently-sized tusk. Another major ivory product was piano keys. As Europe's affluence grew, the demand for luxury items, artworks and ornaments soared. By the 1850s the price of ivory sky-rocketed and one of the results was a huge influx into Africa of firearms. Up until then, the main methods used to kill elephants were poisoned arrows, fall-pits and rings of fire. If the destruction of the animals ramped up considerably, at least the methods of killing became more humane. To meet this increased demand from Europe, the entire West African ivory trade moved operations from Guinea to Cameroon, sending its products across the Sahara in order to dispatch from North African ports.

Naturally, the supply of ivory had been depleted in the coastal areas, and hunter-traders had to penetrate further and deeper into Africa to feed the demand. Zanzibar had become the chief ivory trading post in all of Africa and by the end of the 19th century, was supplying most of the world's ivory, as much as three-quarters in fact. Between the turn of the 20th century and the First World War, the average quantity traded worldwide was 800 tons. This dropped to 100 tons after the War but subsequently climbed steadily again to around a thousand tons a year by the mid-1970s (notwithstanding the odd blip for the Great Depression and the Second World War among others). In the mid-1980s the price again spiked and the results in this modern era, where automatic rifles proliferated, a legacy of the continent's plethora of civil wars, was sheer devastation on the African elephant. The population was halved during the 1980s, an estimated 1,2 or 1,3 million down to 600 thousand-plus individuals. By October 1989, CITES managed to effectively ban the ivory trade when the 101 member countries voted the African elephant onto Appendix 1, the highest level of protection for species threatened with extinction.

Enforcement has proven far more difficult than legislation. The demand for ivory is as high as ever from the Far East in particular, and the ban could cynically be said to have merely driven the trade underground. The animal does show a staggering ability to bounce back, as protected populations recover well in short order due to a number of factors, not least of which is a dearth of their only other natural predator, the lion. That feline is under even greater population pressure than the pachyderm and the small toll that lions take on the elephant populations – mainly preying on the calves – has been largely removed in places. In short order, however, poaching and habitat loss cut swathes through the recovered elephant populations again, in any given place. Of course, for the conservation bodies, countries and hunting concessionaries to come to a consensus regarding endangered species seems to be wishful thinking. Any government that may have common ground with animal protection bodies could find that common ground eliminated overnight when the government is displaced, and it must be borne in mind that Africa's social problems are utterly gigantic. A human life has to take precedence over that of an animal and governments' priorities unsurprisingly lie in this fact.

For Westerners, it's common sense; the world's megafauna species like tigers, gorillas, elephants (and many more besides) are in serious danger of extinction. Anything possible should be done to preserve them. But this is where it gets sticky; it's not quite that easy. For us to berate rural Africans (or Asians, or South Americans) for shooting or poisoning lions / elephants / tigers / leopards / jaguars / whatever just proves how protected, removed or ostracised we are from the reality of developing countries. There are many, many communities in the remote places where it's all people can do to eke a living out of the soil, and they are faced on a daily basis with animals that kill and eat their livestock, consume their crops – often in huge quantities overnight – and worst of all, kill them, either because they are merely another item on the menu, or because they dare attempt to drive the marauders off. This sounds absurd, but it's true. Animals kill thousands of people in Africa every year and none of those human victims are peacefully and humanely put to sleep, either.

This is where the ivory trade has led to, moving towards the end of the 21st century's second decade. It is a tale of slaughter for the African elephant, which has obviously gotten the short straw in its conflict with *Homo Sapiens*. The development of modern technology in firearms, satellite map tracking, transport and flying machines has rendered the contest an increasingly uneven one. The seemingly rash answer is to reinstate controlled hunting. People immediately balk at this; how can killing stop the killing? Well, let me help you better understand the problem…hunting bans actually accelerate the extinction of species. Examples are many and constant; as I mentioned earlier, when Kenya banned commercial hunting in 1973 – Peter Hathaway Capstick used to sardonically remark that the ban was because the hunters were getting in the poachers' way – poaching sky-rocketed and the elephant and lion populations dropped to panic levels: the lion population fell to 10% of its pre-ban levels, where Tanzania's remained constant, continuing hunting throughout.

There are as many other examples as you'd care to mention: in the 1970s there was a moratorium on hunting cheetahs. Namibia – then still South West Africa – had the world's largest cheetah population. The population started to drop drastically, as each time a sheep farmer lost a sheep to a cheetah, he'd shoot it / any other cheetah close to hand, leaving the valueless body to rot in the veld. The ban was lifted, cheetahs prospered and the population grew again, as a direct result of being hunted. Ascribing a value to something – even if only an economic value – is imperative to ensure its survival in this day and age. I know that annoys the preservationist fringe, but that's the reality, particularly in Africa. Robert Ruark wrote on this very point half a century ago. Disturbingly, this applies to the snow leopard, tiger and jaguar as well...we would do well to take note as these species court extinction. Now, to the preservationist-green this still sounds absurd, right? It's actually easy to understand. Right at the outset, understand that hunting (licensed and legal) is distinct from poaching (illegal). The world's hunting bodies such as Safari Club International and the Professional Hunters Association of South Africa – there are countless others – prescribe hunting rules and ethics. These bodies' membership fees and hunting licenses firstly ensure that large tracts of wilderness are set aside and not turned into housing or commercial farmland.

In particular for the elephant, more so than any other species, setting land aside is the first crucial part of the solution. The destruction they wreak on any enclosed area – regardless how large – is established fact. The next level of fees, those for the hunter and his employees, as well as trophy costs, ensure that people are gainfully employed and that the bodies running the concessions maintain fencing, waterholes and other upkeep, including security (read: anti-poaching methods). This ensures that protein-rich prey animals such as buffalo and antelopes are not killed for food by the local populations, who are employed and involved so they have no need to poach for subsistence. Africa's biggest social problem now is corruption. The old colonial governments are all gone; African states self-govern, starting with the French Arab states (Algeria, Morocco) in the 1930s, through the *Uhuru* era of the late 1950s and early 1960s, to the apartheid states (Rhodesia became Zimbabwe in 1980, and the last to topple was South Africa in 1994).

I say topple because I defy anyone to tell me that any African state has thrived since gaining independence. To a one, they have all economically gone backwards at alarming rates. Why? How? Greed and corruption of uneducated and incompetent officials is more than just rife, it's almost the norm. No country, regardless how richly endowed in natural wealth, can survive the inevitable resultant drain on its resources. Driven by opportunistic criminals abroad – the oriental nations driving the illegal ivory trade in particular and the Western nations' misguided donations are the main factors – Africa's powers-that-be are ensuring the extinction of the very megafauna species that make the place unique. Think I'm just ranting? Let me give you examples again; in Tanzania in 2012 there were more than 30 opportunities to create wildlife corridors, linking isolated pockets of game by creating fewer, larger areas to conserve, with the added benefit of opening / re-establishing migration routes. But Tanzania's government refused to act on these, preferring instead to hog its perceived share of hunting income.

The world's huge wildlife societies, and private Western donors for that matter, are being deceived. They believe they are sustaining wildlife, but they aren't; the vast majority of their money is lining corrupt officials' pockets while the species they are convinced their Dollars / Yen / Euros / Sterling are saving, are in rapid decline. Inflammatory? You bet. Can I prove it? Easily; Kenya loses between US$20 million and $40 million a year in hunting revenues. Think they care? Of course not; in one recent year, the Kenya Wildlife Services received US$400 million from European donors alone! The sad irony is that wildlife lovers outside Africa are subsidising the decline in Africa's wildlife. In 2007, a paper was presented by economics researcher and long-time Kenya resident Mike Norton-Griffiths. Although his paper referred to Kenya, it applies to much of the entire continent.

There is a top-down attitude to wildlife: the State is the sole owner thereof. People living among wildlife can't and don't benefit from them in any way, and indeed, should they eradicate a problem animal – which remember, could be eating their crops, eating their livestock and even eating the people themselves – they actually get fined heavily. Does this sound a bit totalitarian, Marxist or Fascist? It should, because it is. Norton-Griffiths said the Kenyan system has failed and continues to fail conservation, mainly because tourist wildlife viewing is restricted to just 5% of the total area where wildlife is found (a mere 23,000 square km or 8,880 square miles). This means 95% of pastoral rangelands are disenfranchised from income generating opportunities. But it's the Western donors that have directly caused the problem, the European ones even more so than the Americans; they don't understand the economics of producing wildlife, focusing on and even becoming obsessed with topical single issues.

Since the 1970s, Kenya has actually shaped its wildlife policies to please the generous foreign donor setup. The hundreds of millions of overseas Dollars perpetuate inefficient and bloated State conservation monopolies. These funds never actually get to effectively conserve the wildlife, the areas in which they live and the human populations both within and surrounding these areas. Hence, many species are becoming ever more endangered, despite decades of towering financial influx. Also in 2007, Pretoria University zoologist Peter Lindsey published the results of a survey, taken from literally hundreds of hunters and safari operators. Each time hunting was banned (starting with Kenya's 1973 ban), there was a proven and marked accelerated loss of wildlife, because *the incentives for conservation were removed.* All of these countries except Kenya subsequently removed the hunting bans, usually within the same decade, and the wildlife recovered. Banning hunting has been shown to increase only one thing: rural poverty.

Overnight, predators become vermin and are shot for killing stock. When the trophy fee is reinstated, this more than compensates for the loss of the stock. It was reassuring to hear Dr David Mabunda, Head of South Africa's National parks, speaking at a film premiere in 2011; he mentioned that South Africa's local hunters (largely biltong hunters) contributed R1 billion to the local economy, foreign trophy hunting another R1 billion. The anti-hunting fraternity wants hunting banned and photographic tourism to take its place, but Mabunda, while acknowledging that photographic tourism doubtless contributed to South Africa's R70 billion tourist industry (no reliable figures being available as to what portion), he prudently added that as a developing country, it would be suicidal for South Africa to ban hunting. He said South Africa doesn't have the luxury of choosing between hunting and photo tourism, and needs both. Wise words; South Africa has a thriving, controlled, regulated wildlife population, as well as a thriving hunting industry employing thousands of people.

At this point in time as I write this, between 2015 and 2018, there are several African reserves and parks bursting at the seams with elephant populations that the areas are incapable of sustaining. Large-scale culling – and this can, as always, be discreet – is inevitable. For example, Kruger National Park can sustain around 7,500 elephants, and currently has around 12,500. Namibia had 4,800 in 1980, there are now more than 20,000. Botswana has at least 160,000 and needs to cull as a priority (it can sustain 60,000-70,000). Tsavo had 11,000 in 2010, up 1,300 in three years. Relocating can be done, which incidentally is extremely risky (elephants can't regulate their breathing when under anaesthetic which is vital to prevent them from overheating, and many die in transit, regardless how much care is taken). But once that has been done, all reserves eventually hit their capacities. The anti-hunting preservationist fringe will then have to watch as ALL the animals in the reserve – elephants and other species – slowly starve to death in the destroyed habitat that always results from too many elephants. It has been noted and recorded with monotonous regularity. Controlled, ethical culling and hunting can and will save the species, if only the world can wake up in time, and harden up just a little.

But it was in no way always thus.

For the modern anti-hunting fringe, set aside the 21st-century prejudices, try to imagine the world a hundred and two hundred years back, where elephants are even more commonplace - nay, even pestilential - and ivory is a sought-after tradeable commodity. One of the reasons it's so valuable is the difficulty in attaining it. There are no modern roads, no vehicles, there are no aircraft, and medical knowledge is positively medieval by today's standards. There are no defined countries, no defined borders, no real rule of law, initially no government and no means of communication other than the spoken word and the tribal drum. There are letters, but this isn't Europe: any written communication could only be attempted in the major towns and even then, would take years to reach its destination, if ever. Firearms are mostly old unreliable black-powder devices.

For anyone to enter this world from outside, much less thrive in it, is scarcely credible. It would take a superman, a human with incredible reactions, incredible strength, remarkable bravery, superb shooting skills, hardiness against strange foods and the most perilous diseases, the sheer luck to match his audacity, an unwavering self-belief and the tenacity of an alligator snapping turtle with lockjaw.

Enter the ivory hunter.

3. William Finaughty

Picture courtesy of the Zimbabwe Field Guide

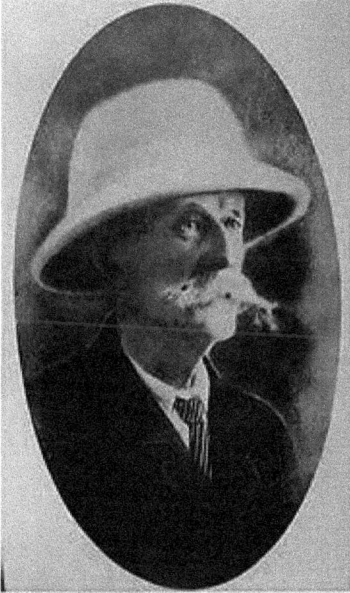

William Finaughty c. 1915 aged 70

Born in the Cape Colony in 1843 of 1820 British settler-stock, William Finaughty was undoubtedly a rogue, a hugely adaptable and resourceful person, a survivor and a good shot, all of which epitomised the ivory hunter of legend. His father was a blacksmith in Grahamstown and the young Finaughty left said town in 1864 (aged 21), to hunt and seek his fortune. It's illustrative of the era, that William had the opportunity and good fortune of being alive at a time where game was plentiful and much of Southern Africa uncivilised if not totally unexplored, as some places yet were. His initial foray was into the Free State, where he recalled the numbers of game as simply staggering. The young William immediately commenced trading in ivory, oxen and goods.

William's second trip into the wilderness commenced in 1865; he joined a Mr. Hartley's shooting party, which was then 10-strong. As William had no horse, Mr. Hartley lent him one, with the proviso that William gave Hartley half of all he shot. The horse was in fabulous condition but was a brute that no-one could ride. It initially unseated William, but he persevered with it and his patience was rewarded: it eventually became that tame and trained that he could shoot from its back, some achievement given that the weapon of choice was the giant 4-bore elephant gun, a black-powder monster that often as not blew people clean out of the saddle. The party moved up into Mashonaland, in what is now Zimbabwe.

The first morning's trip was for elephant; in the early afternoon the party came across four bull elephant that immediately bolted. Finaughty's horse was far fresher than those of the others, and in far better condition since no-one had ridden it, so he outstripped the rest of the hunting party and shot all four bulls. He was well-chuffed with himself and considered this just reward for a horse which no-one else would ride! Later that same week the party came across a large herd and William bagged three bulls, the rest of the party only managing two between them. The next elephant encounter was somewhat bungled, however; William shot a cow elephant and as she fell, he saw that she had a small calf with her. Rather than follow the herd, the diminutive pachyderm chose, naturally, to stay with its mother.

When William rode up, the baby immediately imprinted upon him and his horse, following them; William noted that his horse was none too impressed with this development, while Finaughty himself was a tad nonplussed at what to do. To his astonishment, when he reached the wagons, the same had befallen the Hartleys: a slightly larger calf had followed them "home" too! Sadly, both babies died within three weeks, the gruel and cows' milk fed to them not agreeing at all with elephantine constitutions. People now know that cows' milk cannot sustain elephant calves, as the chemical and mineral makeup differ greatly.

Of note, Katima Mulilo (from the SiLozi, literally meaning "quenches the fire"), a settlement named after the rapids on the Zambezi River which is situated in the fabled Caprivi Strip (Namibia's far north-east extension into central Southern Africa), opened its first shop there in 1940. The shop owner was one William Finaughty (Jnr), William's son. What I found most interesting reading his memoirs was the common practice of chasing down Bushman cattle thieves. The San people are legendary for being Southern Africa's first people, their nomadic lifestyle and ability to survive in the harshest conditions well-documented. Their tracking ability is little short of stupefying, South Africa's military making use of their knowledge to train operatives in survival, bushcraft and tracking insurgents, while the bush war raged in the 1970s and 1980s.

Although the San had been decimated by modern life and forced to those desert fringes by clashes with warlike tribes such as the Zulu, the number of times they stole cattle from the tribes, as well as from the settlers, is remarkable. One wonders if most of the tribal attacks on the Bushmen were actually in retribution; TV Bulpin's brilliantly-researched work *Natal and the Zulu Country* (Books of Africa, 1966, reprinted by Protea Book House in 2013) supports this statement, as the Bushmen were universally recognised as being thieves to be hunted down and killed, and often were. Finaughty mentions catching up with a few such parties who had stolen cattle, cut the animals' leg tendons so they couldn't run off, and eventually eaten them. On at least two such occasions, he and his companions exacted the ultimate toll.

Jamie Uys' epic films *The Gods Must Be Crazy* (1980) and *The Gods Must Be Crazy 2* (1989) show how the Bushmen are confused and out of place in the modern world, so they might be construed as having no sense of right or wrong, or even the knowledge that taking a tribe's cattle could be interpreted as an affront; but the thefts usually occurred at night or when the victims were absent, which suggests they were aware they were thieving. To clinch it, even if they initially had no idea, and felt entitled to take from what they may have perceived as a plentiful supply if they found a large herd, the reaction of the tribes after the first few such losses would surely have indicated to the remaining Bushmen that taking stock animals was wrong and would result in violent reprisal. No, sorry for all the sympathisers the San have – I include myself in that number – but these knew they were stealing.

Back to Finaughty; he left the Hartley party soon after, as Old Man Hartley wanted his horse back, as much due to jealousy as to regret at having to cede half the ivory! Pleasant old guy...William's third trip commenced in April 1866 and he intended that it be to trade, but the solitude of his journey led to him abandoning that idea. He pondered life for a few months and when the Hartley party returned in early 1867, Finaughty joined them again, his memories of his successes at elephant hunting reviving his senses and fanning the flame of that exciting life. This time William took his own two horses and two servants, his intention being to move off into elephant country and break with the party in short order. He soon had a 9-elephant bag, and again the party were annoyed at having been shown up! Predictably, and to plan, William left them.

His success was immediate, eight cows with fair ivory falling to his gun. Realising that this was his calling, William set off for Shoshong, to equip himself accordingly. He bought two salted horses for £60 each; one of these was to become the legendary "Dopper", a powerful bay that became the finest shooting horse Finaughty ever encountered. The horse stood stock-still when required, was greased lightning in the chase, was never nervous and never jumpy. He even held his breath while the hunter lined up the shot! To give an idea of his value and worth, Finaughty used him for three full hunting seasons, then traded him for £300 worth of ivory. Equipped with this wonderful animal and all the other paraphernalia necessary for a long bout out in the "blue", William left Shoshong in December 1867, accompanied by one Phil Francis (a fellow hunter who was later to perish on the Zambezi) and two Cape Colony servants of mixed race.

A quick note here would not be out of place to explain what a "salted" horse is. Horse sickness is a disease endemic to central Africa, but has reached the far north and south of the continent as well. It requires a biological vector for transmission (midges, mosquitoes, ticks), and thrives in the warmth and moisture of tropical climes. Horses that recover are known as "salted" horses as they are generally immune to further infection, and understandably command high prices. During the South African (second Boer) War (1899-1902), it was estimated that at least three in every four horses succumbed to the malady. In his brilliantly-researched work on Steinaecker's Horsemen (Slouch Hat Publications, 2006), the late Bill Woolmore stated the figure at 70-95%, besides 50% of all mules and 10% of all donkeys in the conflict.

In early 1868, the party was joined, by arrangement, by David Napier; he had a large compliment of help, numbering 30 servants. As can be imagined, this body of men consumed a considerable quantity of meat and the hunters were kept busier than they would have liked, shooting for the pot. The party followed the Tati River to where the Simbooki joined the Shashi. One morning at breakfast, and without warning, a horse spooked in terror; the syce reported around 200 elephants visible toward the river. Rushing off with the bare essentials, the hunters approached the river; the south bank was coated with literally thousands of elephants. Finaughty was aghast, calling it "a spectacle of a lifetime." As he was travelling light, Finaughty bemoaned having only nine bullets (one up and eight in his pouch), but he still managed to shoot six bulls and two cows in short order.

As he looked up after dropping the last elephant, Finaughty noticed Napier washing himself in the river. The man had obviously just been put through the mill; his shoulders, chest and back were heavily bruised and one side of his face was skinned. This was nothing compared to what had befallen his saddle, however, which looked as if it had been put through a metal press, and his horse had been tusked right through a hind leg. Apparently, a cow elephant had charged Napier from behind from close quarters and how they got off as lightly as they did was most fortuitous: the cow elephant vented most of her fury on the saddle. The party stayed in the proximity of the herd until the end of March 1868, Finaughty bagging a total of 19 animals for 38 tusks. During this same time, rhino too seemed to proliferate and Finaughty shot many.

Early April 1868 saw the party move into the Matabele country, at the time only the third white party to do so. The previous such had been the Hartleys; there had been no big bag of any consequence on that Hartley trip, but they seemed to have made a positive impression nonetheless: the little village of Hartley on the Umfulu River was named for the party. William found the shooting easy in the Matabele district; the elephants seemed not to react to gunfire at all, which, given that the weapon of the time was the four-bore cannon, speaks volumes. Finaughty later mused how his mind boggled at the bag he'd have achieved, had he had a modern rifle with him then. So ferocious were the dreaded four-bores that Finaughty was knocked down by the recoil on more than one occasion, and twice blown clean out of the saddle! This to a man expecting the power of the shot; unique times!

William considered the two months in the Matabele country to be the best of his elephant-hunting career; he nabbed 95 elephants, yielding 5,000lbs of ivory (over two tons). With the wagons creaking beneath their loads, Finaughty and Napier set out on foot, separately and into the fly country (the areas affected by tsetse fly). In two weeks off in the bush alone he accounted for fourteen bulls and eight cows. He had a few close shaves and one instance in particular cured him of any indigestion he may have had: it was after wounding a large bull in the seasonal Sweswe River, dry and featuring deep sand at that time. The elephant was one of a group of seven feeding off the trees on the river bank. Finaughty's first shot suffered a misfire, so he handed the errant weapon back to the bearer, grabbing the second and wounding the huge elephant, which had by now started to charge the men.

The bearer, however, rather than replacing the first gun's cap with a fresh one, instead managed to put in more powder and a second bullet. Finaughty grabbed that first weapon and was flattened by the resultant explosion; his senses reeling and his ears swollen closed and ringing, Finaughty staggered upright with the elephant almost upon him. He was stuck in the deep sand while the elephant made easy progress, its wide feet acting like snowshoes (or sandshoes in this case) and distributing its weight. By sheer luck, the elephant had to turn to round a small mound of sand and bush, twisting the very shoulder and the socket that Finaughty had managed to wound with the second rifle. Helpless, the great beast stood immobile and an immensely grateful William gave it its quietus. To illustrate how unaffected the elephants were by gunfire in that area, through all this, the remaining six hadn't moved. Where most people could be forgiven for sitting in the shade for a smoke, or even quietly going away to recover their shattered nerves, Finaughty was an ivory hunter; he instead bagged all six.

It is however at this point that William underlined his opinion that elephant hunting on foot is exhausting and dangerous, a far better prospect being to hunt on horseback; as Peter Hathaway Capstick said regarding this comment in his Editor's Note to the reprint edition of Finaughty's book (St Martin's Press, 1991), "Smart man"! By January 1869, William once again headed into the elephant country, this time accompanied by his brother, another gentleman named Gifford and most notably, the young chief Khama, who had heard of Finaughty's exploits and seen his large ivory hauls (Chief Khama was the grandfather of Sir Seretse Khama, first Prime Minister of Botswana and father to Lt-Gen Ian Khama, himself later President). Finaughty mentions the location of this hunt as "100miles (161km) above the Tuli". The Tuli block is to this day an immense and fabled hunting destination. Finaughty stayed in the area for three years, breaking only to replenish supplies, ammunition or to rest and exchange teams of men. While Khama was with the party, their success was much constrained due to constant shooting for the pot: Khama's entourage numbered some 300 people!

Luckily Khama didn't stay for long and the hunters were relieved of their burden as provider to throngs of hangers-on; the area was officially Matabele country, not the neutral piece between the Tuli and the Macloutsie Rivers, so staying was risky for Khama (what Finaughty calls the Macloutsie River is now known as the Motloutse, hard on Botswana's most easterly point, bordering Zimbabwe). Once free of the natives' demands for meat, the team set about gathering ivory. William found and bagged an old solitary bull with tusks of 90lbs a side. The next day William set off with his brother (Harry), and Gifford. They were to have a strange experience; for four days there was heavy cloud and no sun visible. The men lost all bearings, even the river flowed in the opposite direction to their expectations. After following a herd for a time, the deluge set in, and what a deluge it was; as Finaughty notes, a deluge in that part of the world means that ten minutes of the heaviest downpour imaginable results in water on level ground standing four inches deep. He and Gifford sat on a termite heap with their saddles over their heads, looking much like drowned rats, and sat the storm out.

At length the weather cleared, just in time to pitch camp. Harry reappeared, having split from the others just before the rain set in.

The next morning was glorious, and the wet ground made spooring easy. In the early morning, with the brilliant sunshine reflecting off the droplets of water, the men were treated to that classical African sight, a herd of giraffe. This one was particularly noteworthy as there were around 50 animals. Soon the men came upon a herd of elephant, but they seemed to be nervy and moved away. Firing from distance, Finaughty wounded a bull with huge tusks, but it got away. Three days later it was found by some Bushmen (Khoi), and William found himself in the strange position of having to pay for his rightful ivory; the animal constituted his record haul from a single elephant, a total of 250lbs. In all, that herd yielded seven bulls.

Then Harry got lost; for nine days he was in the bush and William feared the worst, but then some Bushmen brought him in. They'd found him 80 miles (130km) from the wagons. He had managed to subsist on some dry mealies (maize or corn), and a meerkat that he'd actually run to ground! Then some Bushmen stole one of the oxen; tracking them, Finaughty came upon the remnants of the thieves' temporary camp and the remains of the stolen ox. The despondent men rested a while, the spoor now cold. Trekking east, they came upon fresh elephant spoor and Finaughty shot five bulls while Gifford bagged three cows. On their way back the men felt that some variety in their meat diet was required and William dropped three buffalo while Gifford got another. During this little excursion, Finaughty was charged by an irate cow buffalo and Dopper had to really motor to get away. Finaughty was thoroughly shaken and this episode prompted him to remark that he'd face a lion before a buffalo any day.

Returning to Shoshong after five months, Finaughty tallied his bag for that period: he had shot 53 jumbos for a total ivory yield of some 3,000lbs (1,35 tons). It was at this juncture that he parted ways with the epic Dopper; the horse went for 900lbs of ivory (then some £300 financial worth). William was truly sorry to see him go but the great horse had taken a physical pounding and was getting on; with elephant and buffalo encounters at close proximity, it's only a matter of time before a second too slow a reaction or a metre lost in the chase will end badly. Finaughty used the proceeds to purchase three other horses for his next jaunt, two of these salted and the third just recovering from horse sickness. Of some note, William was to be accompanied by a little Hottentot named Cigar, who had hunted with Selous, and about whom the great man had written in his fabled work, *A Hunter's Wanderings in Africa* (Richard Bentley & Son, 1881).

This was to be Cigar's first trip into Matabeleland. Also accompanying the party was Chief Khama, again. Soon after they set out, Finaughty shot eight giraffe, leaving Khama and his party to the meat and moving on ahead; it was why Khama had come along anyway! It wasn't long before one of the supposedly-salted horses died of horse sickness; Finaughty groaned inwardly. It was always possible to dupe people regarding horse sickness but it just wasn't done, being rightly considered most unsporting to leave someone truly high and dry in such inhospitable country. It also seemed to devalue the proceeds of the fabled Dopper. The trip was in stark contrast to William's earlier such excursions; for instance, he was now a man of some means and allowed himself such luxuries as jam, cheese and alcohol. He also had two wagons, and the associated double team of men. The party numbered 46 in all.

Five miles after crossing the Macloutsie, the heat was intense and most of the party were resting in the wagons to escape it. Suddenly the driver shouted "Elephant!" and Finaughty looked out to see a herd of 30 animals standing staring at the wagons. He grabbed the nearest pony, no time to saddle up, and slipping a *riem* (leather strap serving as a bit and bridle) into its mouth, raced after the elephants. Three bullets later, William had three bulls to his name yielding 300lbs of ivory, and he celebrated with a bottle of Bass (Bass, still brewed today, was a ubiquitous British colonial African beer, out of Burton-on-Trent; by the late 1870s, it was the largest brewery in the world)! Continuing on to the junction of the Shasha and the Simbooki, where William and Napier had seen the huge herd, the men again found many elephant. Leaving the wagons for a week, the man bagged 8 elephant. One Sunday morning – William tended not to hunt on Sundays, but the rain had fallen overnight and it was a splendid morning, the sun bright and spooring easy in the soft ground – William set out travelling light and relatively unprepared for what lay ahead; he had four bullets in his pouch and one in the gun, a total of five.

As one does, he walked slap into a herd of elephant, the bush close and visibility poor, clumps and spinneys some ten-to-twenty feet (3-6m) tall and interspersed, creating corners and passages all around. William snap-shot a passing bull at some 12 feet distance, the animal appearing and disappearing again like a wraith. He knew the hit was a good one, it being almost impossible to miss an animal as big as a house from a few metres' distance. Following it, the bull lay dead just ahead, a curious lump in the far shoulder. William drew his bush knife and made a slit, his just-fired bullet popping into his hand, still perfect! That day was to be an historic one in the life of William Finaughty; he ended up bagging six elephants with only five bullets! He remarked that he was sorry he'd packed so little ammunition, as shooting was easy that day. After returning to the wagons, he set out for a week, downing three more bulls in that time.

Crossing the Shashani River, William came upon many elephant. On the first day he collected five bulls and two cows. He may then have had a run-in of sorts with a leopard, as it is here in his book that he declares it the second most dangerous game after the buffalo. Perhaps it took one or more of the party's dogs, or stole away with some fowls, or hanging meat. He specifically uses the old Boer name *tier* (tiger). The current Afrikaans word for leopard – luiperd – was then used to refer to the cheetah (current name *jagluiperd*, hunting leopard). This from a man who perennially suffered close encounters with elephants and lions; it's the old hunters and game rangers that respect the leopard the most. Under modern hunting conditions where the hunter occasionally has to go into the thick stuff after a wounded leopard, its cunning makes it a lethal prospect, abetted by speed so great that a fatal shot is often not possible. Men such as Peter Capstick and John Hunter - confessed leopard admirers - would approve.

Finaughty certainly had an eventful life; there was rarely a dull moment. No sooner had his leopard encounter taken place, than three lions killed his horse. Having lost one of his animals not long before to horse sickness, it was fair to say that Finaughty now felt slighted. He tracked the lions down and still seeing red mist, shot all three. Having suffered these financial blows, Finaughty felt there was just time sufficient for a last foray after ivory for the year, and stocked up accordingly. On his second day out, he came upon a herd. The five bulls and five cows he nabbed became his record haul for a single day. Burying the ivory for the return trip, Finaughty continued on his way and over the next few days shot four good bulls, each animal averaging 90lbs of ivory. In early November, William left Shashani and made for Shoshong. *En route*, a fine herd yielded eight tuskers. William Finaughty reached Shoshong at the end of November; it had been a bumper year. 111 elephants had fallen to his guns, a total of 5,000lbs of ivory.

January saw William off again, this time into the Makobbies Mountains. These are the first hills south of the Mangwe River. Following three bulls, William got one with over 100lbs of ivory all-up. He then seems to have had a change of heart, since he returned to Shoshong and sold everything. In April he returned to his old haunts above the Tuli River, this time accompanied by a real greenhorn named Hillier. That young man had run away from his uncle in Cape Town, eventually meeting William's brother in the Transvaal. After a month they were joined by a man named Blanch, and the Jennings brothers. Before long, William had bagged three young bulls and three cows, and a short time later he had three more. Then the party was joined by three Boers: a man named Smidt and his two sons. An interesting aside is that here, Finaughty mentions the party watching a herd of eland eating locusts, and with great relish! A swarm had descended and the hatching eggs made the ground crawl.

Soon they came upon another elephant herd and William bagged 9 tuskers, the Smidts collecting 15 between the three of them. All-up, the short trip had resulted in 57 elephants killed for nearly 3,000lbs of ivory. Upon arrival back in Shoshong, William Finaughty quit hunting; he built three large huts and settled down to trade. He even sold his old gun, which in later years he regretted doing, even making an effort to trace it and buy it back. Its last recorded owner was an elderly Bushman, who had traded it for a tusk; the old gun had seen at least four owners between William and the wizened Khoi. As mentioned before, the savage, venerable four-bore could and did slam people out of the saddle, but as William noted, what could one expect from a handful of black powder and a quarter-pound bullet? The first Boer War intervened and William had an eventful time; among his sorties he could count smuggling cannons and escaping captivity.

One day when peace returned William went out elephant hunting, to try the new breech-loading weapons. He had a 12-bore, but the huge recoil even bruised that seasoned warrior's arm, shoulder and chest, following a trip which gathered him a bull and six cows! After recovering for two whole weeks, William examined the weapon and saw that he'd overloaded the cartridges, and by no small margin. The memory of the 12-bore however seems to have left its mark and he discarded it, preferring instead a Westley-Richards fall-block with almost no recoil. He was very impressed and surprised; the report of the rifle sounded to his four-bore-conditioned ears like a mere cap-gun, yet the results were there before his eyes; with no trouble, noise or pain he (again) collected a bull and six cows. So enthused was he, that on the return trip he got a second bull for good measure.

Around 1880, and nearing 40 years of age, William Finaughty suffered a severe dose of fever, the likely build-up of accumulated years of malaria bouts of varying intensity and severity. This shook him and for the first time in his life he seemed to realise his mortality; I found this a somewhat comical observation, from a person who had nearly suffered death by elephant and buffalo, on several occasions. Neither is very pleasant. But his advancing age – 40 was decidedly middle-aged back in those times, particularly where hazardous pursuits were still commonplace – will have played a role. When young, one is often mentally and spiritually bullet-proof, danger regardless. Whatever the motivations and reasons, the fever left its mark on William and he left to live in Kimberly for two years. He then moved to the rural Transvaal from 1883 until 1887, avoiding the Boers there who had won the First Boer War.

Johannesburg was then the fastest-growing Southern African city, at the peak of the gold-mining boom; among the flotsam-and-jetsam, rich, poor, priests, prostitutes, adventurers and fortune-seekers attracted to the promise of wealth was one William Finaughty. The shenanigans were legendary and many have written about them. William eventually retired to his son's farm in Southern Rhodesia. He told his story to a friend who owned a weekly newspaper, "The Rhodesian Journal" named R. N. Hall. The paper ran the story from June to December of 1911. An American, George L. Harrison, hunting with one of William's sons, William Jnr, in the Kafue River area, heard of the senior Finaughty's exploits and eventually met with the old man in 1913.

Following those interviews, Harrison turned the notes and the newspaper series into the now-legendary and much-coveted piece of Africana, *The Recollections of William Finaughty: Elephant Hunter 1864-1875* (privately printed in 1913). Four years later, William died, aged 74. As he himself mentioned, the hunting he had seen falls to the lot of few men, and he had emerged from it unscathed to boot. Already back then, William Finaughty had noted the continent having changed beyond recognition; I wonder how the old ivory hunter would react to seeing it today.

4. Frederick Courteney Selous

Frederick Courteney Selous wrote several authoritative and excellent works on his exploits and the natural world, but his magnum opus was *A Hunter's Wanderings in Africa* (first published by Richard Bentley & Son of London in 1881). In the very first line of his foreword to the 1999 reprint by Galago Publishing, Peter Stiff made the not inconsiderable claim that Selous was probably the greatest of all the African hunters and explorers of the 19th Century. This is a statement of some magnitude, given the men of the time; but such is the reputation of this man born in London on old year's eve of 1851, that the only change most people would make to that sentence would be to remove the word "probably".

To provide some idea, Selous' real-life exploits inspired Sir H. Rider Haggard to create the fictional Allan Quartermain character; Selous had an entire Rhodesian Army regiment named after him; Africa's biggest game reserve is named after him; Blaser (the prestigious German hunting rifle manufacturer) has a rifle named after him, and they aren't the only ones; he provided an entire collection of wild creatures to the Natural Museum in London; to this day his name saturates the records of Rowland Ward's Records of Big Game; he has an antelope and a mongoose species named after him; and he counted among his friends none other than historic luminaries Theodore Roosevelt and Cecil John Rhodes. During his lifetime he collected every medium and large African mammal species from South Africa to the Sudan, a staggering achievement. Selous is legendary indeed, and as we shall see, with good reason.

He was the quintessential Victorian big game hunter, and like many larger-than-life characters, he was human with all the faults, weaknesses and failings that go along with mortality, but a human with several towering abilities to boot. Selous was born into an aristocratic family, the third generation of part-Huguenot heritage. His father was the Chairman of the London Stock Exchange and his mother a published poet. An uncle was an oil-painting artist, a brother became a famed ornithologist; hardly a low-browed or even average family. I take some solace in the fact that, from a young age, Selous showed great enthusiasm for the stories of the old hunter-explorers, and was besotted with nature from the off: I too have always felt the tug of the wilds and am aware that this adventure-spirit burns strong in many.

FCS's first real brush with danger came when he was just fifteen. *The Times* in London covered the occasion in detail, the event becoming known as the Regent's Park tragedy; on 15 January 1867, the local lake had around 200 ice skaters enjoying themselves on its frozen surface when the ice broke. Forty lives were lost to drowning or freezing, Selous crawling to shore across broken blocks of ice. His first-class education started at Bruce Castle School in Tottenham before he attended the fabled Rugby; his education was rounded off in Germany and Austria, channel-hopping in both directions common among the aristocrats of the times to complete their education. It was on the continent, however, that he was to have another severe brush with trouble, this one more-closely related to his passions and reflective of the times.

Selous had for many years collected eggs and small animal specimens, as have many young boys, particularly of his vintage. While in Wiesbaden, in the old Imperial German state of Prussia, a game warden nabbed him in the act of adding some buzzard eggs to his collection, effectively poaching. FCS knocked the man out, and had to flee the resultant Teutonic wrath to avoid imprisonment, hopping over the border to Austria. In Salzburg he had his first taste of proper hunting, shooting two chamois (a sure-footed wild goat). That decided Selous conclusively and when his schooling officially ended, he returned to England, determined to follow his dream. Although his family had harboured high hopes of his becoming a doctor, Selous – pronounced *Seloo*, after its French origins – never darkened the doors of a tertiary education establishment; instead, fuelled by the works of Charles Baldwin and David Livingstone in particular, FCS's love of nature would eventuate in his name taking its place in the pantheon of great African explorers alongside his heroes.

Fred evidently managed to convince his family likewise, because when he landed in what is now Port Elizabeth in South Africa's East Cape on 4 September 1871, aged just nineteen, his pockets were lined with £400 (back when £2 was a good monthly wage). His goal was the "Far Interior", the area to the north of what is now South Africa. Eventually reaching Kuruman (the last major outpost before the "Far Interior"), Selous must have wondered what lay beyond with more than a smidgen of foreboding, or at least apprehension. I have spent time in Kuruman and it is that brutally hot there, that one overcast day when the temperature unexpectedly *dropped* to 31 degrees centigrade (88 degrees Fahrenheit), it left us chilled and donning jerseys, no jokes. The default temperature over what amounted to several weeks I spent there at different times of the year was 44C (111F) in the shade…and it's a dry desert heat, to boot.

In more latter years I have found the *bushveld* heat glorious, thriving despite my wilting at similar temperatures at the coast; but to a Londoner in 1871, with air conditioning an unknown fantasy, it would have been an intimidating welcome to Africa. There was another dubious surprise in store; *en route* to Matabeleland in what is now Zimbabwe, FCS had acquired two of the notorious four-bore elephant guns, originally made for duck hunting. Ducks must have been mighty critters in those days, or perhaps that was the general term for the odd dinosaur that must still have flitted about Europe: as mentioned in the previous chapter, a single shot comprised a quarter-pound of lead and a handful of black powder, well over three times the charge of a modern 12-gauge shotgun with magnum load, and carrying the related impact. Shooters were regularly knocked down or blown right off of their mounts. The guns most-commonly fired what was effectively a .935-.955-inch calibre ball (24-25mm).

Early in 1872, Selous reached Matabeleland, and its fierce ruler, Lobengula. It was here that the young man's appealing demeanour and searching, hypnotic blue eyes first weaved their magic; Lobengula granted him free rein to hunt whatever and wherever he chose. Lobengula found it amusing that someone so young had designs on hunting elephant, and actually granted the rights in the mistaken belief that the youngster would be driven from the hunting grounds in short order upon meeting his first African big game. Lobengula was an easy person to rub the wrong way; his capital, Gubulawayo (today's Bulawayo) means "the place of killing", and wasn't lightly named. So much as a sneeze in the king's presence was instantly punishable by having the person's head smashed in with *knobkerries* (war clubs with a round head at one end), which would certainly put a stop to one's sinus problems...

Regardless, Selous now had a mandated run of the area and set about realising his dream of becoming a hunter-adventurer. He met a Hottentot hunter named Cigar, the partnership destined to become a fabled one. On their first day out, a bull eland fell to their guns and they feasted on the animal's fine, fat brisket before drifting off to sleep. Before sunrise on the second day, they were off, and it was soon patently obvious from the damaged foliage that they were in elephant country. Crossing an open space around midday, the party ran across the spoor of an old bull and swung into pursuit. After an hour of spooring, the great beast appeared before them like a grey mountain, fanning its ears in the extreme heat and quite oblivious to the men's presence. Backing off a bit to shed their trousers (facilitating silence and running ability), the men again approached.

Side-on to the giant animal, the men got to within 60 paces when it sensed or saw some movement, advancing a few steps towards the party with trunk outstretched, searchingly tasting the air. The men froze and as the elephant slowly turned away, Cigar whispered to FCS to put a hole in the great beast. Selous obliged; aiming for the shoulder, the roar from the huge gun brought a matching bellow of anger, fright and pain from the pachyderm, which decamped forthwith. The men followed on the run, scared to lose the huge quarry, Selous simultaneously scared for another reason: he was acutely aware that his gun was now empty! As the elephant slowed, Cigar too fired at the animal, at which the great bull turned and came walking toward the men, ears splayed and trunk searching. That act alone would unnerve the brave, but Selous, hastily reloading, got to within 20 yards and perforated the bull again.

Down the elephant went, and although he tried, couldn't rise. A last shot in the back of his head did for him. It was Selous' first 'phunt, his tusks long, white and nearly perfectly-matched (61 and 58lbs in weight). The day was yet young, so the men chopped the tusks out and buried them, intending retrieval on their way back to the wagons. It being Selous' first elephant, he sampled the creature's heart, roasting pieces on a forked stick. Forever afterward he pronounced it the African hunter's Holy Grail. Early the following morn, the party came upon elephant spoor, and after hours in the energy-sapping sun, caught up with the herd, sensibly fanning themselves in the shade of a clump of trees. Only mad dogs and

Englishmen...this Englishman shot a young bull, Cigar again affording him first shot. As the herd decamped – the young bull actually joining them until his brain ran out of oxygen – Selous reloaded on the run and potted a cow elephant that dropped as if electrocuted.

Rushing on, he managed to nab yet another young bull. As he lay panting, exhausted and recovering from the exertion in the shadow of his last victim, Selous could hear Cigar and the rest of the party firing. The ex-jockey and his men had accounted for six members of the herd. Cigar recounted how, when he'd hunted with Finaughty, he'd been petrified of elephants, especially following a particularly close scrape. Selous had nothing but praise for the little man, and found him fearless. Obviously a brave individual, the Hottentot had real, justified fear to overcome and appears to have done so. Finaughty hunted on horseback, considering ivory hunting on foot too dangerous, and it speaks volumes that Selous stated that he never saw Cigar's equal as a foot hunter. When the men returned to the cow elephant that Selous had shot, she had vanished, leaving a small piece of broken-off tusk in her stead! Selous was gob-smacked; his shot had obviously stunned her, merely knocked her out. But gone and still alive, she was!

The following day started in much the same way as had the previous: early in the day the party ran across some spoor and after tramping for ages while the sun turned them medium-rare, eventually came up with the herd. Selous' luck got no better, however; he wounded an elephant, but it ran off and got clean away. Cigar meanwhile accounted for three young bulls. It was late in the day, so, exhausted by the heat, thirst and exertion, the men camped near the carcases; but the peace and restorative properties of sleep were readily denied them by the cacophony emanating from the lions and hyenas that had descended on their elephants. *En route* back to the wagons, Selous accounted for two more elephants while Cigar got three. All in all, Selous was delighted with this, his first jaunt out for jumbo, and couldn't wait to set off again in kind. It was now late October, the heat always worst before the rains come, oppressive and crippling.

After restocking and replenishing supplies, Selous set off with Cigar on 2 November 1872, their second sortie out after elephant. The omens were good; late on that first day they came across a small herd of bulls, collecting two apiece. A couple of days later the men were headed for a river, the heat brutal. They were almost there but pulled up for a breather. What should saunter out of the bush but a large herd of elephant! Parched fatigue momentarily forgotten, the men raced to intercept the herd, Selous snap-shooting a cow which dropped like a rock. It was *déjà vu*, however; Cigar alerted him to the fact that his "dead" cow elephant was in the process of resurrection! It seems FCS had a knack for rendering cow elephants unconscious. One presumes he went for headshots, but given his then-relative inexperience, wasn't hitting the brain, four-bore shoulder-artillery notwithstanding…

Annoyed, Selous turned to finish the job, getting up close before the cow charged. He turned her with a headshot, then finished her with the classic heart-lung shot just behind the shoulder. Following the sound of the shooting – the rest of the party up with the herd – Selous came upon a highly aroused young bull, likely wounded by Cigar; it was looking for someone to punish but as the youngster froze, it turned away, offering the shoulder shot again. Selous took it, and the animal took off like a rocket, running a full 200 yards (180 metres) before succumbing. The rest of the men joined Selous and with the thrill of the chase over, the thirst which had driven them toward the river returned with gusto. In short order they set off thence again, but reaching the river, found it bone-dry. Their disappointment can be imagined, and there was no recourse but to walk down the riverbed until water was found. The sun had done its parching work however, and the men trudged on, unrewarded.

At last, around midnight, they came upon a deep hole with a little water, and feverishly gouging the hole bigger with assegais meant that within an hour, everyone's thirst had been slaked. The party slept where they lay, a shelter not even contemplated and even a fire scorned. The next morning the men were all gathered around something in the sand, and repeatedly exclaiming "Hau!" (a shortened version of "Hawu!", and pronounced "How"), an expression of surprise, shock or realisation used by the Africans but well-known to all ethnic groups throughout Southern Africa. Selous sauntered over to find out what it was and the clearly-visible spoor of a large lion showed that he'd approached to within a few steps of the slumbering men before walking off, doubtless peeved at having been thwarted in his quest for water. Sometimes one needs a slice of luck, and it doesn't require advanced cerebral activity to deduce that, had the lion been of a slightly different persuasion, FCS may have ended his still-fledgling career right then and there.

Within a week the heat and drought were broken as the rains mercifully descended; that same riverbed was now a river several feet deep and the landscape was transformed from a baked, dusty semi-desert to a sprouting, green woodland with standing water anywhere one chose to look. Nature can often be cruel in her irony and the men now had trouble staying dry, their supplies, equipment and themselves soaked almost constantly. Selous shot three elephants in this time, one a fine bull with well-matched tusks of 50lbs a side. They then left the district until the rains had ceased and lobbied Lobengula from April to be allowed to hunt. The chief at last relented, although it was already June (1873) before they were given their leave to do so. Selous brought three bulls to book, all with fair ivory, and as usual all were acquired at the cost of great physical toil. Coming upon a large and oft-used elephant pathway, the men set off after several bulls whose spoor was fresh.

Tracking hard all day, the men made up time on the bulls until, late in the afternoon, they spotted two giant elephants under a *mopane* tree, some way down the side of a slope. The larger bull had the biggest and best ivory Selous ever saw, even in all his years' experience thereafter. This animal fell to his shot after a short dash, and after a further chase, the other bull too was collected. Exhausted and again tormented by maddening thirst, the men eventually found water and once again collapsed, hydrated and fed. This time having the sense to move away some distance from the water, the party slept almost comatose, until roused around midnight when some lions - which had come to quench their thirst - saw fit to test their newly-hydrated vocal cords. The ravine resounded with mighty roars; normally Selous liked to lie and enjoy the noise (while nearby…outside…!), but this time he so needed to sleep that he had the men roll large rocks down into the ravine. The lions either kept quiet, moved off, or both, and the party resumed their slumber!

One day Selous got a taste of the four-bore elephant gun, one he'd rather not have gotten. In an eerily-similar incident to one that befell William Finaughty – and must, upon reflection, have befallen many if not most of the early ivory hunters – Selous' gun misfired, and instead of merely replacing the faulty cap with a working one, the bearer loaded the still-loaded weapon with another ball and a second handful of black powder, while Selous, oblivious, anchored the animal with the second gun! It seems that Finaughty had been slightly luckier than Selous: he was merely dazed and knocked over. When the latter grabbed his first gun and pulled the trigger, he was lifted from the ground by the resultant blast, to fall face-first into the sand, his cheek split open like a grape and gushing blood, while his shooting arm was rendered useless. The stock of the weapon was shattered, even though it had been bound by elephant ear skin (applied wet, the skin is like an iron band when it dries). Using his bearer to help aim, Selous killed the wounded beast, marshmallow arm notwithstanding.

The cut in his cheek mercifully healed of its own accord, which was fortunate; Selous had no means of closing it and it didn't get infected. But the shoulder was worse-hit; it was ten days before Selous could shoot again, and three whole months before he could hold his arm out straight from his body. Nice little guns, four-bores…Selous then got a chance to see the fabulous Victoria Falls, or *Mosi-oa-Tunya* (the "smoke that thunders" in Kololo or SiLozi). Now a UNESCO World Heritage Site, the Zambezi River tumbles some 350 feet (over 100 metres) at over a thousand cubic metres *a second* (38 thousand cubic feet a second), and that's average flow. Rainy season is naturally far higher. Although neither the highest nor the widest falls in the world, it is classified as the largest, the width of over 1,700 metres (5,600 feet; more than a mile) resulting in the biggest sheet of falling water on earth. For perspective, it's twice as high as Niagara, and Horseshoe Falls will fit against it twice with room left over. It's a fantastic sight, the spray, noise and sheer magnitude making a human feel very small. Back in 1874, it would have been even more mind-blowing; Selous was suitably awestruck.

I've tried to focus on Selous' elephant-hunting sorties in this chapter, but his legendary status was rounded by some equally-dangerous exploits against the other members of Africa's Big 5. In May 1874 on the Nata River, a huge bull buffalo charged Selous and his normally-reliable mount moved at an inopportune time. Trying desperately to rearrange things, Selous pulled off a shot at the bull just before it hit, flicking both man and horse into a graceful arc as if they'd been ragdolls. Selous, horse and gun landed in different directions, the horse hitting the ground running. From the ground Selous saw it was mortally wounded, its entrails hanging out as it ran on adrenalin. But right then he had a bigger problem, a large, black one with a massive horn-boss, standing mere feet from him. That he'd missed the snap-shot was evident in that the bull didn't process him into a bloody mess, merely charging once on his way by. Selous flung himself to the side and 'only' collected a thump to the shoulder which drove his elbow into Mother Earth! When he'd recovered his gun, he put the poor horse out of its misery.

FCS then took in the Chobe River, where the ivory hunting was again good, if exhausting; foot hunting was brutal compared even to horseback-shooting of the day. The overwhelming impression reading *Wanderings* is of hard slog, thirst, exhaustion and unreliable or inconsistent old ammunition. The old hunters certainly worked hard for their dues. It is reasons such as these that place Selous and his contemporaries above the modern hunter. Come August 1874, Selous found himself on the south bank of the Chobe, and an odd experience befell him. Early one afternoon, the party came across the spoor of a herd of cow elephants. Leaving the bulk of his men to set up camp, Selous set off after them with just two gunbearers, Arotse (FCS used the then-phonetic "Arotsy") and the classically-named Hellhound. Coming up to the herd, which was peppered with several really small babies, Selous shot first one cow, then after much running and several follow-up shots, another.

Standing at the second cow, which had displayed such refusal to shuck off the mortal coil, despite having had a finishing shot administered to the base of her skull, Hellhound alerted Selous that the cow was opening her mouth. FCS fed her another dose, this time from so close that smoke curled out of the entrance wound. The men returned to the first-killed cow, removing the heart and some fat (much-prized by Africans) before making for camp. Pre-dawn was just breaking when the party returned, and leaving three men to remove the first cow's tusks, Selous proceeded to the other; but in its stead was a large imprint in the sand and a gout of blood emitted by the trunk! FCS was forever more at a loss to explain how this animal had soaked up 5 four-ounce bullets to the body and two to the back of the head, yet soak them up it did. When it's not your time, and all that…

Selous then experienced a very busy September month, which included him coming upon a huge herd of elephant, quite one of the largest he'd ever seen; he reckoned it may have numbered 200 animals. The bulls were easily discernible, towering over the majority, which was comprised of cows and juveniles. He had several very fruitful days' hunting, the only thing more impressive than his haul being his ability to stay alive despite a sobering number of misfires. The ammunition of the times, you'll have heard by now, was shoddy at best, and Selous himself attributed a disturbing rash of misfires to grains of dust and dirt causing the caps to not ignite. This was a huge factor in the high mortality rate of the ivory hunters; those who survived understandably became legendary. Selous then reached a personal milestone in shooting his first lion, which was perhaps the more remarkable that it had taken that long, given where he was operating.

Indeed, after seeing three lions early in the piece - he'd heard their nocturnal vocalising many times, some of those times recounted above - he hadn't seen any in daylight since. He shot a lioness in fine condition in early December 1874 before making for the Tati. Here a trader brought a number of letters from England, Selous' first for nearly three years. He made for Durban via the Transvaal and Natal territories, embarking for England in April 1875.

* * *

Returning to Algoa Bay in March of 1876, Selous made at once for Matabeleland, a four-day trip by ox wagon from the coast. He had many adventures meeting traders, encountering giraffe, seeing many types of antelope and had several encounters with lions, one of which sadly resulted in the loss of his horse, Bottle; but it was September 1878 before he next came across any elephants. He had just met up again with old friends Cross, Clarkson and Wood, who just a few days previous had bagged eight bulls, and the men set out for ivory. Selous felt the old excitement unique to hunting jumbo; his previous months had hardly been relaxed, but there was something about gathering ivory…

The party headed for the "Hill of the Stump-tailed Bull", so-named for an elephant shot there years before that had an odd stump tail, by none other than the Hartley Party of William Finaughty fame (see the previous chapter). Given the practice of taking the tail to claim a carcase, and the fact that many elephants that were thought to be dead, sometimes rose and departed, merely stunned, this is most likely the way in which the bull acquired his stump; or is that, lost his tail? He would have been a feisty customer, and it must be said, somewhat understandably. The party had thought the area free of tsetse fly, but it wasn't long before six tsetses settled on the horses, the men catching them before beating a hasty retreat back to the wagons. An inauspicious start!

On 17 September they crossed the Umbila River, immediately coming upon the fresh spoor of five or six bull elephants. Following, the men noticed around noon that the great beasts suddenly cut into the fly zone, likely scenting or hearing the pursuit at some juncture. As if to underline the change, the men soon killed a fly that settled on Clarkson's mount. Coming upon a dry watercourse, a large herd numbering perhaps 60-70 animals became visible on the far side. The relaxed herd seemed to tolerate the men until at length, the men ever nearing, a large bull turned and faced them, breaking branches and spreading its ears in warning. As Clarkson lined up to fire at the bull, it turned away, revealing another stump tail!

This was Selous' first elephant hunt on horseback and he'd been told to fire from the saddle, the theory being that in case of a charge, there would be insufficient time to mount and make one's getaway before 5-to-7 tons of grey-brown wrath descended. Sounds reasonable! Selous' horse however hadn't read the script, walking forward each time the reins were dropped and refusing to stand still. Exasperated, FCS chased up close to the fast-departing herd – the rest of the party now firing – and dismounted, sending a quarter-pound of vindictive medicine into the shoulder of a young bull. The bull ran 200 yards (180 metres) before falling, stone dead. Things happened quickly; in rapid succession FCS accounted for a fine cow and another bull for a total of five shots, as fast as you read this.

He then experienced the flip-side of that coin when his next target – a bull – soaked up six bullets before charging so determinedly that Selous' exhausted horse only just managed to get away. FCS felt that had the 'phunt not been as hard-hit as it was, he'd have caught the horse; which would've meant that we'd never have read *Wanderings*, and Selous and horse would've joined so many other ivory hunters and their steeds in becoming indistinguishably mingled with Africa's fine red earth. As this last bull fell behind Selous, Wood and Cross appeared driving the vanguard of the herd before them. FCS licked his lips at the bounty that was surely about to befall him; the herd was exhausted, and milling around, made easy targets. But never underestimate Africa…

With plenty of ammunition left (Selous' colleagues were now out), FCS could be forgiven for anticipating a windfall, but he had counted without the large cow elephant he first selected and approached. She obviously felt otherwise. Putting his first shot in just behind the shoulder, like the manual says (wouldn't that make for entertaining reading, if there were such a thing as an ivory hunter's guide from those days…), FCS quickly put his next one in between her neck and shoulder, as she was winding up to charge, facing him from 30 yards (27 metres) distant. Selous was about to reload when charge she did; frantically digging his spurs into his exhausted mount's ribs produced a mere walk, the nag just starting to break into a canter when the elephant hit them.

The phenomenal impact of the blow slammed Selous and his horse to the ground. Coming to his senses amidst an overwhelming smell of elephant, Selous was pinned down, luckily not mashed flat then already, but unable to move. Mustering the strength born of mortal urgency, he wrenched lose, looking up on all-fours at the elephant's rear legs to left and right. Her forelegs bent, the great cow was earnestly engaged in flattening the man with tusks, trunk and chest, but unbeknownst to her he'd gotten free. Quietly as possible yet with the alacrity required in such a situation, the man scooted, taking care to stay behind the animal's rear end each time she turned, scanning for him, head held high, and hell-bent on skewering the tormenting human.

Moving off a way, Selous came upon Cross' gun-bearer, and so fortified crept back to find his horse. They found him sans saddle – which must be what the enraged cow elephant was trying to prove could be blended with the ground – but he sported a large gash in a rump, clearly made by a tusk. Regaining his rifle, Selous approached the cow to within 50 yards (45 metres), dropping her with another textbook shoulder-shot and finishing her with a final round in the back of her head. Taking stock as the action suddenly ended, FCS found that – understandably – he'd been through a bit of a physical ordeal. One eye looked as if a heavy-weight pugilist had landed a haymaker; one side of his chest lacked skin and his neck was vying with his back in the pain-and-stiffness-stakes; but given where he'd just been and what he might have looked like, his escape was a fortunate one and that fact wasn't lost on him.

As so often happens when the adrenalin comes down, the men realised they'd not had water all day. That, plus the exertions of the hunt in the tropical climate, meant that a tormenting thirst was now their lot. Reaching the river after two hours of torturous hiking in the gathering dark, they found it…dry. Following the course for another mile or so (1,6km), they at last hit pay-dirt, the muddy waterhole a literal lifesaver under the circumstances. With no food or blankets, a large fire had to suffice in the comfort stakes. Selous syringed his poor horse's wound out twice a day and despite the severity thereof – the elephant's tusk entering near the anus and running obliquely into the poor animal's rectum – it made a full recovery within two months.

The hunt had yielded the party 21 elephants, for a total of 700lbs of ivory (some 320kg). An interesting footnote to that hunt, and Selous' miraculous escape: the cow that FCS had thought to be the one which tried to flatten him, actually ended up being another which Cross had wounded earlier; thus, the actual culprit escaped. Although Selous was convinced she'd soon succumb – both bullets he'd fed her having been fatal shots – she was not found and could not be tracked. Pity anyone she ran into…

After a few more similar adventures, Selous made his way south to avoid the First South African (Boer) War, which ran from December 1880 to March of 1881. He was prophetic in roundly condemning it as deplorable, and that it would leave a legacy of hatred for generations to come by splitting Dutch and English colonists in the country, and his greater criticism was unfashionably aimed at the Empire. He then finished *Wanderings* with a wonderful paragraph, stating that his reward for the book and the information shared within would be ample if his notes provided "amusement or instruction to any sportsman-naturalist" or assisted any roving spirit to head for Africa! Take a bow, Frederick Courteney Selous; I would safely say that you could count yourself as compensated! That effectively ended Selous' career as an ivory hunter, but he continued for many years collecting wildlife for the British Museum, and accompanying people as a guide and professional hunter.

The East African campaign of the First World War finally claimed the life of FCS, where Africa's deadliest animals had failed, despite some hair-raising attempts. The British had formed a formidable Legion of Frontiersmen, mainly comprised of settlers and professional hunters, but the fact that tropical diseases was by far their biggest killer didn't hide the fact that the brilliant German strategist von Lettow-Vorbeck's divisions beat the British forces lined against him all over the wilderness. Near Beho-Beho in German East Africa (now Tanzania), Selous' division was surprised by a superior number of Germans and the legendary frontiersman, then aged 65, was shot and killed. He was buried at Beho-Beho, the gravesite in what is now Africa's biggest game reserve: the Selous.

5. Arthur Neumann

Arthur Henry Neumann was a timid, introverted and solitary little man, a seemingly-odd combination for an elephant hunter in the black-powder era. He wasn't really strange, and Raoul Millais (the son of Neumann's best friend, the famous hunter and artist John Guille Millais) recalled him as being jolly, lots of fun and good with children. But he recoiled from civilisation, cities, too many people and noise. In later years he displayed what modern psychologists would call paranoia, convinced that the entire planet was against him. When he committed suicide at his lodgings in London on 29 May 1907, he had been planning to return to the East Africa he so loved. It is rumoured that he was rejected by a lady whom he fancied, which drove him to end his life, despite the potentially happy outlook of returning to the open spaces and wilderness. This all indicates severe depression as well.

Like so many people that have been in combat or have hunted in the remote places (and Neumann had done both), he found it impossible to ever adjust to daily civilised life, and the injuries he'd sustained – which as we'll see were considerable – might have started to cause him increasing discomfort by his mid-fifties. It was a sad end for a man that never received the fame and recognition he deserved during his lifetime, or for some time afterward. This was for several reasons, principal among which was the timing of his epic record of his ivory hunting exploits, *Elephant Hunting in East Equatorial Africa* (Rowland Ward, 1898): the Second Anglo-Boer War greatly affected its sales. This was unfortunate, as it was obvious from the off that it was a high-quality work. Alexander Shand of the Edinburgh Review wrote in 1899 that the exciting tales of close calls were told in such a simple, straightforward way that the work was implicitly believable.

First editions are extremely valuable collectors' items and for many years the book was very rare. In later times he has gained in the estimation of historians, but that has been tempered in modern times by the current shock and aversion, and the very concept of ivory hunting being perceived as mass-slaughter. What Neumann was, was one of a very elite group, even among the esteemed company of the ivory hunters in their heyday; these included Norton, Anderson, Pearson, Hunter and Rushby. But beyond these, with Bell, Sutherland, Banks and perhaps Stigand, Neumann formed a very special group. Born on 12 June 1850 in a small village called Hockliffe in Bedfordshire, some four miles (6.4km) from Leighton Buzzard (itself a town between Luton and Milton Keynes), Neumann's early life is largely undocumented, aside from establishing that from an early age he yearned for the silent places, and took an interest in hunting the local cats with his dogs!

Aged nineteen he made it to Port Natal (now Durban in South Africa) and tried farming, trading and gold prospecting before fighting in the Zulu War of 1879, for which he was decorated. By 1890 he was appointed to the General Africa staff for the Imperial British East Africa Company, and from Mombasa spent the next year in the interior. He then returned to Zululand as a magistrate, but was back in 1893 to commence his dream of an elephant hunting career. Already aged 43, he was aptly armed with a .577 express double rifle and a .450 single, both black powder jobs from the house of Gibbs, and he added a Martini-Henry, a breech-loading single-shot weapon much in use during the British reach for Empire, of .577/450 calibre, necked down to reduce the powder pressure. From his military exploits and his prior visit to the East African interior, it was evident that Neumann was a fine shot: his Swahili moniker was *Nyama Yangu* (my meat), suggesting that when he lined up, the targeted animal checked out…

Neumann saw his first elephant fully four months after leaving Mombasa, and though not the ideal animal (it was a cow, and with small tusks to boot), Neumann felt it imperative to drop the animal and not botch his first elephant in front of the men. Patiently waiting a full fifteen minutes for the cow to turn, offering a temple shot, Neumann sent a .577 express pill into her head between the ear and eye. The great beast fell as if pole-axed. That the others were unaccustomed to people – or more-specifically, to gunfire – was evidenced by the fact that they moved only a short distance before again settling. Gingerly following, Neumann came upon two more elephants, the first facing him. Her chest was exposed as her trunk tasted the air, searching for the scent of danger, trying to discern from whence the shot had emanated; so, Neumann shot her, adding the second barrel into her side as she turned.

The animal made 50 yards before falling. Going on, a third elephant fell to another temple shot. Soon coming up to another two or three, Neumann felt he was warming to his task and approached less pensively, when he received his first piece of evidence of the danger inherent to the pastime. The closest elephant charged, dropping to a headshot when a mere 6 yards off. He then learned a vital lesson to immediately feed another dose into an elephant stunned in this way, when the creature rose and decamped before offering another chance, as Neumann worked his way around for a clearer shot through the dense cover. The wounded beast then stood some 60-70 yards away and screamed her pain and defiance, the enraged sound chilling the listening men to the bone. Trying to approach and finish the job, Neumann took a snap-shot at yet another passing cow, hitting it, but both this animal and the beast with the head-wound got away with the rest of the herd.

Neumann regretted the two wounded escapees, but as he said, ivory hunters needed to maximise shots and take every chance that arose. Still, aside from the poor animal's suffering, it didn't bode well for anyone those elephants may have happened upon…Neumann was to become known as probably the least-discerning of the great ivory hunters. Bull or cow, big or small, Neumann considered it worthwhile. He actually hated the word 'sportsman' when referring to ivory hunting, preferring the name hunter. He did thus remove some of the romantic fluff and take away the uncaring, trivialising term that ivory hunting was merely a sport, a game, and not the dangerous killing job that it actually was. After this first foray, Neumann lamented the fact that his feet were in great pain, a real liability for a hunter on foot. Gratefully using the resultant two days off to rest his hind paws, Neumann agreed to a ceremony with the local tribe (the Mthara), whereby he effectively became their blood-relatives.

The next day Neumann resumed his search for ivory, shooting three cows and a young bull. Cow tusks were then known locally as *kalashas*, the quality usually better than bulls' ivory, being softer, if available in smaller packages. Neumann saw some progress, in that these tusks were better than his previous batch. This was a positive, as he mentions the huge expense inherent to such a foot safari (a large number of porters was essential, as much for the group's protection as for their main purpose, that of transport. A smaller party was susceptible to attacks and raids. Distances covered were great, so time consumed was accordingly much. Disease and injuries resulted in further delays. Obviously, the onset of motorised transport greatly facilitated the safari industry…). Then Neumann shot an impala, remarking, as many have, how the northern sub-species have much longer and wider horns than those from South Africa and its neighbouring countries.

This is true, and is instantly apparent; it is also the case with the Cape buffalo: the biggest horn bosses are from East Africa, the animals themselves being equally massive in the body. Next, Neumann enjoyed his red-letter day, one of those days when the stars align and everything seems to fall into place, the extraordinary becoming commonplace. He moved into the Janjai district, the one adjoining that of his Mthara friends. Waiting in the early morning hours for the guide to join them at the appointed place and time, Neumann set off after a cow rhino with quite the best horn he ever took, a perfect forty inches long measured along the front curve. Returning to the meeting spot, guide now in tow, he then felled four elephants in short order, the first two dropping as if pole-axed to headshots.

His halcyon day was then tempered somewhat, when he was attacked by a swarm of bees that had taken up residence in one of the hollow tubes of wood that locals leave in the trees for that very purpose, thus ensuring themselves of a regular supply of honey. Neumann didn't marvel at their ingenuity; instead, he offered a few choice sobriquets and backed off sufficient to at least satisfy the bees that he had no designs on their golden riches. Bees sufficiently lulled, he returned to the fray. When his .577 ammunition ran out, he switched to his Martini-Henry, and by the time the day drew to a close he had nabbed a further seven 'phunts, for a then career-high day total of eleven. The party then moved into a more thickly-wooded area, rich in butterflies, and Neumann added to his impressive collection.

The heat was crippling, and the party quickly wilted, having badly misjudged their water supplies and the next likely source. Many have perished in these very circumstances, but necessity is the mother of invention; with their water stocks long-depleted, Neumann shot two zebras, the water in their stomachs saving the men's lives. The presence of lions was obvious, the odd glimpse complimented by the occasional carcase of a recent victim. Lions drink often and readily when water is available, but are hardy and many prides survive in the harshest places. Indeed, they thrive in dry times, the prey animals weaker and easier to catch around the ever-shrinking waterholes. The next morning the men returned to the zebra carcases, and two lionesses had annexed them. Neumann shot the first, and she thrashed about angrily, biting and raging as lions often do when hard-hit, but not incapacitated.

The second, a fine young beast in her prime, searchingly raised her head to see what was happening, and she also received a .450 slug for her troubles, where the neck meets the torso. She expired as if a switch had been flicked. The first however, a gnarly old cat well-past her prime, required three more bullets to shuck her mortal coil. Skinning the cats in the extreme heat, the men noticed a pride of 13 more lions, among them a massive male, and the huge herd of zebra they were trailing – several hundred strong – was ample evidence as to why the big cats proliferated.

*   *   *

Moving into Ndorobo territory, Neumann was guided by one of these adept hunters and at last accounted for a large bull elephant, this time staying close and behind the animal even after it was wounded, so it couldn't find him and erase him. Its ivory was only average but Neumann felt happy and relieved; it had been some time since he'd accounted for his previous elephant. Neumann was then treated to one of Africa's realities, which was often witnessed by all the early ivory hunters, to their initial astonishment: the Ndorobo hunter fetched his family, and these literally moved their quarters to nearer the carcase. For several days following, there was no hunting as the Ndorobo literally swarmed all over the carcase like ants, as Neumann wrote 'wallowing in gore and thoroughly enjoying themselves.'

After these few days off, Neumann set off after more white gold, but unable to find his Ndorobo guide, he took two younger volunteers from another family that was nearby. In short order he shot two cows and a fine bull, the bullets audibly hitting the elephants' thick skins in the hanging heat, BOOM-*whock*. His temple shots were improving, the second cow and the bull dropping like stones, while the other cow required only one follow-up round. The bull was short in stature but sported a fine pair of tusks. Neumann managed a stern shot at another cow as the herd fled, but although she (and the herd) escaped, Neumann got her ivory anyway when some Ndorobos found her dead a few days later. Neumann gave the carcases to the Ndorobo clans in exchange for great gobs of delicious honey.

Neumann felt a longing to hunt up in the Lorogi Mountains, and asked the Ndorobo – who had gotten sleek off the bounty of his success – to guide him there. They however tried to dissuade him, the higher climes evidently cold, wet and unpleasant. Neumann relented (this time at least), having acted against local advice before, and remembering that it had been to his detriment. Leaving El Bogoi and crossing the little Seya River, which drains the Lorogi range, Neumann almost fell victim to what would have been a wholly-unpleasant death by fall-trap. The Ndorobo never used them around El Bogoi, so it wasn't uppermost in his mind as he spoored along, eyes fixed onto the track in a forested area. Presently, Neumann felt his forehead come into contact with a cord strung across the trail, freezing him mid-step. Slowly looking up, he saw, poised and suspended above him, the massive and heavy harpoon shaft.

Neumann was grateful that the owner hadn't set a hair-trigger, lest the wind set it off, and he hadn't moved the cord sufficiently to dislodge it, for which he was suitably glad! That month ended up being a fairly successful one, Neumann gathering ivory steadily, but of particular note was one sortie after some huge bulls. Having returned to the El Bogoi district, Neumann was breaking his fast one morn when three young Ndorobo brought news of elephants in close proximity. Setting off immediately, Neumann was soon able to hear the pachyderms, and the breeze being favourable, was able to approach with little difficulty. Two or three massive bulls stood together, the deep internal rumblings of communication clearly audible, the air thick with the strong, unmistakable scent of elephants while the great beasts fanned themselves with their ears and simultaneously cooled their blood.

Neumann got so close that as he looked through a gap in the foliage, the view was of an elephant's shoulder, a textbook shot with nothing else visible, so close was he. Kneeling for a better angle, Neumann touched off, then immediately followed the now-rapidly-departing jumbos. A short way ahead, the victim stood immobile, and two further shots did for him. The men took his tail and were just eyeing the first shot – just above the heart – when the giant animal got up! Neumann quickly fed it two more bullets and it fell again, this time conclusively. Neumann measured the huge animal, which yielded 70 and 80lb tusks, but although he followed the others – five or six bulls, as it turned out – the wind swung and he had to be satisfied with just the one for that day. The next day involved cutting out the tusks and the usual consumption of the carcase by the Ndorobo.

Off again the following dawn with two Ndorobo youths and his bearers (Squareface was lead bearer, tasked with carrying the .577 double; Juma, the second bearer, lugged the Martini-Henry *coup-de-grace* weapon; while Ismail carried the axe and other bric-a-brac), fresh spoor was soon found. Evidence of the pachyderms' path was lined by chewed clumps of sisal, which the KiSwahili speakers termed *mkongi*. Neumann named it vegetable bayonets, which is a fair description! He mused that where it proliferated, it might be a successful undertaking to commercially farm the plant. He has subsequently been proven correct, sisal production in Kenya and Tanzania exceeded only by that of Brazil, which is far and away the world's leading producer.

Presently, two large bulls were visible in the thicket of the valley below as the men crested a rise. Neumann managed to get right up to one, putting a .577 surprise through its lungs. He then left it, knowing the shot was a telling one, and set off after the second massive bull. This first one was found the next day near Neumann's camp, in which direction he had oddly gone after receiving the bullet. His single tusk displaced 75lbs. Of interest, Neumann examined the skull and discovered that the animal had never had a second tusk, there being no socket on the other side. Coming up behind the second bull, Neumann mused on the curious contrast between an elephant's impressive, majestic, intimidating front end, and the almost comical, baggy stern. Soon however, his time for an inner chuckle was over: the wind turned and the bull did likewise.

Neumann had determined to try both barrels simultaneously when confronted by his next bull, so with the giant beast's chest exposed, he did just that, touching off both triggers. The result of firing two barrels of a black-powder double, as we've learned, was predictable: the bull was hard-hit, and Neumann received a massive smack in the face. Doubtless nursing his battered features while muttering some hair-raising sobriquets, Neumann followed and gave the now-standing bull another shot in the chest (one barrel this time!), and as he contemplated another, the bull charged. Neumann and Squareface dodged off the path and the bull bore down on a fleeing Juma, Neumann putting the second barrel into its ribs as it thundered by. After a short time, the huge animal succumbed, and though a bit smaller in stature than the previous bull, yielded more white gold (84 and 70lbs).

The first three bullets had formed a triangle on its chest, two of these puncturing the heart. Peter Capstick wrote often and well on the vigorous tenacity with which the Big 5 – indeed, most African animals – cling to life, and these two bulls killed by Neumann underline that, and chillingly so. Despite receiving close-quarter, lethal shots from a heavy-calibre black-powder weapon, the animals still decamp, or charge. The great Tony Sánchez-Ariño wrote that an animal only dies when a vital organ is destroyed, and he was spot-on; but two things are clear: 1) modern ammunition is heaps more effective, consistent in performance and reliable than that of days gone, yet 2) despite doing everything right, these huge and mighty creatures can still easily have enough gas left in the tank to blend the hunter intimately with the soil.

After much fruitless time was spent searching for elephants, Neumann finally had a chance to try his new battery, a .303 Lee-Metford and a 10-bore by Holland. He collected five elephants with only one escaping wounded, for a return of eight shots, two of these being follow-up shots to finish wounded animals. Although both weapons were effective, the 10-bore was a brute, kicking like a donkey while emitting smoke akin to that emanating from the Flying Scotsman. Neumann bemoaned the accident that resulted in the loss of his old .577. Moving to higher ground, Neumann noted the Grevy's zebra, Waller's gazelles (gerenuk) and ubiquitous mimosa trees with their feathery leaves. He also noted where elephants had passed, the forest absolutely wrecked in their wake. Seeing some elephants in the distance, the men made a long detour to finally come out above them, looking down over the valley to a stunning view. Neumann was reminded of scenes from old books on South African hunting, where he'd cut his teeth, the entire vista teeming with wildlife. Elephants filled every open space.

Neumann soon came across a family of elephants enjoying the water in the stream, and seemed at this point to experience the hypnotic effect that elephants can have on people, and which at some stage appears to have touched most of the great ivory hunters. A bull and cow stood touching each other's faces and mouths with their trunks, and so tenderly that Neumann was transfixed. At length, Squareface sidled up silently beside Neumann, whispering to him to fire. This shook Neumann from his reverie, and it seems almost as if he had to mentally remind himself of why he was there. Neumann shattered the peaceful scene by sending two 10-bore shots into a bull, following up with a .303 into a rapidly-departing cow. Another cow stood on the far bank, and although it was further off than any elephant he'd ever fired upon, Neumann dropped her with two shots from the .303, its accuracy and penetrative ability a feature of the model.

Running about as if in a frenzy, Neumann must have felt like a kid in a candy store, and admitted to balancing most precariously on the edge of losing control. The overload of elephants, whatever direction you turned, was almost too much to bear. Contrary to his nature, he lost his cool and felt that had he been calmer, he'd have collected yet more ivory, for fewer cartridges spent. Neumann then experienced what could be termed a close call, if I may use massive understatement. With bedlam humming about him, now ducking under boughs, now leaping broken branches in the path, the sounds of elephants moving through scrub all around, Neumann watched the swaying bushes and the glimpses of elephant between them, through it all the heat stifling. He stood in the path, having just pulled off a snapshot at a half-chance, when the loudest, shrillest scream rent the air asunder.

Being deaf in his right ear, Neumann had great difficulty pinpointing a sound's source, and that was the case here; but where this disability is an impending death sentence in this most perilous of professions, it likely saved his life on this occasion. Neumann took the scream to have emanated from the beast he'd just wounded, and he reacted not at all. Then he felt a slap on the back, just below his right shoulder. Slowly turning his head, Neumann looked up at a huge black head and gleaming tusks directly above him! The animal was obviously trying to discern what he was, since he'd not reacted at all to its scream, such as a human would normally do. Then things happened fast; showing admirable restraint by not soiling himself – which under the circumstances, most people would feel him quite entitled to have done – Neumann instead flung himself to the side, throwing up his rifle as he spun, but the elephant disappeared into the bush before he could draw a bead on it, the huge critter likely as adrenalin-charged as the man. Neumann was totally unhurt.

Towards the end of the day, he added three large bulls, all in the muddy bog, which brought the day's bag to twelve animals. As previously alluded to, Neumann felt he could've done better, and made a telling comment which clearly indicates the sense in using double rifles with automatic ejectors; opening the 10-bore to extract the fired cartridges each time was difficult, and dangerously time-consuming, when time is what one least has. The return to camp was a five-hour slog, but the full moon made it tolerable. Reaching camp at 1am, Neumann cleaned his rifles first - the mark of a consummate professional - and after a bath and meal, finally retired at 3am. The men had been at it for eighteen unbroken and strenuous hours. The next day the party rested, the bull Neumann had first fired upon the morning before, found dead. That brought the previous day's tally to 13 animals.

The following day, a still exhausted and ailing Neumann (malarial fever is a recurring nightmare when one is fatigued) added three cows to his bag before sending men to El Bogoi with a load of ivory, the party's carrying limit now reached and breached. A few days on, on 9 October 1895, Neumann and a small party set off to climb the range which contained the head of El Bogoi, actually resting at that streamlet and slaking their killing thirst. The climb was immensely taxing in the heat, there being no track or trail at all, but once atop, the going was easy in the damp, cool still. Huge moss-covered trees dangled long vines, the flora totally unlike that on the flats, and Neumann didn't like it at all, describing the scenery as 'cold, damp and gloomy'. After a night there, he was even more damning, using 'dismal and depressing' as adjectives after listening to the strange calls of the night creatures.

It is weird how strange natural sounds can exacerbate one's loneliness; the sounds of birds in particular, to which one is unaccustomed, render an unfamiliar place all the more alien. I recall the same when we'd emigrated to Australia, and some years later, after familiarity had rendered us oblivious to the effect, some friends too emigrated to the city we'd moved to. They noted the strange bird-calls waking them on their first morning, and feeling totally alienated. Exercise may have raised Neumann's spirits, as it does, because after a day's fruitless tramping, he now considered the forest beautiful and interesting! The party moved down to where the hills met the sweeping savannahs, using the less-steep western side of the Lorogi Mountains. Neumann loved this altitude, it most reminding him of South Africa's *highveld*, from whence I originally hail. It is indeed a most pleasant climate.

He wandered over to explore Kisima Lake, shooting two Jackson's hartebeest *en route*. The party then crossed back into the territory of Lesiat, Neumann's old Ndorobo friend. Immediately, the weather was noticeably hotter. Neumann exchanged as many beans as Lesiat's wives could carry, for a huge and ready supply of honey. It was clearly late spring, as Lesiat said it flowed like water at that time; but true to Ndorobo nature, what the tribe really sought was meat. By the end of October, Abdulla and the main porter caravan had still not returned from delivering the ivory, and were now a full ten days late. As agreed, Neumann moved on to Mount Nyiro, to await them there. Due to the regular rains, the undergrowth was far heavier than had been the case a year previously, and the going consequently arduous. Camping in the shadow of Mt Nyiro, they were eventually joined by Abdulla and the main caravan, who'd suffered the loss of two donkeys on the way. One succumbed to thirst after having been lost for a few days and the other – Neumann's cherished favourite – provided a dinner for some lions.

Before setting off for Lake Rudolph (now named Lake Turkana), the world's largest alkaline lake, Neumann had a lucky escape from a puff adder, whose head and neck he'd pinned to the ground – totally inadvertently – with his boot, while about to sit down! Holding it there, he blew its head to perdition with his light rook rifle, which he was carrying at the time. As he commented, although one may suffer many misfortunes along one's way, there are also some fortuitous escapes, some of which we may not even be privy to. At length, Neumann set out for Lake Rudolph on 2 December. On the way he shot his first topi, a fine and fast antelope related to the hartebeest, and largely the northern version of the tsessebe found in the continent's south. Once at the lake, the men soon revived and were replenished by the plentiful change in diet of fish and goose. Despite being absolutely inundated by mosquitoes, when elephants were found, Neumann was able to flatten three huge bulls in swampy ground. Two of these exceeded 100lbs a side, both sides; a good morning's work.

The party had intended to move on up the lakeshore, but the locals assured them a large elephant herd was nearby. Despite mosquitoes in biblical numbers, they stayed on another day. The promised bounty eluded them the following day (the mozzies must have paid the locals off), but in ample compensation, Neumann saw a type of hartebeest unknown to him. He didn't shoot a specimen then, but later managed to procure the skulls of both genders and a skin; this resulted in the Neumann's Hartebeest (*Bubalis neumanni*) being added to the annals of natural science! At length the men reached Kéré on New Year's Day, 1896. Here Neumann intended to stay for some time at least; but it was here that the safari was to receive one of its hammer blows. Late in the afternoon, Neumann went to bathe, his man-servant Shebane (pronounced Sheh-bah-neh, after the phonetic) carting the chair, towels and fresh clothes as usual.

The river there ran large, deep, smooth-surfaced and dark, and as they sauntered to the water's edge, a local native tending his crops said something to them. As neither Neumann nor Shebane understood, they ignored the man. Having bathed, dried off and dressed, Neumann then sat in his chair and laced his boots, not two metres from the water's edge. The sun was just setting when Shebane, a dozen or so yards off, shed his clothes to wash himself. Neumann noted this because the black man had never done this before while with Neumann. Turning back to his laces, Neumann heard a cry ring out, and looked up to see a sight which was to remain with him for the remainder of his days. Shebane was held as a dog holds a stick, in the jaws of a massive crocodile, which was gone under the swirling water quicker than thought, and Shebane - who had already ceased to cry out, likely instantly dead from the massive jaw pressure - was gone with it.

A horrified Neumann was now thoroughly depressed, Shebane having been a dear and valued member of the safari. Neumann then realised what the local man had been trying to tell them, and found out that such crocodile attacks were rather a feature of the place: while they were at Kéré, a local man was taken a short time later. It's a sure and safe bet that Neumann took no more bathing sessions in the river. It had been quite a start to the year, and it wasn't about to get any better. On 9 January, the party started back for Bassu, now having supplies and food sufficient to undertake such a venture. And so, to 11 January 1896, a day which would alter the fulcrum around which Arthur Neumann's life revolved: the events mentioned earlier in the chapter on The Ivory Trade...

The men set off early as usual, mosquitoes all over the place while birds flitted back and forth through the dawning light. The party entered the encircling forest along the swamp's edge, the bush dense and leafy. Soon they came across an elephant path, fresh spoor clearly visible along it. Ahead, the progress of the herd could be marked by the loud splashing as the animals moved through the marsh. Neumann was carrying his Lee-Metford, loath to use valuable heavy cartridges on these smaller cows and young as the party came up with the herd's rear-guard. They walked on unperturbed, sometimes standing to look on unalarmed at the men's presence. Seeing no bulls, Neumann was just wondering which cow to pot when one decided for him, charging.

Neumann swotted her in the chest, and she dropped instantly, never to rise again. In short order, he was then charged by a small vicious cow, but the men managed to evade her, before he shot a second small cow. A young bull appeared, Neumann potting him. The beast made his escape, but Neumann ignored it, knowing the hit was a fatal one. His men found it some days later, near where he'd fired at it. Neumann mentioned that this herd in that area were accustomed to people fleeing from them, and as a result had come to expect that reaction from people, making them more aggressive and consequently, much more dangerous than was usually the case.

Almost immediately after hitting the young bull, the same small, vicious cow appeared, and she was still fighting mad; she charged again, with the same venom as before. Peter Capstick wrote that the most terrifying sound in hunting is not the elephant's enraged scream; it's not the grizzly's roar from close-quarters; it isn't the bellow of a Cape buffalo in murderous mood; nor even is it the bowel-loosening grunts emitted by a charging lion. It is the dull, metallic click of a misfire while experiencing a charge. It usually marks a most decisive and unpleasant full-stop to one's mortality on this fair planet; the true sound of death. Neumann experienced this noise of finality now, turning to flee like chain-lightning before the furious cow elephant.

Amazingly, he managed to work the magazine on the run, firing behind him without daring to look back, but again the rifle was silent. Neumann flung it aside and dived off the path, his final card the hope that the cow would dash by. Turning to face what was coming as he fell, Neumann landed on a pile of brushwood which supported his back and head and likely saved his life. The elephant arrived as he landed, the first impact effectively the world's biggest head-butt. A '*knut*' from an elephant would make a festive night in Newcastle or Glasgow look like a tea party, and it somewhat understandably resulted in much of the skin from Neumann's face deciding it had business elsewhere, his head falling backward and fortuitously, away from any further, more serious damage.

Next, the furious animal drove her short left tusk through the man's right bicep, then through his right ribs and she concluded festivities by crushing his ribcage with her head. Neumann quite reasonably thought his time had come, and whether it was the smell of blood or the presence of her calf was academic; the cow chose suddenly to leave him. When she had charged, Neumann's men had understandably scattered like chaff before the wind, and finding that he could actually stand up, Neumann did so, calling to them. Soon his three bearers were at his side, Squareface literally weeping at his plight. Juma however berated the gunbearer for his weakness (!) and Squareface turned off the waterworks. The men helped Neumann to a tree, binding his wounds as well as was possible.

Neumann then sent the steadfast Juma off at a run to summon more hands so that the damaged hunter could be borne back to camp. The rifle – which had landed Neumann deep in the proverbial in the first place – was undamaged but for some indentations caused by the cow's toe-nails when she trod on the stock. I'm sure a part of Neumann wished that at that time, it was warmly nestling in Hell's remotest depths, but the other part of him was grateful it still functioned; the herd still surrounded them. Neumann noted his good fortune at being near a lake, the fresh water to drink, bathe his wounds and cool his head a great comfort. The men carried him past the clearly-audible herd, Neumann terrified lest one charge, which out of the necessity of self-preservation would likely result in the wounded white man being dumped in the path by the men.

The fall would likely drive a broken rib into a lung, but a charging elephant would finish the job far more quickly once it got to him. Camp was however reached without incident, where Neumann's wounds could be properly washed amid an atmosphere featuring more mosquitoes than air. His suffering was intense, but his good fortune was the more remarkable: no limb was broken, no artery severed, his right lung – almost unbelievably – was intact. Neumann was grateful for getting off that lightly. He had been under no illusions, philosophically musing that the profession was likely to result in an accident, the more so the longer one pursued it. So many things could go awry in the close cover of Equatorial Africa while pursuing jumbos, that to eventually retire unscathed was highly improbable.

He wrote that some may consider it just retribution, which would certainly be the general consensus today, with the salivating green fringe so prominent; but he harboured no ill feeling against the cow, considering her actions those to be expected in what was effectively a combat situation. Neumann then had his men carry him to his main camp at Kéré, sending word to Mombasa lest he not recover. His convalescing was to be long and painful; without surgery or medicine, and with fever ever-present, he had to rely on keeping wounds clean and a powerful, healthy constitution to heal. For weeks he hardly slept and for two full months, could lie on his back only. Apoplectic with boredom and pain, and desperate for a change in scenery, Neumann had his men cart him off back in the direction of the lake after a month.

They left on 5 February, reaching a sandy ridge with a pleasant breeze in the Reshiat district early on the 8th. There, Neumann was able to stand, walking slowly unaided and even managing to shoot some doves with his rook rifle. Buoyed by this success, he gleefully bearded a topi, with Juma bearing the .303, to his joy felling it at long range with his second shot. As one often does, however, Neumann had over-exerted himself and suffered a relapse. His next month was marked by crippling fever and violent dysentery. By the end of the second month after being gored, Neumann at last felt he was well on the road to recovery. He'd had a sturdy, well-ventilated hut built on the highest part of the rise, and named it 'convalescent camp'. He recovered with no further relapses, hampered only by mosquitoes at night and flies by day.

The area seemed to feature lots of bugs, but very few butterflies and no bees at all, which meant no honey. There was however easy access to eggs and milk, which obviously played a considerable role in Neumann's healing. At length, just over three months after sustaining the injuries, Neumann's side wound closed. He felt well enough to leave the cherished recovery spot on 17 April 1896. Soon the party came upon a lone bull elephant in thick cover, and Neumann's still-painful body and more painful memories of recent suffering oddly appeared not to be uppermost in his senses! He neared it and soon could sight only a leg as he crouched. Intending to cripple the elephant, he fired, scuttling away with an alacrity that he recalled as most impressive, along the shrub tunnel. The bullet didn't have the desired effect – not sure how he thought a .303 round into the lower leg would disable a large bull elephant – but in short order, Neumann must have had severe *déjà vu* fit to loosen his bowels: the elephant charged down the tunnel path, screaming shrilly.

Ever the hunter, Neumann still maintained the presence of mind to fling his rifle to one side, ensuring its safety, before flinging himself off the path into some bracken. This time his luck held, the bull veering the other way after the herd. Neumann was crestfallen at the day which drew a blank, but the next day he changed tactics. He hunted with Juma only, as the heavy black-powder weapons were still beyond his health to fire, and the quieter, calmer Juma was more easily adaptable to the slow, deliberate stalk than was Squareface. Results were dramatic and immediate, Neumann downing two large bulls in short order, granting Neumann some mental respite from failure and actually invoking a feeling of glee at his long-awaited success. The next day he used the same tactics, collecting three more bulls with his careful-stalk-and-careful-fire method. Feeling on top of the world again, Neumann shot a large male oryx and hung the meat as biltong, one of the finest foods there is.

The party reached El Bogoi on 3 June 1896, the bulk of the men taking the ivory on to Mthara on 6 June. It was here that Neumann pricked his hand on the thorn which was to ignite a bacterial nightmare in his right arm. At length it disgorged putrescent black matter and shrank to a shadow of its former self, but at least the pain eased. Lions were ever-present, a man-eater taking two honey-gatherers in separate incidents before another narrowly mistimed its attack on one of two men while he tended a fire, the cat actually landing in the blaze and upsetting the cooking pot. The combination of bare flames and boiling water made the lion's appetite disappear, at least at that point. The two men slept in trees for the remainder of their journey. Then the party itself was attacked, the donkeys targeted in the kraal. One was killed and Neumann cursed his useless right hand, being incapable of holding the rifle despite the lion presenting an easy target in the moonlight. The next night another donkey was taken, members of the party now panicked and predicting the worst.

Neumann recalled how Lesiat so dreaded the area due to the lion attacks. Neumann, however, had an affinity for his donkeys, animals he'd always been fond of. This turned out to be unfortunate for the lions. Tracking the lions to their lair, Neumann set a trap-gun, and one – an old, maneless, mature male – duly sprung the trap and shot himself. Neumann actually had the second beast plumb in his sights when the errant Lee-Metford again failed him. Not to be thwarted, Neumann reset the trap gun, and that night the second male – a far larger, younger animal – activated the trap, shooting himself too. Gradually, Neumann's hand healed and the party headed for Mombasa and home. As a last hurrah, Neumann again decided to go via the western side of the Lorogi Mountains, hoping for some final windfall in choice ivory. Shouldn't have done that...the safari's trials and tribulations to date notwithstanding, Africa had a further toll to exact.

This time, the two Ndorobo guides took the small party via a longer route into the mountain forest, leaving less daylight by which to build a sturdy *boma* against the area's active, local man-eater. That task was rendered impossible when the clouds burst, water hammering down and rendering all building impossible. When it relented, Neumann was left feeling exposed and angry. The men lit a large fire, bedding down around midnight. Neumann awoke from a fitful nightmare wherein a lion had attacked the camp, and stepping outside his tent for some fresh air and to calm down, saw the Ndorobo guard awake and alert. It's disturbing how often this very dream visits men as a premonition; Neumann was just drifting off again when he was jolted awake in no uncertain terms by the soundtrack of a real attack. Instantly, no-one was sleeping. The men fired guns in the direction of the departing lion, its spine-chilling grunts and growls clearly marking its path. The lion had taken Squareface, Neumann's lead gunbearer. The white man glanced at his watch; it indicated 1:15am.

Daylight broke and found Neumann up and tracking the man-eater, accompanied only by Juma. The blood trail led to a mass of squabbling birds, clear evidence that the lion had departed. The remains of Squareface were revolting, tragic, and something not easily forgotten. Despite all Neumann's considerable successes, Africa had exacted a heavy price. The lion made good its escape in the thick forest, free to roam again and free to visit death and destruction upon the people of the western slopes of the Lorogis, as lions have done for millennia.

*   *   *

Arthur Neumann spent the next two years in Britain, recuperating and enjoying his fame. He spent some considerable time at the Macleod home of Dunvegan Castle, where he wrote *Elephant Hunting in East Equatorial Africa*. The Second Boer War started in 1899 and Neumann joined the fledgling South African Light Horse. British victory was attained in 1902, but by then Neumann was gone, already back in Britain sometime during 1901. He then returned to South Africa, after a government post there, but was thwarted, so headed for Uganda instead, to visit a friend. He next cropped up as buying a Rigby double rifle in London, the intention being to return to Africa and hunt near the Abyssinian border. According to his biographer Millais, Neumann returned to the vicinity of Mt Kenya sometime in 1902 for some five years, occasionally venturing north to hunt bull elephants.

In September 1906, under pressure from those lobbying against uncontrolled hunting of big game, Neumann returned to the UK. He initially stayed with Millais, and it was from this time that Millais' son Raoul remembered him so fondly. Neumann had become increasingly solitary and although he had set the wheels in motion to return as a government official in the *Gwaso Nyiro* area of the East African Protectorate, he left a brief note and committed suicide at his lodgings in London on the 29th of May, 1907. He was 56 years old.

6. Chauncey Hugh Stigand

Chauncey Hugh Stigand is usually recorded in the annals of history as a soldier, explorer and colonial administrator, and that he was; but he was also so much more: at heart, Stigand was an adventurer, hunter and sportsman. He was the embodiment of that free spirit that sought the wide-open spaces, the remote and silent places, no matter how savage, rather than civilisation's banal malaise. If his name sounds flouncy by modern standards, rest assured that the man was anything but. Born in a small French coastal town called Boulogne-sur-Mer (his father was vice-consul there for Britain) in 1877, he was schooled at Radley before joining the military in 1899.

Stigand's first port of call was Burma, next stop Somaliland, before joining the legendary King's African Rifles in East Africa. In 1910 while serving with the Egyptian Army, he was the officer who received control of the mythical Lado Enclave from the Belgians. But what most interests us were his ivory-hunting exploits, mainly garnered during the years 1900-1913 and covered by Stigand, who wrote prolifically, in his stand-out work on the subject, *Hunting the Elephant in Africa: and other recollections of thirteen years' wanderings*, published by Macmillan and Co in 1913. Stigand built himself into a physical brute of a man, to the point where his feats of strength – even as an 18-year-old – were displayed at carnivals.

This continued into his military days to the point where he was probably the strongest man in the British Army. This was no mean feat, as that army was then the world's largest and most powerful. Today, the equivalent would be the strongest individual in the US Army, and Mother Green has some veritable monsters in her ranks by anyone's standards! As if that weren't enough to stand out, C.H. showed an uncanny knack for mastering local languages, back when it was considered beneath most officers. This was obviously of great help militarily, and certainly for a hunter in the wilds; at his peak, Stigand spoke twelve languages to translator levels.

Well before then, however, a landmark meeting occurred in Chauncey's life, when he was a mere sprite of six or seven: the Stigand family travelled to Trieste and met Sir Richard Francis Burton, the legendary Victorian intellectual who had 'discovered' Lake Tanganyika, at least to the modern Western world of the time. The lake is exceeded among freshwater lakes in depth and volume only by Siberia's Lake Baikal. Chauncey was captivated, Burton's legendary presence leaving an impression on him that would drive his African adventures. During his preliminary military training he met Sir Henry Morton Stanley (who had found Livingstone), and this further bolstered his desire to go to Africa.

Stigand starts off his fabled book by pondering the lot of the (then) modern hunter, and his musings ring even truer today. He considered ivory hunting to be in a class by itself, even when compared to hunting other members of the Big 5, but bemoaned the time of his birth, quite rightly noting that by the time of his tenure, licenses had become exorbitant and limited. Also, the great herds had retreated into some of the continent's most inhospitable terrain, whereas early hunters had unlimited numbers of jumbos to pot at their leisure, in most agreeable climes. The only plus-point vis-à-vis the pioneer ivory hunters was the reliability, lightness and accuracy of modern rifles and ammunition.

This is even more so the case today, and is indeed a giant factor; many of the first ivory hunters received the Deep Six due to faulty weapons, or unreliable and inconsistent ammunition. Surrounded by huge numbers of elephant, one needed a rifle to function, and the fact – mentioned already – that they often didn't, made this a lottery with some very high stakes, and some correspondingly-low probabilities of reaching retirement age intact. Thinking of when he'd hunted in pleasant climes, Stigand recalled his first foray after elephant in the Aberdares, which came in 1906. He actually found it uncomfortably cold. It was dangerous, low-visibility hunting, the ghostly forms appearing and disappearing in the mists, bamboo and thick foliage.

Guided by some Kikuyu honey-gatherers, C.H. made good, collecting a few bulls, but there were none of the gluts of plenty that had fallen to the old masters. Back in 1904, the climate was very different as Stigand crossed the Zambezi from the Southern Rhodesia side (later Rhodesia and now Zimbabwe), to the Northern (now Zambia). He and his trio of trackers soon came across a small herd. The young bull charged the men, although Stigand had hoped that he wouldn't have to shoot it. He had no choice, dropping it and adding a second round into its forehead as it rose. This second shot too wasn't fatal and C.H. found himself in a footrace with death. In desperation he flung himself into the many boughs of a fallen branch as the pachyderm closed the gap in strides, the elephant pushing and kicking him while drops of its blood spattered his bush shorts.

Emerging at the other side of the vegetable maze, Stigand's stalwart tracker Matola was on hand with the second rifle and Stigand gratefully put a round through the furious, stamping elephant's brain. A short while later, C.H. had an extremely close call – if I may use his levels of understatement – with another member of the Big 5: the rhinoceros. Today this prehistoric monster is courting extinction and isn't noted for being too bright; it is possible that evolution may catch up with the creature, and the planet will unquestionably be the poorer; but Stigand's encounter underlines a point which Peter Capstick used to stress, and one which forever renders the question as to which member of the Big 5 is the most dangerous, as impossible to conclusively answer: the difference in terrain can fundamentally alter the danger of an encounter, and with them, the hunter's chances of survival...

In Nyasaland (now Malawi) and Northern Rhodesia, Chauncey pointed out that the thick *miombo* scrub makes an encounter with a rhino – or indeed, all of the Big 5 – a very different prospect to coming across them on the East African plains. The hunter who has been tagged by a member of the Big 5 is likely to rate that one as the most dangerous, and somewhat understandably. In 1905 while after elephants, Stigand came across strange tracks, the thick grass still springing back and leaving the treads indistinct. While pondering their source, Stigand soon received an answer in no uncertain terms: the steam-engine puffs and snapping bracken preceded a rhino's head exploding into view mere feet away. Chauncey fired as a reaction, the animal swerving aside but immediately replaced by a second rhino! Plunging out of the way, Stigand suffered the usual fate of those fleeing in thick cover: he tripped headlong.

The huge beast kicked him on its way by and to C.H.'s horrified astonishment, swapped ends in a flash. Chauncey found himself soaring upwards, recalling relief, as he landed flat on his back, at the sight of the rhino's disappearing rear end. Reaching for his precious rifle, Chauncey noticed his torn-off finger nail, which immediately started smarting, as such injuries are wont to do upon discovery! Checking his rifle over for damage, Stigand was surprised at the reaction of his men, who had started reappearing: they were uttering cries of horror. Following their gaze, Chauncey glanced down at himself; his chest sported a huge hole - right over the spot where the heart supposedly resides - while both chest and shirt featured scatterings of what he called mincemeat. This discovery diverted his attention from the finger nail, but then the sounds of rhinos returning reached the party!

Chauncey's men helped him up and put the rifle into his hands, but the rhinos soon ran off again without putting in a second appearance. C.H battled to sleep that night (makes sense!), until around 2am when Captain Mostyn arrived from Fort Manning with assistance. He had brought Ghulam Mahomed, an Indian Hospital assistant. That stout soul stitched Stigand's wound up so well that our Chauncey felt well enough to undertake a 240-mile march (380km) – albeit still in bandages – and complete it in ten days! With all due respect to Mahomed, and Stigand was very complimentary regarding his medical work, Chauncey clearly wasn't your average man…

It will come as no real surprise that Stigand considered the finest elephant country he ever saw to be the fabulous Lado Enclave, specifically the southern part, and he mentioned the south-east edge of the Welle district, just after the Belgians had abandoned it. In 1908, Chauncey had been fortunate enough to obtain a permit to the Lado from Brussels. Although a legendary elephant haven, the area was sparse as regards other game, so food was scarce. Hardly any of the countryside was cultivated, so the hunting party had to trade meat for flour.

Right by one of the Nile's headwaters, Chauncey suddenly had a taste of what the old ivory hunters must have experienced; an unrestricted license and an absolute plethora of pachyderms all around. In chest-high grass, the party was spooring a large herd, judging by the myriad tracks. Presently, a local hunting party could be heard shouting from the opposite side of the valley, which resulted in the herd doubling back on Stigand's party. Suddenly, the world was a swirling mass of elephants, the 300-strong herd milling about in family groups of 20-30. Stigand admitted to a feeling of sensory overload, and rushed hither and thither, firing like an automaton.

Exhausted at length and flinging himself prostrate to drink from a muddy pool, Stigand rose to tally his bag, eight elephants killed and only one lost wounded, which took some doing, given the circumstances. The native hunters then got what they'd come for, descending with joyful cries on the great heaps of meat. Stigand, dog-tired, took his chance to retire to the comforts of his camp. The next day Stigand actually had to send for his canoe, so much ivory was there to be carried, and he was disgusted by the scene of the butchery as men swarmed over tons of bloody red elephant meat. There were however no paddles, so the ivory haulage was slow and laborious.

En route – slowly! – to Wadelai, where Stigand had arranged to meet an acquaintance named Hart at a specific date, he shot an elephant and managed to trade some of the meat for a paddle, rendering the canoe useful at last. Stigand rested a day at Wadelai, the old Belgian station overlooking the river, and used the afternoon to train his men how to use the dugout canoe. While passing a group of hippo, the bull raised himself up out of the water – a clear threat display – before submerging, a path of rippled water showing his passage as he bore down on the canoe. Chauncey readied his rifle to convince it otherwise. Suddenly there was a tremendous crash and the canoe was lifted a yard out of the water, falling back upright, and to Stigand's surprise, unholed.

The departing hippo's path was marked by the water rippling in the opposite direction, and the steadfast Stigand felt the animal had merely enjoyed a joke at the men's expense. The reality is very different, as many people die in Africa each year in this very way. The rock-solid canoe doubtless saved lives; a modern one would likely break up, depositing the men into the river, where thrashing and yelling in the foam churned up by a territorial bull hippo usually results in serious injuries and/or deaths. Chauncey commended the canoe's loading capacity, often loading it with half a ton in addition to its crew. The following day saw the party depart, the canoe carrying the ivory and some food while the porters went by land.

The hippo encounter still fresh in his mind, Stigand dreaded losing his ivory to any other violently-inclined hippo that might object to a canoe making advances on its harem, so he travelled in the dugout himself, rifle at the ready. He also rigged a buoy of sorts, attached to the canoe by a length of rope, to indicate where the vessel was if it were to suffer some terminal attention from Africa's notoriously evil-tempered river-horse. Chauncey felt grand as they cruised effortlessly down the Nile, memories of traipsing through tropical Africa a stark contrast to this ease of travel. The party struck shore at a little Madi village, where the only resident reacted to Stigand's question as to where the elephants were by pointing inland.

This was enough for Stigand, who promptly appointed this individual as tracker. Elephant spoor was found soon after setting out: jumbos had raided the village crops in the night. Tracking was good and the going was easy; around 3pm the reluctant tracker pointed a small herd out to Stigand, the best part of a kilometre distant. He then collapsed under the nearest tree, his job clearly done by his estimation! This had been Stigand's first exposure to the Madi tribe, and it never ceased to amaze him how timid and ignorant of the ways of elephant they were, despite living in close proximity. The man refused to go any nearer, so Stigand approached alone.

Taking cover behind an ant hill some 50 yards away (45m), Chauncey noted that none of the beasts carried decent ivory, but his porters needed meat. Choosing the largest, he shot it and returned to camp, intending to trade some of the meat for flour. All went according to plan, as by the time they set off, the party numbered several hundred people, all carrying varying quantities of flour. But Chauncey had reckoned without his Madi tracker; having made a point of noting the way, given that individual's poor bush craft, Stigand noted immediately when the old man set off insistently along a different path. Deferring to the man who one might expect to have local knowledge, Stigand duly went along, but it wasn't long before it was clear they were lost.

After many wasted hours, during which time most of the people had drifted off home, Stigand brought them back onto the actual path, but as it was late, they had to make for camp. Stigand was not thrilled, as one might imagine, but happily learned that his porters had found the dead pachyderm in his absence and secured the tusks. Loading the canoe with the meat they'd also recovered, Stigand sent it over to the Uganda side of the river and traded it for flour there. While waiting upon its return he again set off after more ivory, and striking spoor of a large herd, tracked them for some hours. At length, closing to within 30 or 40 yards (some 27-36m), what should happen along but two of the benighted Madi, happily chatting at the tops of their voices and blissfully unaware of anything around them.

Of course, the herd decamped, and Chauncey took until well into the afternoon before catching them up again, in a marsh. Two Madi lost their nerve, fleeing with loud splashes through the marsh. By now I'll wager that Stigand loved the tribe…immediately, a large cow-elephant came investigating, and this being in the Congo – unlike in Uganda – cows were considered fair game. Chauncey dropped her but this resulted in the herd departing again. This herd was one of the largest he ever laid eyes on, considering there to be some 500 in the Sudd and 200 more on the opposite slope, all-up some 700 elephant in view.

*   *   *

Chauncey listed the Big 5 in his order of danger as follows: lion, elephant, rhino, leopard, buffalo; but he qualified the statement firstly in that his list was based on his own experiences, and secondly, the relative scarcity of buffalo in some areas following the Rinderpest epidemic. He also mentions that lion and buffalo in particular are peaceable when unwounded, but exceedingly dangerous when wounded, and thick cover – into which both invariably retreat – exacerbates the danger they present. There are other factors too which he felt had bearing, such as how careful, or careless the hunter. Chauncey poignantly remarked on how Africa is such a land of contrasts; the extremes of heat and cold, altitude and flats, swamps and deserts. He also believed that one cannot fully experience or appreciate the relief and exhilaration of a welcoming fire, warmth, food, water and comfort unless denied these; that is indeed so.

Stigand digressed from his ivory quest to discuss and encounter one of my favourite subjects: lions. He noted his first contact with a wild one being in Somaliland in 1899, which was exceptionally thrilling with an animal one has been taught since childhood to hold in awe. The Somalis say a lion makes a man jump three times: the first time is when you hear it, and those who have heard a full-blooded roar at night will attest to that; the second is when you happen across its spoor, even if you're looking for it; and the third is when first you sight it. Stigand also noted something that Craig Packer was to verify using data analytics nearly a century later: man-eating epidemics often break out in the rainy season, and Stigand mentioned Nyasaland in particular (now Malawi), although this holds true for most of the continent. The grass is long, which hides the lions, but hides the herds too. Puddles and bodies of standing water abound, so game doesn't need to converge on one of the few waterholes in any given area.

Lions raiding a village – either for stock animals or for people – tend to do so on pitch-dark nights, and are adept at avoiding the hunter. Stigand also notes the rampant superstition, whereby Africans are loath to provide information which may assist a hunter, lest the lion avenge himself on the informant. At the aptly-named Simba station in what is now Kenya, Chauncey was mauled by a lion, which he matter-of-factly recounted. As lions have done since the rail was laid in the 1890s from Mombasa to Uganda (the fabled Lunatic Line), these animals used to drink regularly from the pools which formed under the water tanks used to refill the locomotives, especially in the dry season. Chauncey clearly wasn't having one of his brightest moments, seating himself on a girder a mere 6-7 feet (2 metres) above the ground. By-and-by, a lioness padded out of the surrounding grassland, sauntered up to the pool below the man and started to slake her thirst.

As Stigand shifted, the cat started, rushing off a short distance but offering a better shot. Stigand duly ventilated her and after a dash of 200 yards or so (180 metres), she dropped dead across the track. As Chauncey contemplated descending, he decided the better of it as two huge male lions appeared from the grass, across the track and right by the dead lioness. Both approached the dead animal, sniffing, pawing and scratching before lying beside it, whining. They then rose again, sniffing and scratching about. This went on for half an hour or so, followed up by alternate roaring for maybe a further 30 minutes. By now, Stigand's backside was likely numb on the girder, but descending wasn't top of his to-do list, especially when both males headed towards the water tank.

As the first neared, Chauncey fired, the bullet later found to have broken the animal's lower jaw on its way down into a shoulder. The lion collapsed where he stood. The other, having frozen at the report, now came on as if nothing had happened! He paid for his remarkable reaction – or lack thereof – with a bullet, bouncing about for a time before dashing off into the grass, where he was found dead the following morning, 100 yards (90m) from the line. By now the cat which had temporarily occupied the water trough below Stigand had revived, and Chauncey punctured him once more before he too departed the scene. The moon had by now disappeared and it was dark, as only African nights can be. Stigand made for the station, returning with his orderly and a lamp. Passing the place where the last-hit lion had entered the grass and seeing nothing, Stigand went on to the lioness before returning.

By now a small crowd had gathered at the water tank, as Chauncey again passed the spot where the lion had gone into the grass. He fancied he could see the animal, and indeed it transpired that he could, but the darkness fooled his eyes into thinking it was further off, and lower than it actually was. Suddenly, the non-descript tawny blob was airborne with a loud roar, the orderly and Matola scattering behind Stigand. The man's left arm was the first thing the lion encountered as the rifle went off into its chest, its right forepaw over his left shoulder while it set about chewing that left arm to pulp. With no real alternative, the now-prostrate Chauncey used the only recourse at his disposal, his free right arm, and started beating the lion with his fist. This is usually futile, but Stigand was unusually strong and the fear of death was undoubtedly fuelling his adrenalin.

The lion by now also sported three bullet wounds, so after a last shake for good measure, the animal suddenly upped and left. Stigand immediately reloaded and followed, but saw nothing. With classic understatement, he then thought the lion best left alone (you think??), returning to the party at the water tank before getting his wounds well-syringed out with disinfectant. The paw over his shoulder had left him three long claw-marks for posterity while his left arm featured eight large holes and a severed nerve in the wrist. His clothes were soaked in blood. Chauncey then had six hours to kill until the Nairobi train arrived, and the bumpy journey did nothing for his comfort with wounds that had by then cooled and stiffened.

Stigand commended the treatment in Nairobi hospital – where, by grief, they will have seen some classic injuries – and despite his arm swelling enormously while assuming several interesting shades, that limb was saved. The severed nerve in his wrist was the biggest injury, and it was a full seven months before Chauncey could use the wrist at all. It took a full two years before he could hold a rifle steady to his satisfaction. None of this prevented him, however, from shooting his next lion some nine months after the attack; you see, Chauncey was keen to see whether or not he'd lost his nerve on lion, but happily reported suffering no mental nervous reaction…

As for the cat that worked Stigand over, it wasn't done yet. Chauncey gave his orderly strict instructions to climb the tank in the daylight so the animal could be seen, then fired upon from that vantage point. Under no circumstances was anyone to approach before doing this, and Stigand repeated this three times for emphasis. Did his men listen? Nope; what do you think happened next? Spot-on! The lion was still alive, and by then, one can understand, really loved people as a species. A group approached it, and to top it all, the only armed *askari* was at the back of the line, from whence he could contribute not at all. Chauncey's orderly led the line, and it was he who received a first-hand demonstration of how a lion's claws work. He eventually managed to crawl away; the next train was stopped and the lion – having truly done his bit to enhance the reputation of *Panthera Leo* – was shot from the guard van.

Chauncey's next sortie after lions included a suicidal venture into a cave after a large, wounded, black-maned male. Advancing a short distance, he made out a blob which could have been a rock or the lion, he couldn't be sure; his eyes had adjusted to the gloom as much as they were going to. Whispering to his man that accompanied him (Husseni) that he, Stigand, wasn't sure what the blob was, he then asked his companion if he knew. When Husseni answered in the negative, Chauncey said he thought he might fire at it to make sure. This he duly did, the report within the cave's confines deafening the men. Nothing happened; nothing moved, so presuming the object had indeed been merely a rock, the men advanced. Chauncey poked the object with his rifle as they neared, and it was the lion, now stone-dead! Of anything one may choose to label Stigand, a coward was surely among the least-likely options…

Stigand and Hart had been forewarned by the Belgians that the Lugware tribe (pronounced Loog-wah-reh) were hostile and warlike, and that a large troop escort was advisable if one were to risk hunting in their territory. Both however found them as hospitable as their poverty permitted. They in fact considered someone who provided meat as a godsend. They were more savage and unrefined than the average tribe, no question; but friendly enough. Not long after entering Lugware territory, Stigand dropped a massive bull after a very lengthy and tiring trek in its wake; but the tusks were disappointing at only 40lbs (18kg) each side. Stigand didn't shy away from recording his failures, and many were the days of tramping through thorn scrub and blazing sun over exhausting miles, for no reward at all. A particularly-frustrating episode occurred one day thanks to Stigand's temperamental Mannlicher, which had shown a tendency to misfire since it had been accidentally submerged while crossing a river some time before.

The striker spring rusted, and misfires while one is charged by a bull elephant are anything other than helpful. Spooring a few bulls, a huge one with giant tusks emerged right where Chauncey positioned himself to intercept it. The Mannlicher however misfired twice, a third shot working but striking the elephant too far back. The shot nonetheless brought the great beast to his knees. Trying to anchor his prize, Stigand lined up again, but the errant Mannlicher again failed to function. Apoplectic, Chauncey raced to get the big bore from its bearer, but in his absence the elephant disappeared. As can be imagined, he then spent some time roundly cursing the firm of Mannlicher, his inept men that should have been by his side, and the world in general. The huge tusks had been well over 100lbs a side easily, Chauncey reckoning them to be 120-130lbs a side each. He was understandably furious after twelve hours' hard slog in the heat, to come so close before being foiled.

The long trek home in the dark failed to lighten Stigand's frame of mind, and his dinner of beans with red millet flour – which might have been so different a repast – didn't help either. The following day, Stigand determined to track the bull he'd wounded, and took Maliko with him. Maliko had been one of the men who'd not delivered the day before, and he clearly felt obligated to right the wrong. Despite his obvious terror – he was of a timid disposition – he followed Stigand over hill and dale, through all the thick stuff into which wounded elephants invariably retreat. The men breathed a sigh of relief as they emerged from some very thick scrub, but their respite only lasted a few minutes; the path wound down into grass and reeds so thick, that the stalks met overhead, the men effectively in a tunnel. Rounding a corner, they came upon a tree under which the huge pachyderm had stood a while. Chauncey breathed another sigh of relief that the animal had left: a chance encounter at such close quarters with a wounded elephant would likely have had dire consequences for the men.

They burrowed on through the reeds, Maliko shivering in terror beside the white man, until they rounded a corner and were blocked by a huge black mass not 5 yards away! Stigand, steadfast soul that he was notwithstanding, considered this the closest he'd ever been to an oblivious elephant, and that he'd rather never repeat the experience. In modern terms: he got the fright of his life! The animal's tusk was in the way of a heart shot, and Stigand didn't dare move, so he shot it just aft of the ideal spot, at which the creature decamped, to the obvious relief of the men that he'd not charged, or confusedly picked their direction upon fleeing. Chauncey afterward wondered why he'd not shot it in the head, but I think he can be forgiven, as he was a mite close for fully-rational thought! Reloading on the run, Chauncey emerged from the thick reeds to see the 'phunt crossing the valley not far distant.

He did however notice that the beast did not seem to be the one he'd wounded the previous day, which was a pity. Closing every few moments when the blazes of scrub would momentarily open, Stigand fired into the animal's stern a few times until with a scream the huge beast doubled back and tore down the path. Stigand hurriedly crouched behind a tiny thorn bush not two feet high and hoped against hope he'd escape attention. The elephant thundered by, Chauncey glancing up to watch the huge ear pass literally directly over him. The elephant stopped some 20 yards on to test the air, and as Stigand manoeuvred for a shot, reloading simultaneously, the great creature disappeared, never to be seen again. This illustrates the difficulty and hardship often involved to secure ivory; sometimes after much time and effort, and trying to ensure one didn't lose a wounded elephant, precisely that would happen.

Stigand mentioned that in his experience, a wounded elephant – unless it had been seriously wounded and was found dead nearby the next day – travels hard and fast through the thickest bush available, twisting and turning to purposely shake off pursuers, then will go for some 40 miles (64km), where it then stops to recover until healed. With modern lenses on, the number of people endangered within that radius would be considerable, even if the animal does actually recover. Even if it does, it has its elephantine memory to fuel revenge on any people it may encounter. All of this is the reason why the hunting bodies prescribe the following-up and killing of wounded game, especially dangerous game, as an unconditional priority. Stigand trailed the creature some more but he then developed a huge abscess on his leg.

This eventually burst, at least partly relieving his pain, but he had no choice but to abandon the chase. His men carried him back to his camp at Mt Gessi. There, Stigand received word of a fellow officer – a Captain Halkett – who had been given a thorough going-over by an elephant. The officer had been charged in thick grass, stabbed through the thigh by a tusk, then was literally flung away. When he landed, he wished he hadn't, his shoulder taking the full impact. There was no medical treatment available at all, so Halkett lay in a critical condition and in waves of understandable agony until the steamer arrived to take him to Butiaba (on the eastern shores of Lake Albert in western Uganda). He was then carried to Entebbe (the seat of government in Uganda until independence was gained in 1962; the capital since then has been Kampala). Halkett was obviously lucky, but he was doubtless as hard as the men of the times: he recovered fully and by Stigand's account, was soon as fit as ever! The men of the times were a mite tougher than the contemporary model, methinks…

Chauncey's abscess eventually cleared up, so he set off on the Dufile Road (pronounced Doo-fee-leh). Since the Belgians' departure, the track had become overgrown. Eventually coming upon the old Belgian station of Arenga – which the natives had torched – Stigand joyfully found some tomatoes; he seems to have loved this versatile fruit as much as I do, as he mentions happily finding it on more than one occasion. Coming across it would have been doubly-pleasant after subsisting on flour, millet and game meat for months on end. The party entered thick grass and Chauncey then gathered ivory in a most unusual and amusing way; his one puttee came loose, and as it was a lengthy and difficult process to tie up again, Stigand left it to drag for a while. The spoor they were following told of a large herd.

Eventually, Stigand "met a sapling", to use his own words! Propping his foot in the fork a metre from the ground, he commenced retying his puttee. Of course, it was then that the large black head of a bull elephant chose to reveal itself some 30 yards distant, the wind blissfully blowing the man's scent straight into the bull's face! The strange pantomime got even funnier, Chauncey selecting to fire from that very position; the 'phunt disappeared. Chauncey probed hither and thither, but seeing nothing, went straight to the spot where the great head had disappeared. Nearing a black heap, Chauncey saw his elephant, dead, and with fine ivory to boot! Perhaps fate was repaying him for his last few failed sorties…there was an interesting surprise for Stigand upon arriving back at his camp: Husseni had bought him a baby serval, but sadly the creature died before long.

Chauncey mentioned – as have many closely associated with the bush, and in hunting and other conservation roles – that to truly appreciate the wilderness, one must take interest in the small things as well as the big. It is often easier, as small things abound, right at one's feet or outside one's door. Large creatures must often be sought at great distances, with much effort, and often at similarly-escalated levels of associated danger. Chauncey named the impala as the prettiest and most graceful of all African game. My ex-wife would approve; she shares Chauncey's view. The impala is unquestionably a stunningly-beautiful and gracefully-proportioned animal. He wistfully imagined keeping a herd, which he felt would tame quite easily. The herd which lives in Skukuza, Kruger Park's capital in South Africa, is indeed quite accustomed to people and the brazen tameness of the chinkara gazelles in India suggest the animal may indeed tame easily.

The honey guide is legendary across much of Africa, as well as in Asia, where the bird also occurs. Its symbiotic interactions with people, and with other animals – most often the honey badger – are well-documented. The bird's scientific family name, *Indicatoridae*, reflects its habit of showing man or beast where a store of honey is, in exchange for the grubs and beeswax. Stigand credited this relationship developing over time to the bird's intelligence; he felt that these birds long ago watched honey-gathering people and learned that they can get nests down, open them and chase off the hive's original occupants. He also considered that the bird must have thought people rather stupid, as they'd often wander about and miss hives, occupying themselves with all sorts of other nonsensical tasks; so, the bird deigned to start showing the daft humans where a goodly supply of honey was, from which it would also clearly benefit. Many observers, over much time, as well as what we know about the intelligence of many bird species, show that Stigand was likely spot-on. A supply of honey is a glorious thing when one has been out in the 'blue' for a time, subsisting on corn meal and lean game meat.

And so, to the First World War, where Chauncey spent the first year – 1914 – in trenches in France, the boom of artillery overhead, the mud, slime and putrefying human matter underfoot. He was luckily then considered too valuable to waste away in French trenches, his African experience much-needed as the East African Campaign escalated. Chauncey became Major CH Stigand in 1915, before being sent to Darfur in 1916. He was made Governor of the Upper Nile Province from 1917-18 and then of the Mongalla province (in South Sudan), in February 1919. Unlike many, he had survived the war, but a life of living by the sword most-often has but one ending.

In October 1919, while attempting to suppress an uprising of Aliab Dinka tribesmen at a place called Pap between the Lau River and the White Nile, the British force was ambushed by far greater numbers of the enemy. Chauncey Hugh Stigand was killed by multiple spear-wounds to the chest. This phenomenal man, a towering physical presence, a wonderful intellect with a giddying ability to combine it all as the ultimate woodsman and diplomat, was survived by his wife Nancy (an American from Washington DC) and their infant daughter, Florida. He was just 42 years old.

7. Denis Lyell

Although often mentioned in the same hallowed tones as Sutherland, Bell, Stigand, Rushby, Banks and Neumann, Denis Lyell was more an overall adventurer and hunter, rather than specifically a great ivory hunter, and in this way was much like his hero F.C. Selous. He was, however one of the most valuable of the early hunters in that he was a prolific writer. He thus provided much evidence of the ivory hunters' craft, environs and existence, while few others did, even those who were far more committed ivory hunters to the exclusion of all else. What's more, he was descriptive and could arrest one's attention in much the same way as the three great American writers in this genre – Hemingway, Ruark and Capstick – did. He wrote eight excellent works, but his magnum opus was *The African Elephant and Its Hunters*, first published in 1924 by Heath Cranton Ltd. It would turn out to be his most important book.

Born in Calcutta, India on 6 February 1871, Denis David Lyell was the eldest son of the Scottish merchant James Carmichael Lyell and Kate Harriette Latham. Soon after his birth, the family returned to Scotland where Lyell grew up, in Monifieth House just outside Dundee. He was interested in the outdoors from an early age, and as have many thousands since, became captivated in his teens by the writings of big-game hunters. In 1893 (aged 22), Lyell headed for Ceylon (now Sri Lanka) and after a year made it to the Indian mainland. It was here where he received his baptism of fire, exposed to tiger hunting. The lure of Africa however won him over and by 1899, aged 28, Lyell arrived in Mashonaland, in what is now Zimbabwe.

He set about traversing the sub-continent, making a name for himself as a superb professional hunter. His forays were marked by stalks on foot through heavy foliage, which required very accurate shooting at close ranges, with very little or no margin for error. He spent some time in a clerical role in Nyasaland (now Malawi) for the King's African Rifles. Lyell suffered the fate of being born a few decades too late; the halcyon ivory-hunting days which were experienced by Selous, Baker, Gordon-Cumming, Finaughty and Cornwallis Harris were over, and Lyell bemoaned the fact. He did however benefit from the great strides made in modern firearms and ammunition, before the advent of which, those legendary ivory hunts were little better than a high-stakes lottery.

I wrote these last few lines with a huge sense of nostalgic regret, as I have often bemoaned being born too late, for these exact reasons. As Lyell was born almost a century to the day before I was, the feeling of regret feels somehow more acute, if bathed in irony. I am however heartened that Lyell refused to accept that things were 'over', and pursued his passion regardless. He did after all join the pantheons of great names in this most perilous of professions. Lyell did state right from the off that hunting the elephant varied widely based on habitat, and that most of his experience had been gained in Nyasaland (now Malawi), north-eastern Rhodesia (now Zambia and the northern parts of what is now Zimbabwe), and Portuguese East Africa (now Mozambique). Selous had gained most of his vast knowledge in what is now Zimbabwe.

Lyell idolised Selous – which was quite natural and understandable – and first met the master in 1906. They became firm friends, both intelligent and articulate, both avid readers and writers. Of interest, and his views hold water and seem reasonable, Lyell considered elephant hunting in his time – around 1900 – to be far more dangerous than it was for the old masters, great advances in guns and ammunition notwithstanding. The animals were by then more aggressive due to years of persecution and had retreated into thicker cover. Readers of really old hunting fare will have marvelled, as the authors themselves did, at how scores of elephant stood out in the open and didn't even move when one of their number was shot. This often allowed the hunter to shoot every animal present.

Of interest too was Lyell's assertion that an elephant was nowhere near as intelligent as a dog; and that an Indian elephant's intelligence far exceeded that of the African. He also doubted that the African pachyderm had ever been successfully tamed in the past, or that it would in future. He has since been shown to be way off the mark on all those counts. People have trained African elephants, several tours now offering elephant-back safaris, and we have the now-ancient story of Hannibal who crossed mountain ranges with African elephants during the Punic wars with Rome. In addition, the elephant is now thought to be the mental equal of whales and dolphins, with only the great apes thought to be closer to human intelligence, and far superior to any dog.

Regardless, context must be lent to the time – over a century ago – and the man, who made a living shooting elephant as a commodity, not studying them as research subjects. Lyell noted something not always immediately obvious when crop-raiding elephants are discussed: over the course of one night, a hungry pachyderm can eat a family into poverty, that is known; but before the harvest, each animal can trample six times what they consume. The damage can be imagined, and Lyell considered that the natives' plight could easily be sympathised with. He did, however, consider confronting and attacking elephants during night raids, and particularly if armed with rudimentary farm implements, to be deadly-dangerous, especially before the harvest, when the grain stands twelve feet high.

This is all true, and is the main reason elephants account for some 500 people a year. Lyell considered the close thorn scrub encountered in Zambia's Luangwa Valley as possibly the worst place to track elephant, and Peter Capstick would and did attest to the difficulty and danger inherent to that exercise; but many would elect the Sudd, the nightmarish swamp alongside the Nile in South Sudan as worse. There, apart from the terrain which stops man but not elephants, there are clouds of blood-sucking insects to literally drain one's life-fluids, while simultaneously injecting several things known and unknown to science!

There are perhaps two other places on the continent which are at least as bad: the thick forests of the Addo in South Africa's south-east, and Zimbabwe's notorious *jesse* bush. It's a moot point as to which is worst, but all four of those territories render shooting the creatures over the open plains of East Africa to something akin to murder, particularly with today's rifles, ammunition and scopes. Lyell actually considered elephants to avoid swamps, as their great weight and struggles if caught seem to exacerbate things when stuck. This seems reasonable, and maybe Lyell was right; but desperation to avoid hunters could explain them occasionally frequenting wetlands.

That renders the swamp a sort of last stand or last resort; small wonder an elephant in that cornered frame of mind is a dangerous prospect. To support his statement, Lyell cited examples where native tribes drove herds into such terrain and could than take their time spearing the helplessly-stuck animals to death. In November 1906, Lyell was camped in what is now the north-eastern part of

Zimbabwe, at the Rukusi Stream. He had just awakened when his man-servant's smiling face parted the tent flaps with a happy greeting, the ritual morning cup of tea in tow. Lyell dressed quickly, the fresh morning reflected in the dew drops on every leaf and blade of grass. Although many people aren't hungry first thing in the morning, it is always a good idea to eat regardless, should a long day's walking lie ahead; particularly when one is after elephant.

Lyell customarily consumed several salted eggs and several cups of sweet tea. The men were readying a plentiful water supply, because as Lyell correctly mentioned, the sun in the latter part of the calendar year in central and southern Africa can be terrific. A goodly supply of ammunition was likewise set aside for the trip. The trackers had their usual implements, travelling light with a spear each and maybe a light axe, their job too vital to risk them being encumbered with heavy loads. Tea, rusks or biscuits and biltong are always good types of food for the trail, as one may out of necessity be required to sleep out in the 'blue'. As the sun showed itself over the horizon to the east, the party was off, transitioning from human to game tracks. Once well-clear of the human habitations, Lyell tested the wind using his small calico bag filled with fine flour. The downside, which he observed and I have often pondered myself, is the unpredictable changeability of the wind at that time of year, the swirling dust-devils hypnotic in the lazy afternoon hours, but aptly named, as they trick and bedevil the hunter.

After traipsing for quite some time and distance, the men came to a pool in the rocks overhung by trees, scenic and easily approached due to the soft, sandy banks. As Lyell scoured the bed for signs of elephant spoor, his eye caught a ghost of movement beneath a bush, which he took to be a python; but in a flash, a leopard flowed up the bank and was gone into the thick grass. From Lyell's telling, there is every possibility the men would have missed the cat entirely had it merely frozen. Not for nothing did Peter Capstick consider the animal to be wrapped in the best camouflage in nature. After a full two hours' march, the men espied what they'd set out after: the tracks of a good-sized bull elephant in the sand where the animal had watered in the night. The spot featured rhino spoor as well, and Lyell wondered if the two animals had encountered each other.

The water was cleaner than that from the village, so the five men slaked their thirst before dumping out the bottles' contents and refilling the vessels from the pool. The weather was now as hot as the proverbial as the men readied themselves for business, Lyell's rifle barrel too hot to touch. Mafumba spoored well, the bull unhurried, and the men followed him easily, his passage visible by the damage to trees he'd sampled on his way. A small puff-adder had been summarily flattened by one of the great beast's feet, Lyell noting this as unusual, since elephants don't usually take a toll of smaller creatures. Most in truth get out of the huge animals' way when they hear or sense them approaching, which isn't difficult; but puff-adders' stock-in-trade comes from lying doggo in paths, the reason they bite so many people across the great continent of Africa each year.

By 1pm the heat was oppressive, the men seemingly no nearer the great elephant, so the party rested. Once rejuvenated by water and tea, they again sallied forth some 30 minutes later. Soon it appeared they were suddenly gaining, the elephant likely resting out the heat of the midday for longer than half an hour; its dung was progressively warmer and fresher. For some time, the ground had been sloping upward, and when they reached the highest rise, the valley set out below held scattered green trees, likely denoting the presence of water. By general consensus, the men felt that the bull would be there, among the trees. Passing through some long grass, Mafumba suddenly dropped down, one arm held behind his back with fingers snapping for attention. Instantly, no-one was drowsy. The party dropped to a man, an elephantine rumble clearly audible.

Lyell felt the rumble to be a warning, not the relaxed and pleasing sound which often emanates from a peacefully-feeding herd. The wind was favourable, so the huge animal had likely heard its pursuers, but not scented them. The terrible heat seemed more acute in the still tension, sweat beading off the men. Slowly edging out of the grass, which stood some ten-to-twelve feet tall (3-3,5m), the men saw the elephant under a tree almost facing them. Lyell harboured no hope of dropping the beast with a head shot from his .256 Gibbs, so he exchanged it for the .400 Jeffery which Mashila had borne all morning. Lyell loosed off into the bull's chest, the powerful solid almost collapsing the huge animal onto its hindquarters; but he recovered and set off, post-haste. Lyell seized the smaller weapon and peppered the elephant's head as it fled, one of the rounds penetrating the brain. The animal dropped as if poleaxed and never moved again. His ivory totalled 90 lbs (41kg).

Resting exhausted and hot beside the carcase, the men knew they needed to replenish their water supplies; none knew this country, but Mafumba said he'd once been there years earlier. His sub-conscious mind served him well, for when he made for a bamboo thicket some three-quarters of a mile distant (1km), it yielded a small stream. The ravenous, meat-hungry men were allowed some of the trunk for their dinner, and they gnawed well into the night. Lyell marvelled at their capacity for meat, as he had many times previously; he considered it likely that each man could get outside 12lbs (some 5kg) at a single sitting, and had seen it too often to be wrong. The night passed comfortably but for the raucous cacophony put up by hyenas; they had taken a lot of meat from the trunk where the men had cut it, but the rest of the elephant was untouched. Most importantly, the ivory was intact.

Around the end of the dry season in 1905 – "winter" in central-southern Africa; the inverted commas because it's hot and dry, as opposed to hot and wet – Lyell found himself in what is now Zambia, in the fabled Luangwa Valley, Peter Capstick's old stamping ground. He was camped at Kazembi's village, sat in the valley between the Luangwa River and the Muchinga Mountains. The tsetse flies were omnipresent, Lyell hoping against hope that he and his men wouldn't get sleeping sickness. Supplies were running low and Lyell shot a waterbuck for his men, as well as an impala for himself. The waterways were clogged by *matete* reeds, which proliferate throughout the region; John Taylor recalled them in what is now Malawi. Lyell sent some men to Nawalia to fetch any mail, and happily there were some letters from home, as well as two 'Field' magazines.

Lyell was grateful for the fresh reading material as his copy of Selous' fabled work "A Hunter's Wanderings in Africa" had been read so often, it now assumed a pliable, rag-like appearance. The book was his 'bush Bible', and no-one in history could have criticised him for that! Finding elephant spoor one morning, the men followed it through the notorious *matete*, before heading through light woodland, which was at least easier going. It then however headed back into the thick stuff, until around 10am the men rested awhile, baked and parched. Lyell read some of the letters from home, chuckling to himself at the surprised reaction his family would have displayed, had they seen the filthy retinue that opened the letters, as well as the wild, remote surrounds! The tracker, Chikamagombe, soon felt refreshed sufficient to take the spoor again.

Soon the men closed with the bull, a great, grey mass against the sky. Lyell had a superb black-powder double ten by Purdey, but preferred to carry his trusty .303, not least because the cloud that hung following a black-powder shot wouldn't clear in the absence of a stiff breeze. Through a gap in the foliage, Lyell put a .303 surprise into the animal's shoulder, its loud grunt indicating a palpable hit. Following, a half-mile elapsed (some 800m) before the elephant was found, standing hard-hit beneath a tree. Lyell shot it in the brain and it went over like a stone. In short order, Lyell had his men start a fire and brew up a kettle of tea, while the crew beamed in anticipation of the windfall in meat and fat.

On another occasion – precisely diarised as 16 October 1905, in fact – Lyell awoke with an attack of ague, a legacy of constant, repeated and unhealed malaria. He contemplated staying in camp, but decided to get up and go out. It was as well that he did, as he was rewarded with the biggest, bulkiest bull that he ever collected. The sun was already well up when the men set off headed west, toward the Muchingas. After just 90 minutes, one of the leading men stopped, pointing out a great, black-grey mass among the trees. The first task was to establish that it was indeed an elephant, and not one of the numerous large rocks which abounded. The glimpse of a tusk soon allayed those fears and the men approached quietly.

It soon became evident that the elephant was enormous, and on cue the wind began to blow erratically, to worsen the elephant's already shifty, distrustful demeanour. Lyell realised that he'd best shoot before the creature got their scent and left, which at best would add hours of hot spooring to the equation. Resting the .303 against a sapling, he aimed for the earhole, the little bullet winging its way into the elephant's head with an audible crack as it struck bone. The elephant stumbled but didn't go down, Lyell putting a second shot low into its shoulder. The huge beast rushed off full-tilt, but made just 50 yards (45m) before crashing to its knees. Lyell added two more bullets to the earhole and the great bull was his. The party returned to the village, Lyell's men singing all the way. Shaky with fever, the hunter retired to his stretcher, having secured a noteworthy prize that day.

Many hunters have marvelled over the manic and often-entertaining goings-on that constituted the cutting up of an elephant carcase, and Lyell recorded this huge bull's sub-division to show how amusing the process could be to a European. Africans love meat, and will go to extraordinary lengths to secure it. Upon the death of the elephant, the cry of *"Nyama!"* (Meat) went up, Lyell likening the response of everyone within earshot to that of vultures. People working the fields dropped hoes and other tools, rushing for blades of all sizes. The men flocked to the carcase, followed by the women, many with infants tied to their backs. The men sliced off huge slabs of meat, tossing it to their womenfolk. Then the fun really began; a full-blown catfight broke out as women squabbled over the choicest bits, yelling 'like demented fish-wives'. People who have lived long in Africa will relate, the noise overwhelming.

To their credit, despite the apparent heatedness of discussion, rarely did the women come to blows, but it did occasionally happen. The men swarmed the carcase, Lyell likening it to ants, as have many other ivory hunters. Incidental cuts were inevitable and didn't halt proceeding in the slightest. Any injuries sufficiently severe to require treatment or staunching were so dealt with, before their bearer returned instantly to the fray. One man was brought to Lyell with a sharp blade buried some two inches deep (5cm) in his backside; when Lyell extracted the weapon the man dashed back, scared to miss out, with no more than a grunt of satisfaction! After some hours in the sun, a few interesting physiological phenomena revealed themselves. As combat soldiers and medical students will be well aware, a body's stomach and intestinal gases swell these organs immensely in the heat.

If left for several days, these gases become noxious as the flesh putrefies; but after only an hour or two, they instead become a source of merriment where elephant carcases are concerned. Now and then, someone would inadvertently puncture the stomach or intestine. This was not only accompanied by a hiss, not sounding unlike that emanating from a burst pipe or a steam train, but also by a sudden emission of fluids and related matter onto the culprit and his immediate surrounds! The first elephant of the season is ritually disembowelled, the men then literally stepping into the body cavity with the intention of coating themselves in the animal's blood, for good luck. This blood has to dry on the body, and Lyell recounted the smell as being confronting and not for those with weak stomachs.

Often, meat that eventually makes it back to the village huts is sky-high, sufficient to shock the colonial European of the day, for whom 'high' meat – read rotting, in various states – was often consumed as an emetic. Lyell recalled being shocked at what rural Africans considered still edible, seeing them occasionally eat meat seething with maggots, and even green with putrefaction!

Denis Lyell considered Arthur Neumann to have been outright the greatest elephant hunter who ever lived, no doubts. He also rated Sir Alfred Sharpe as the best such ever to hunt in Nyasaland (now Malawi). Lyell recalled some of the sorties of his friend and collaborator on some works on African fauna, C.H. Stigand, as being of note. As we well know, Chauncey did indeed build up a catalogue of exploits of some note. Lyell was a confirmed 'small-bore' man, a firm believer in accuracy over brute force. He tried and used myriad calibres, but categorically stated that no-one really needs anything over a .350 for any game, noting that African game is far more tenacious of life than any other, so his statement applied worldwide. In theory he's spot-on; in practice, however, weeding wounded game out of the thick stuff, especially the Big 5, requires something over a .400, as the time and space available to drop an animal which moves like a streak, stone-dead, is very short. It takes but little imagination to work out what remains of a man when a wounded and angry member of the Big 5 arrives. 'Remains' is very much the operative…

Lyell does correctly pre-empt the above paragraph by mentioning that no responsible hunter should fire unless certain of a killing initial shot. Tony Sánchez-Ariño has laboured that very point. Lyell considered a good magazine rifle as superior to a double, for reliability reasons, and the latter's occasional tendencies to jam. He did concur with most experienced hunters' view that the most dangerous of the Big 5 depends much on personal experience and circumstance; as Capstick opined, often it is the one that catches up with you! Using Nyasaland and Northern Rhodesia for his barometer (now Malawi and Zambia), Lyell discounted the rhino as it hadn't killed many hunters there. As was the fashion and custom of the time, the leopard wasn't even discussed. He does note that where elephants and lions seem to leave soon after attacking, a buffalo often smashes a man long after he's down. Willard Price wrote that a buffalo doesn't just want you dead, he wants you flat.

I do recall from my time in Kenya that the locals considered buffalo and lion to be the deadliest. Lyell considered this to justifiably be the Kenyan view based on the large number of hunters lying in Nairobi's cemeteries, whose gravestones cite death by these two animals. He stated that the lion is far faster than elephant or buffalo and is able to take cover more easily. A mauling can also account for one, due to the septic teeth and claws. Without stating it in those words, he thus leaves one with the impression that a lion is the deadliest prospect to face out of the Big 5. Lyell did however consider the elephant as the greatest quarry for man to hunt, and that when elephants one day may be no more, the planet will be much the poorer. Lyell admired the then-recent works of a man who is the subject of the next chapter, and it makes sense that he'd feel a certain affinity to another small-bore advocate. His accurate shooting was also much admired. That man has become an absolute legend, even in the esteemed company in this book: a certain W.D.M. Bell.

The Great War changed Denis Lyell's life irreversibly; he was back in Britain and had just married Marion Brown of Dundee when he was sent to serve with the French Red Cross, under the auspices of the French Army's 45th Division. As they did so many others, the wholesale slaughter, constant shelling, trenches, rats and other horrors of war greatly affected Lyell, who felt the world had gone mad. He emerged unscathed from the conflict – which was something in itself, especially considering his role there – but the mental damage was telling. His great friend Selous was a casualty in 1917 and as the conflict finally ground out, both Lyell's nephew and Selous' son were killed. The 1920s found Lyell more prolific in his writing, the pages an obvious escape from his tortured mind.

Although Lyell truly loved his wife, he was the embodiment of his breed, the ivory hunters; his soul yearned for the wild, open spaces and its uncomplicated freedom. In his final years he moved homes several times, clearly unsettled and not at true peace. He breathed his last (aged 75) in September 1946 in Peebles, a small town in Tweeddale in the border country of Scotland. It was a year after the Second World War had ended, and the great old hunter would have been dismayed as, just two decades on from the Great War, the world went even crazier.

8. Pete Pearson

Picture courtesy of Tony Sánchez-Ariño

Tony Sanchez-Ariño will be well-known to most readers of this genre, and rightly so (stick with me; this is indeed a chapter on Pete Pearson!). Not only has he written prolifically, but Tony is now utterly unique in that he is truly the last of the great ivory hunters, having consorted with and met most of the protagonists in this volume, while hunting alongside them in the annals of history. In 2020 Tony celebrated his 90th birthday, having shot his last tusker – number 1,317 – at the age of 83. I could have nobody else write the foreword to this book and to my delight, Tony readily agreed to do so, providing some remarkable photographs to boot. To compile an exhaustive list of the ivory hunters is impossible, many of them outright poachers and/or people on the run from the law. The occupation being as hazardous as it was, many hunters died in the remotest places, often lost to history. Most never wrote of their exploits, great hunters not often being great literary heads as well, which is a pity. Those that did harbour talent at both pursuits have provided us with an array of invaluable literature, luckily capturing some of humankind's most remarkable times for posterity.

Tony wrote a near-exhaustive work on this most amazing league of adventurers, his renowned *Elephant Hunters, Men of Legend* (Safari Press, 2005) worth its weight in gold. Nobody in history is better-placed to pen such a work. Tony himself is included, as seen by Harry Manners, but to justify Tony's amazing career would easily fill an entire volume based on his terrific longevity and fastidious record-keeping, a job well beyond your humble servant. I wanted to write on those ivory hunters only that spoke to me in some way; each of the men mentioned here did. Then Tony prodded me to include one more, and I have a good idea as to why. Peter C. "Pete" Pearson was a contemporary of Robert Foran, Bill Buckley, "Deaf" Banks and "Samaki" Salmon to name a few, but the source material on him is relatively scant. Pearson himself, while most efficient, was brusque, distant and uncommunicative. He declined to record his trophies and didn't write much in the way of logs or journals, a few letters and the recollections of others comprising all we have to go on. Tony's suggestion was also made in the knowledge that, having grown up in South Africa, I now reside in Australia, the Great Southern Land which birthed Pearson.

Having lived in Australia now for the better part of fifteen years, I believe Pearson's brusqueness to merely be a feature of Australians, many of whom are loath to tout their own achievements. It's a character trait which is very much in evidence, and I find it even stronger in New Zealand. The confident, aristocratic ivory hunters from England and Germany, for instance, would seem brash and boastful by comparison. This is precisely the sort of detail which I'm sure Tony felt I might be able to brush this biography with, lending some different perspective. The 1934 article on Pearson in the *Ararat Advertiser*, titled "Pete Pearson Elephant Hunter And Game Ranger" and housed at the National Library in Canberra, indicates that Pearson was very pleasant, accommodating and always willing to assist others!

Peter Pearson was born on the 16th of January in 1877 in Melbourne; educated at the exclusive Caulfield Grammar School, he however felt incapable of settling in to an urban lifestyle and left to seek his fortune aged 18. For five years he traversed his huge homeland, counting among his ventures surveying in Victoria, shearing in Queensland as well as New South Wales, and mining at the fabled Broken Hill (now world-renowned as the world's largest global mining conglomerate, BHP).

The year 1900 found Pearson aboard a ship headed for the Boer War in South Africa; his arrival itself would be inauspicious and yet, a measure of the man in overcoming it. For some reason not recorded, the ship dropped anchor a mile from shore (1,6km). This suited Pearson not a bit, and his requests to dock were laughed off (there was likely a valid reason for this, but if a young Pearson was aware thereof, he was unimpressed). The other deckhands were highly amused at his suggestion that he's swim to shore, which might in itself have warned him; the suggestion that sharks were about definitely should have, but with a wave the young hothead leapt overboard, fully confident in his swimming ability to swim the distance, nuts to the sharks. Having completed some 200 yards (180 metres) distance, Pearson turned about to wave to his erstwhile companions again. His confidence waned a tad when they all pointed at something in the water. Pearson's gaze followed their directions and he did later admit to a thrill of advanced apprehension: knifing through the water towards him was the triangular fin of a shark, stereotypical but still remarkably effective at curing indigestion!

Sometimes one is the bat; sometimes the ball. Providence can lend a hand just as easily as it abandons one. Pete Pearson's luck was most decidedly in; a mere few yards away, a waterlogged native boat bobbed into view, as if sent. The watching men were treated to an impromptu race as Pearson dashed to the craft, the shark closing the gap all the while. A grateful Pearson got there first, but the boat was slippery as an eel and he fell off once or twice before finally making it aboard. No sooner was he on board, than the perilous craft rolled, Pearson again in the drink with a shark, and who knows how many more unseen besides! He reboarded in haste and managed to balance this time. Looking about him, however, Pearson saw how many sharks had been watching from below: circling the unsteady craft were no fewer than ten sharks! It was clear Pearson was not meant to shuck the mortal coil that day; a piece of driftwood happened by and leaning watchfully to reach it, the man now had an oar of sorts.

For half a mile or so, Pearson edged closer to shore, the sharks in close attendance. When he reached the breakers, he dived in and was washed gratefully ashore. Although a brave man, this encounter forever stuck with Pearson. Years later he'd relate how the sharks circled menacingly, ever closer, and this was his abiding memory of the sea. There is next to no information on Pearson's Boer War exploits, other than that he joined a cavalry regiment towards the end of the conflict. When the conflict ended, Pearson headed for British East Africa, arriving in Mombasa in 1903. Before long he decided to hunt elephant professionally, acquiring a .577 Nitro Express double rifle as his tool of the trade. This was the archetypal weapon for the ivory hunters, large enough to settle the hash of any elephant, even effective against charges from close proximity. Pearson settled on the Masindi district in what is now Uganda, but it soon became obvious that the permitted quota of three elephants a year was never going to suffice to earn a living.

In early 1904 in Kampala (now Uganda's capital, back then not much more than a fort and surrounding settlements), Pearson met Bill Buckley. Buckley, then already a famed ivory hunter, told Pearson about the fabulous Lado Enclave, a largely unregulated area of the Congo Free State, hard on the west bank of the Nile with Kero marking the northernmost point, Mahagi the southern.

The Lado Enclave is well known as the ivory hunters' Shangri-La, a pure paradise of free-for-all. The situation largely came about because of two factors: Belgium's inadequate administration and policing of the territory, and their mistreatment of the native inhabitants. This allowed the Lado hunters – some 25-30 of them operating at any one time – to earn the loyalty and friendship of the locals by offering them the meat from the elephant they killed, in exchange for 1) warnings and information regarding the movements of the Belgian patrols, 2) essential food supplies besides meat, and 3) porters to transport the ivory back to Uganda, on the Nile's east bank and under British rule.

Buckley didn't have to spend much time convincing Pearson; the pair set off and the partnership was notable for two things: its success in commercial terms – the men seeing one herd of 2,000 animals the one day – and the fact that this was the first and last time that Pearson partnered anybody while ivory hunting. Always the loner, Pearson's reserved and unsociable nature likely made sure of that. In his defence though, he liked to work alone and merely needed to learn the ropes; Buckley would have been as fine a teacher as could be hoped for. Pearson set up in Koba, the British administrative post on the Nile's east bank, opposite the Lado's southern point. He occasionally set off from Nimule, much to the north, but largely counted Koba as his base. He wrote several letters while at Koba, in the lulls between hunts; what is of note in his writings is the shocking conduct of the indigenous tribes, as well as the Europeans' disdain for them, which at the time at least is somewhat understandable.

One letter dated 13 November 1908 has Pearson mentioning the game abounding in the Lado, including elephant, hippo, rhino, lion and leopard beside the antelopes, which were too many to mention; but he also remarks that the tribes inhabiting the area only respected the white hunter because his rifle could provide copious quantities of what Africans value above just about anything: nice red meat. The deal suited both parties, as the ivory hunters only wanted the tusks and perhaps someone to help transport same. The tribespeople had no use for ivory and work was work; the meat was their incentive. So powerful an incentive, that in this same letter, Pearson noted the propensity toward cannibalism, particularly in poor crop years. The problem was not as severe as further west, but was present nonetheless. George Rushby experienced the phenomenon too, discreetly burying the piece of human flesh he'd been gifted, when nobody was looking.

Pearson recorded what many of the old ivory hunters marvelled at: the swarming of an elephant carcase by the tribespeople, once the hunter had taken the tusks and allowed free rein. He strongly advised anybody with a delicate stomach to preferably be elsewhere, once the locals descended upon a fallen pachyderm. Throngs of people would follow the hunters, often hundreds strong; at the kill, they would ascend trees or melt away into the undergrowth, emerging when it was over. They set upon a carcase with all manner of home-made cutting instrument, bickering and squabbling all the while over the choicest bits; Pearson noted the tribespeople often coming to blows, purposely cutting each other and a few deaths were not uncommon: he had witnessed three people killed while fighting over meat. Their favoured parts were the entrails, a theme common to both male and female tribespeople, with Pearson witnessing eight or more individuals fighting over the choicest entrails while *inside* the huge carcase.

The cannibalistic tendencies already alluded to were apparently far more prominent to the west, principally by the Bacongo tribe (now Bakongo). Pearson wrote that it was actually considered etiquette, should a tribesman die, to send the corpse to the neighbouring village for a feast! This was then readily reciprocated, so readily in fact that should someone fall deathly ill, the only reason the witch doctor would be summoned was to speed them along to death's door!

In another letter toward the end of 1910, also from Koba, Pearson recounted an event which provides an insight into life in the Lado; from this it's clear that a Shangri-La the Lado might well have been from an ivory-hunting perspective, but it certainly wasn't a free one…returning one day to his main camp in the Enclave, Pearson and his men found it looted of everything valuable, then burnt to the ground. This would have been hard enough to bear, but some of the men left in camp had been killed for consumption. Yep; literally taken away to be eaten. He wrote the letter six days after his return, and the following day Pearson was to take his remaining men – in the custom of the villages – to exact revenge and exterminate some of them! What is staggering, is that a) this was perfectly expected and accepted by the tribesfolk, and b) that Pearson openly pens it in a letter. Pearson drily remarked that this sort of thing happened from time to alleviate boredom, particularly in the dry season, when no crops can be planted!

The tribespeople consider humans as meat, so Pearson opined that the locals don't mind the reprisal, killing another human not meaning the same to them as to Europeans. Should revenge or reprisal not be exacted, the original perpetrators view it as one being quite content to be harvested, so would come again! Pearson was known to the locals, who expected him to exact revenge, and he was philosophical about dying during such a revenge raid: an arrow in the back was better than ending up a meal, although that may have happened regardless, had he copped death by arrow…Pearson gathered his scattered staff, burnt down half a dozen villages where evidence of cannibal feasting was found, with six people murdered in retribution. The Pearson party thus returned 'happy and satisfied', justice having been served by accepted tribal standards! Pearson's party was adjudged to have won this fight (their opponents' casualty list outweighing their own). This was important, because had they suffered more deaths, the victors were then entitled to raid again, killing further!

Pearson realised that his letters were to Christian, European-heritage audiences and went to some pains to explain his conduct, understanding that his relatives' reactions to this report would be shock at the punishment meted out. He does however make some sense, given where he was: he mentions that nobody in advanced Western societies is shocked when a schoolmaster flogs a boy, or a judge sentences a man to the whip (good grief, how times have changed, even these viewed as barbaric and totally unacceptable now…), saying his relatives should not think it a crime when he takes a life that has threatened his own. He reminded them that the Lado was a district where there was no law. The only law was that of the jungle: the weakest go down. In 1910, Pearson's party ventured into an area where no white man had ever been and encountered vastly superior numbers of volatile tribespeople. He tellingly - and with patent obviousness - recounted the opponents as being too strong, and having to give best. The cannibals dined off the best of Pearson's men and returned one as a curio, heavily mutilated: the man's nose and lips had been cut off.

The ivory hunters counted all this as par for the course, the risks to balance the gain, or rather the cost of such a windfall. In those years, ivory was both plentiful and valuable. Pearson considered 1908 to have been a prosperous year; his best day's yield in that year was ten elephants, the tusks of which were valued at £310. In 2019, that was worth in excess of £37,500 which provides some idea as to why the entire market existed.

*   *   *

Pearson continued to hunt the Lado Enclave until 1910, when the territory returned to British rule (following the death of King Leopold II of Belgium). He then went to the Belgian Congo, where the plethora of elephant herds had the authorities (in the Belgian- and French-controlled territories) issuing commercial hunting licences for between 20 and 30 elephants. Pearson started hunting the Ituri Forest (later to be fabled as the home of the okapi), but it was so densely overgrown that he left for the areas around the Uele (pronounced Ooh-Eh-Leh) and M'Bomou Rivers. He then tried out the Ubangi-Shari district (then part of French Equatorial Africa, now the Central African Republic).

The *Ararat Advertiser* article records one comical instance, which in retrospect, must have taken place often back in those days, indeed all over the globe, and particularly relating to the colonial times: Pearson was trailing a small herd of elephants into unfamiliar territory, when he happened upon a notice board informing him that he was now in German East Africa. A cursory search revealed several similar such boards, but Pearson being the ivory hunter that he was, loath to pass up the promise of tusks for which he'd already come some distance, he merely moved all the boards on a few miles each time. Eventually he'd managed to move the entire border 35 miles (56km) further east than it originally was, and so it remains to this day! Pearson's sardonic fatalism, which is often a feature of people living in constant proximity to violent death, was evident when recalling some close shaves with death by elephant: he opined that "one expects to be scorched, if not burnt, when playing with fire." Indeed…

As 1914 rolled around, the clouds of war had gathered, a war unlike any before it. The British government felt that the German authorities in German East Africa might arm the local tribes and sow discord among the tribespeople. The British Army decided to enlist men with extensive knowledge of the East African bush, as well as the experience of dealing with local tribes. Among these were the fabled F.C. Selous and P.J. Pretorius. Pearson too readily enlisted, and was given the honorary rank of Lieutenant in the Intelligence Department. Again, his war exploits are lost to the winds of time. When World War I ended, Pearson returned to hunting, initially in Tanganyika (the former German East Africa); here licences for up to 25 elephants were available, but over time, these too were eventually prohibited.

Pearson returned to Uganda. Despite the windfall in earnings during his time poaching in the Lado, Pearson had not managed to invest any of his money and began to feel the pinch. He was reduced to eking out a living from the ivory harvested via the few licences he could get shooting elephant in the British territories. In his defence again, there were many expenses to offset the average safari, especially large and lengthy ones. There was indeed big money to be made, but distances were enormous, and in those days before the automobile was commonplace, all transport was by porter (much if not most of tropical Africa was beset by malaria, or by the tsetse fly; this meant that horses or stock animals could not survive, and in areas where they could, they were susceptible to theft by tribespeople or attack by lions). Each protectorate required the payment of licenses.

Government super taxes and export taxes were levied too; as often alluded to elsewhere in this book, the hunter could easily walk 20-30 miles (32-48km) on the spoor of a single bull elephant. Eventually closing with the quarry, one careless action by the hunter or his men, even a twig inadvertently snapped, could result in the entire herd decamping and the entire day's tracking wasted. Often the herd would take cover in 5-6 metre-tall (16-20 feet tall) elephant grass, the hunter needing to stand on his tracker's shoulders just to see. From this precarious perch a shot was often required, and somewhat understandably, results could vary. Unreliable guides / trackers / porters were commonplace, desertion a common feature of the times. To add some spice, one must bear in mind that all of this took place in the wildest parts of Africa, where elephants are merely one of the large-and-hairies capable of shifting a hunter – careless or otherwise – into the next world.

The ivory trade, and particularly the hunters' side of things, could hardly be described as steady, budgetable income. There were times of plenty and times of famine. As did many of the adventurers thus employed, Pearson experienced leaner times. To supplement his income he commenced trading, as did many others, William Finaughty a fine example. This too, however, was beset with problems, the logistics of remote and undeveloped Africa hardly a setting for efficiency. Money was not used; barter was the legal tender, a cow being the standard unit of exchange. Donkeys were in high demand, often brought in from Abyssinia (today's Ethiopia and Eritrea) and the Karamoja region. The trouble was trying to ensure them safe passage through extremely hostile territory: if bandits didn't get your donkeys, lions would. The central trading post in Uganda was Mbale, the government station.

As the centre of the agricultural district, it became a veritable bazaar, abuzz with Indian stores and outfitters for expeditions into the 'blue' (from 'the wide blue yonder'). The biggest problem besetting the place was however the climate; the area was swampy as it lay in a valley. Heavy rains would drain into the valley and the resultant mosquito problem brought about an all-too-predictable result. For a time, Pearson persisted with Mbale as a trading base, then made for Karamoja, using cloth, beads and other such goods to secure cattle from the tribespeople. He always did a brisk trade with them but on one occasion, departing after having acquired numerous cattle – and strangely, given his propensity to work alone, he was with another white trader, most likely for safety reasons – headed in the direction of Mount Debasien (now known as Mt Kadam for the person who first scaled it, Sailesh Kadam; at 3,063 metres (10,049 ft), it lies just north of Mt Elgon). The area was very rocky and covered in thorn bushes, most unpleasant country through which to traverse.

Before long, Pearson realised that he'd been duped, the cattle all developing huge tumours under their ears. The men were headed for the village of Menimani, in earlier times a trading stop for Swahili and Arab traders along their slaving routes, with the intention of trading the cattle for local donkeys. The exchange then was a good one for the cattle owner, the going rate a cow to six donkeys. But the hundreds of villagers who'd hopefully made for Menimani were sorely disappointed, Pearson's cattle clearly diseased. Securing the few donkeys that he could with the even fewer healthy cattle he had, Pearson returned to the Kenya region of British East Africa, doubtless in a foul temper. The return trip itself was anything other than fun; donkeys show a tendency to escape and return to their original homes given the chance, and as mentioned previously, it was also open season between thieves and lions. Months of discomfort, long distances and hard work for nought.

Pearson recalled an instance that he considered to be the closest shave he ever received, in a quarter-century of hunting Africa's darkest, wildest places. Given that it stood out in a quarter-century of hunting Africa's darkest, wildest places, it would be noteworthy indeed. It was 1906 and Pearson was on a trading expedition to the interior; this was during his Lado tenure, so he was likely taking ivory out or bringing supplies back in. Regardless, the men were walking through the jungle when a lion sprang out, landing within feet of Pearson. That alone would indeed be memorable. As often happens at such times, Pearson's rifle was with his bearer, some distance behind. Luckily Pearson's immediate companion at the time was armed, and that stout soul dropped the lion stone dead with a shot through the heart. At that distance, anything other than an instantly-fatal shot would've been the end of both men, in most inventive ways too. When it isn't your time, and all that…

Pearson was to be a convert to repeater rifles; as mentioned earlier he commenced his ivory hunting career with the potent .577 NE, adding a Mannlicher 6,5 x 57mm for small game. Later he tried a .404 Jeffery, a .416 Rigby, and a .425 Westley Richards, but his favourite – indeed his favourite weapon, period – was the .375H&H Magnum. He was to use a custom model by John Rigby for many years. Never one to keep records or brag about his exploits, Pearson did once mention to the Prince of Wales (later King Edward VIII) when asked during their Uganda safari in 1928, that he'd shot three elephants in the Lado with tusks exceeding 150lbs (67,5kg) a side, both sides. His largest is credited as being 155 and 153 pounds (70 and 69 kg). What is conclusively recognised, is that Pearson collected the all-time record tusks for a female elephant, now housed in the Natural History Museum in London. They displace 55 and 59 pounds (25 and 27 kg) respectively.

*   *   *

In 1924, the government of Uganda created the elephant control section of the Ugandan Game Department. This was in direct response to the destruction of agriculture by elephants, which was resulting with monotonous regularity in the death of both people and pachyderms. The protectorate was divided into four large districts, with a designated white hunter and several native staff to oversee the game in each. Three of these four were "Samaki" Salmon, "Deaf" Banks and "Pete" Pearson, all famed ivory hunters. This was a blessing of fiscal security for Pearson, after twenty years of adventure. Pearson's area – the largest of the four – was the West Nile province, some forty thousand square miles (some 102,000 square km) which included the southern section of the old Lado, an area he knew intimately. By all accounts, Pearson finally found the tranquillity he craved and delivered sterling service.

Pearson's area contained some 12 thousand elephant; as elephant control officer, he and his team accounted for around 200 head a year, maintaining the population level. Pearson described his duties in a letter to relatives. He had some 500 miles of roads (800km), traversed (gratefully I'm sure) in a Hudson Super Six, which was incidentally a noted performance car for its day. Pearson's had a box body, which accommodated all his camping equipment, supplies and four employees in addition to the large Australian himself. Thus equipped, the party could survive for three weeks out in the 'blue'. Every so often (every 15 miles or 24 km) there were excellent administrative camps to rest at. A day's tramping after a herd involved six or seven hours' hard tramp, Pearson remarking that the bush was quite unlike the Australian equivalent. Equatorial Africa features dense undergrowth with grass often 20 feet high (6 metres), meaning the hunter needed to close to within ten feet (just 3 metres) of his quarry in order to shoot. Elephants at these distances are an interesting prospect.

In 1924 Pearson joined "Samaki" Salmon in accompanying the Duke and Duchess of York (later King George VI and Queen Elizabeth, the Queen Mother) on safari. The pair were clearly successful, as 1928 saw the same team looking after the Prince of Wales on the Uganda leg of his safari. The Prince's brother, Prince George, went to Tanganyika at the same time. The safari was arranged by the Governor of Uganda. One of the royal party was Sir William Gowers, and he was on hand to eye-witness a remarkable act of bravery by Pearson, on the very last day of the safari. The party was following the tracks of a bull elephant near the famous Murchison Falls when they were charged by a different bull. With no time to think, Pearson grabbed the Prince and flung him into the safety of a thorn bush. Then Pearson and Salmon fired simultaneously at the elephant, which crashed down a later-measured 4 yards (3.7 m) from the Prince. Sir William later wrote that "it was an exhibition of presence of mind, quickness and courage which I am glad to have been privileged to witness, and which none of those who saw it will ever forget."

The Prince presented Pearson with a royal tie pin and cufflinks in grateful thanks, but he also asked Pearson if there was anything special which Pearson might desire, within the Prince's power to give. Somewhat oddly, Pearson requested that when he died, a small monument be erected to his memory in Bakumi, which is on the escarpment overlooking Lake Albert, on the road between Masindi and Butiaba. He might have had a premonition, because in little over a year, Pearson was dead, victim of stomach cancer. He died in the hospital in Kampala on 10 September 1929. He was 52 years old. Pearson had mentioned his wish to the governor and Sir William took it upon himself to erect the monument. He consulted the Prince of Wales and set up a fund for those who wished to contribute to Pearson's memorial. Many did, the Prince of Wales among them, and the monument was erected. Tony Sanchez-Ariño has often stopped by the monument to honour one of the most fabled members of what Theodore Roosevelt called the Company of Gentlemen Adventurers: the ivory hunters of the Lado Enclave.

9. Walter Dalrymple Maitland Bell

Picture courtesy of Royal Aero Club

By now it will be patently clear that the ivory hunters of legend were anything but ordinary men; even in a time when men were men, and merely recording one's hardships was viewed as whining, these men stood out as more resourceful, braver and more absolutely free than anyone. In any given pursuit, it is normal for one person – or, over time, a very few – to stand out above the rest. In this most select group of veritable supermen, that one person would be 'Karamojo' Bell. As so often turns out to be the case, the exceptionally-gifted are adept in several spheres, and Bell was an adventurer, hunter, soldier, sailor, painter, writer and decorated fighter pilot, and was accomplished at all of those before he departed the mere mortals in 1954.

Walter Dalrymple Maitland Bell arrived kicking and screaming in 1880 to a wealthy family of Scots and Manx ancestry, on the family estate Clifton Hall in Linlithgowshire. The building, near Edinburgh, is today a school, which counts among its pantheon of famous former students the legendary Formula One racing driver, Jim Clark. Bell was the seventh of eight children and was just two years old when his mother died. His father Robert ran a successful business in coal and shale oil, but died when the boy was just six. This left Bell to be raised by his elder brothers, and it wasn't long before all the discipline problems associated with an absence of parental love and guidance became apparent. Bell ran away from a string of boarding schools and one difference of opinion resulted in Bell clouting his school captain over the head…with a cricket bat!

Aged just 13, he ran away to sea; Bell was headed for Tasmania and work in a starch factory, but within two years he was back in Scotland. Next, he was sent to school in Germany, but the free spirit loathed confines as we already know, and boarding school is nothing if not confining; add Teutonic discipline to the mix, and the outcome was predictable. Bell fashioned a homemade kayak and set off down the River Weser! He was headed for the sea but the makeshift craft foundered. The only way Bell could afford passage back to Britain was by selling his shotgun; he'd sooner have sold a limb, but had no choice. He was now 16 and his brothers had obviously heard enough of his pleading and nagging: they bought him a single-shot .303 Fraser and a second-class ticket to Africa!

Bell was in heaven, stepping off the German freighter into British East Africa at the fabled port of Mombasa. In those days before the Uganda Railway was completed, caravans to the interior were the norm, and Bell planned to work for one; but since most were run by Arabs, any whites seeking to join were seen as spies. Nature lent Bell a hand though; groups of Indian rail surveyors in mule-drawn buckboard wagons were being constantly preyed upon by lion, the mules and men alike. Eventually these men went on strike until armed guards could accompany them. As he had his own firearm and ammunition, Bell was hired on the spot for one of these guard roles, with Voi his temporary headquarters. It wasn't long, however, before Bell's heaven soured.

The neat little Fraser rifle immediately jammed its just-fired cartridge cases due to the pressure of the early cordite expanding the cases; the errant case could only be shifted with a ramrod, as if single-shot weren't already enough of a handicap. As Peter Capstick wrote in his brilliant *Death in the Silent Places* (St Martin's Press, 1981), this perhaps made Bell a finer marksman, knowing that his first shot absolutely had to kill, full-stop. He was however realistic enough to recognise this fault in his weapon as a likely fatality-in-waiting for him, and swapped the weapon for a black-powder, single-shot, falling-block .450. The Greek trader who thus acquired the .303 thought he'd scored, while Bell knew better; but the Greek had been shrewd too: the hollow copper-point .450 cartridges, of which there was a plentiful supply, were duds, and Bell had a lucky escape during his first foray with the .450, after lion of all things.

The shots failed to stop the lion, and both Bell and the African with him were fortunate that the errant ammo at least damaged the animal's jaws. When the predator retreated into cover, the African summoned a lynch mob, which descended on the compromised *Simba* with such venom and fervour that Bell – who later wrote that he seemed to be the only frightened (or was that sane??) person present – had some difficulty getting in the final, fatal shot. This sortie ingrained in Bell two things: 1) use solid bullets over expanding ones; and 2) good-bye, .450! He acquired a British Army .303 Lee-Metford magazine rifle, using 215 grain round-nose solids, and thus found his sweet spot. He became a lethal protector for the men on the surveying jobs.

One lasting impression from Bell's preference for light bores, is the fact that so many people would follow his methods and tendencies, to their extreme detriment; many were killed. It is possible, with immensely-powerful, large-bore rifles, to knock an elephant out with a head-shot which misses the brain. Several have been knocked down in this way, and were thought to be dead, by many hunters; only for them to later recover and leave, sometimes killing whoever was in the way in the process. I have mentioned before the habit of claiming a jumbo by cutting off its tail; oftentimes, an elephant so claimed was merely knocked out and recovered to wander with the extreme pain of a removed tail, which would smart long after the headache from the gunshot had worn off. Bell would almost always hit the brain, which is fatal with the smallest calibre, provided it can penetrate that far.

Many of the hunters that tried to emulate him weren't such lethal shots. A near-miss with a .577 or .600 Nitro Express will at least drop the animal; using a .275, for instance, and *not* hitting the brain, is a one-way express ticket to a premature grave, and that was the destiny of many a hunter, provided enough of them could be scraped together to bury…to provide some context as to how tiny the margin for error is when small calibres are used against dangerous game, it is now illegal to hunt the Big 5 with anything smaller than the ubiquitous .375H&H Magnum, and rightly so. Even that brilliant calibre, with its excellent penetration and thought to be the round which has felled more members of the Big 5 than any other, is usually considered too small for Group 4 dangerous game (elephant, buffalo, rhino) due to the fact that the hunter may encounter these animals in a charge, or in such close proximity in dense cover that an instantly-fatal shot is imperative.

Meanwhile, Bell kept trying to make contacts to gather sufficient native manpower for an elephant safari; with his own funds depleted, bankrolling such an expedition was out of the question. No word was forthcoming. Nairobi was reached, then left behind, when at length, news arrived of a German explorer following up the line. Bell was galvanised and thrilled; a chance, possibly...? The man was headed for the border country between Uganda and Abyssinia (now Ethiopia), where elephants were supposedly that plentiful, they almost grew on trees. Rumour had it the Teutonic adventurer was a man of some means, and Bell was ecstatic when his application to accompany the party as hunter was granted, but the proviso to his joining was to be a costly lesson for the youngster: he was to give a month's notice to the railways while the German assembled the safari in Entebbe (then Uganda's capital).

Bell counted down the days, resigned and awaited his summons from across the wide blue expanse of Lake Victoria. The weeks went by with no word; by now skint again, Bell brokered a deal with a local tribe whereby they house and feed him in exchange for his killing the local hippos that spent their nights consuming the tribal crops, and their days and nights killing the odd person foolish enough to confront them, or just in the wrong place at the wrong time. The area was a hotbed of malaria, and in short order the young Scot was struck down. Feverish and suffering, at last word reached Bell that the safari had left some time before. Bell was devastated, and with no alternative, headed back to Britain, this time in steerage, but not totally scuppered: on the credit side of his ledger, he now had some idea of where the great elephant herds were still to be found, and he had some African hunting experience in his pocket, to boot.

None of these, however, literally lined his pockets, so outfitting a safari meant asking his brothers for money again...funny how life sometimes replays events, and Bell must really have thought he'd been here before, especially when he was denied, yet again. The adventurous spirit received news of the gold rush in Alaska's Klondike region, but the news was already old. Bell nonetheless made his way via Canada, armed with (surprise!) another Fraser rifle, this time in .360 calibre with 160 rounds. During the journey over the frigid waters of the North Atlantic, Bell met a fellow Scot whose brother ran a paying claim on the gold fields. Bell first took up work here, and the pay was good, but soon left to pursue the more-lucrative (and adventurous!) meat-hunting. Next stop, Dawson, a last vestige of civilisation to which meat and furs were sent from the remote regions beyond.

The trusting young Scot appears not to have learned his lesson, soon befriending a dog-sled owner named Bill, no surname provided; this often happened in the gold camps, people preferring to remain anonymous in case they struck it rich, or to hide a dubious past. Also, it must be remembered that the poor young Scot was likely lonely. The men worked an area some 200 miles (320 km) from Dawson, Bell shooting while Bill sledded the meat back to the outpost. This went on all winter, until the thawing snows started spoiling Bell's latest meat stockpile. No sign of Bill, whose last trip had been a particularly heavy-laden one. At length the Scot hiked the 200 miles back to Dawson; of course, no-one along the way knew of this particular Bill, and once again Walter Bell was left high and dry, this time with a considerable sum actually owed him. Salvation arrived, although as it so often does, it was in a strange form and it appeared debatable whether it was salvation at all.

The Boer War broke out, which meant little to anyone in the Klondike, Bell included, but for one significant detail: it was in Africa! There were five thousand men competing for five hundred posts, but Bell's shooting – a perfect score – ensured that he'd be among the 500. Strangely – or perhaps not, many combatants finding it difficult to recount wars, the mental wounds still too raw – Bell was vague and didn't dedicate much space to the conflict in his writings. The tedium and marches resonated with him and clashes were often volleys of fire between groups who couldn't see each other. Bell was even captured, but well-treated as he was young and a Scot, which puzzled the Boers. Lightly guarded, he and a fellow prisoner disappeared one night and returned to British lines, where they were even promoted to scouts, supposedly now wise in the ways of the enemy!

The war ended with little fanfare from Bell, and with discharge he headed back to Britain. It had taken fifteen long years, but he was now 21 years old, and as such had come into his inheritance. He immediately set about outfitting a professional hunting trip to Africa. It had at long last come to be, via the roles of scholar, sailor, guard, hunter (in both Africa and North America), miner, labourer and soldier. This should inspire those who dream; persistence pays, and there are many paths and means to get to where one's heart desires to be. Bell continued his now long-standing alliance with Daniel Fraser, the Edinburgh master gunsmith. As was all the rage at the time, Fraser was promoting the power of the Nitro Express double rifles; but the brutal power was lost on Bell, the ultimate small-bore advocate. Instead, he chose two ex-military .303s, sported up for hunting. He added a Mauser pistol; more of that little weapon later!

Bell then travelled the legendary East African route: docking at Mombasa, then taking the Uganda Railway all the way through what is now Kenya, to the end of the line, Kisumu on Lake Victoria, his heart singing. *En route*, he'd sought advice on where best to embark from, and made for Entebbe, having heard that Uganda was now the area to be. At a place called Unyoro (now known as Bunyoro, a kingdom in Western Uganda; at the height of its powers, it controlled the Great Lakes region), Bell readied himself, but Africa got in the first blow: he was struck down with severe dysentery and had to get hold of a man named Ormsby, whose name and details had been provided to Bell by a mutual friend, should he require assistance. In this case, Bell certainly did! Ormsby, a colourful character involved in gun-running among other things, duly nursed the young Scot back to a semblance of rude health. Bell then set off; at last!

Bear in mind that until this time, Bell had never even seen elephants, but fittingly for a man who would become known as the greatest ivory hunter of all time, his first glimpse was something special: eight big bulls gathered around a mud wallow. And it was here, right from the off, that the second great pillar of Bell's legendary ivory hunting status would be cemented (the first being his propensity toward small bores). A soldier had once assured Bell of the brain shot on elephant for quick instant kills; he instructed Bell that the great beasts' brains were nestled in the very roof of their heads. But by the time the sixth bull so shot had ambled off unperturbed, even feeding again as it walked, Bell suspected that he'd been told a fib! He next potted the creature just behind the shoulder, intending a heart shot. The dying beast went ballistic, its vocalisations clearing the area before even this accomplished marksman could loose off again.

Bell now determined two things: 1) to prevent this cacophony by always hitting the brain, and 2) to conclusively establish where that organ hid itself inside an elephant's noggin! Back to Ormsby's for a large logging saw, and after his men had removed the head and skinned it, Bell had them cut the skull in two, top to bottom, lengthwise down the middle. Making precise sketches – and Bell could sketch; his books provide ample evidence thereof – Bell noted the brain cavity, largely in the skull's centre, just above and ahead of the earholes. And thus was the greatest brain-shooting ivory hunter birthed, his real magnum opus being to hit the disturbingly-elusive target from the rear flank. It would become known as the 'Bell shot', copied often, but never again mastered by anyone. Most stopped trying after failing at it, provided they survived in the first place. Bell's first-ever ivory weighed 81 and 78 lbs, a fine first harvest.

Civilisation's inexorable march was putting pressure on the Mohammadan trading caravans, whose main commodities were ivory and slaves. They retreated to ever-wilder haunts, one of the most remote a piece of north-east Uganda known as Karamojo (today called Karamoja, a five-district strip which was under British rule between 1916 and 1962). Due to its savagery and sheer isolation, it was also home to huge numbers of giant tuskers. Bell was drawn as if by a magnet. To this day, the area has been a byword for violent conflict and unrest, and is immensely poverty-stricken as a result. By now Bell had retained a .303, swapped the other for a .275 Rigby, kept the wicked little Mauser pistol and added a .450/.400 double rifle. He would need them in this land, where the notorious Karamojong had to murder someone to achieve manhood.

All this was bad enough, but the victim could be anyone, of either gender, asleep or awake, old or young. Bell encountered this tribe early on, having just crossed the Turkwell River (now spelt Turkwel). They were surly – to be expected – but readily told him of four bulls nearby, hoping to watch the Scot make a fool of himself with his puny rifle battery. Their eyes widened and attitudes did an about-face when the young Scot shot two of the *atome* (pronounced ah-too-meh, elephant in Karamojan) over their hearts after a long trek. News spread of the *Longelly-nyung* - 'red man', whose lethal little guns provided unexpected entertainment along with the resulting protein windfall.

It was during this time that Bell slaked his thirst, and that of his men, by having the tracker, Pyjalé, open the water stomach of a just-killed jumbo one day when far from base camp. It was brutally hot and the men's water supplies were depleted, leaving them staring at the very stark reality of death by thirst. Bell recounted the water as being clean, odourless and admittedly a bit warm, but life-saving nonetheless. I mentioned how hunters have been saved from dying of thirst in this way, in Chapter 4. Hunting along and impressing the watching hordes, Bell reached Mani-Mani, 150 miles (240km) beyond the Turkwell. The awaited conflict materialised, and Bell benefitted from a misunderstanding to draw a line in no uncertain terms with the Karamojong, and the slave caravan traders who would stop at nothing to maintain their way of life.

Well aware of the ever-present threat of murder, Bell learned that five of his men were missing among the maze of huts in the area. Bell took five of his askaris (each fortified with a .577 Snider carbine) and promptly took a great portion of the Karamojong cattle herd. This was tantamount to sacrilege and in short order, some 400 spearmen appeared in protest. Bell's party stood their ground, and his reputation had already preceded him: several elders started to throw grass in the age-old submissive plea for mercy. Bell demanded his porters' safe return, threatening to kill all the captive cattle and send off some of their tribesmen to happier hunting grounds along with them. The porters promptly reappeared; they'd merely gotten lost, but the message was clear: Bell was not someone to be trifled with.

Bell did make mention - as have many white men before him and many since - of the phenomenal recuperative powers of the bush African. A man who had suffered a gaping wound under his arm from a spear thrust, calmly sauntered up to a white doctor and raised the arm for inspection. With each breath, a flap of lung appeared and disappeared through the wound. "Take him away!" ordered the sawbones; "there is nothing more to be done; the lung is involved (exposed to the elements, a sure sign that fatal infection would be along shortly)!" Three weeks later, Bell noted, that same man was up and about again, healed for all intents and purposes! He marvelled at the resilience of the African, with a defining coverall, Bell believed, being his wondrous capacity for enjoying life. Makes modern man reflect a little, doesn't it...?

Bell's description of his meeting with the slave lord, Shundi, makes for captivating reading; his harem alone numbered some 80 women. This giant, who rose to prominence despite being a Kavirondo slave himself, is amazing enough – realising that the Koran forbids a Muslim from keeping another Muslim as a slave, Shundi had the smarts to convert to Islam himself and was free – but he is also thought to be the master of the man who shot the tusker with the heaviest ivory in history, on the slopes of Kilimanjaro, a man named Senoussi. Most records wrongly attribute the slave as being owned by the mythical Tippu Tib. The caravan traders clearly saw Bell as a spy and a threat, and so sought to do him harm. Their chance came soon afterward, and it would bring the deadly little Mauser pistol to the fore. The dry season was now in its crushing pomp; animals and people were desperate.

Bell hastened to the wells when summoned; some of the Karamojong were preventing his cattle from drinking, merely laughing when Bell sought answers. Having his men again herd the poor bovines nearer, three of the spearmen actually started to beat the herd animals in the face to drive them off! Bell's Gaelic blood flared up; snatching a war club from one of the 40 antagonists around him, he brought it down with all his strength onto the head of the nearest man. The blow would normally have split a man's skull like a grape, but the club actually shattered, while the would-be victim grinned broadly at Bell! The Karamojong wear a clay headdress moulded with their hair, and it hardens into a veritable helmet; if Bell didn't know this before, he did then. As is the African's wont, the men present burst out laughing at the unexpected event, and Bell was about to succumb himself when he noticed one of the spear-wielding heroes piercing the groundsheet which created the waterhole in a small depression. The temperature of Bell's blood instantly reverted to boiling; enter the little Mauser…

Back then, a gun's effectiveness was measured by the extent of the noise, the magnitude of the cloud of black powder and the size of the hand-cannon itself (and as mentioned before in this book, hand-cannons are what some of the old elephant guns unquestionably were). The Africans believed the hole caused by the bullet merely allowed the fire to enter, this latter actually causing a person's demise. Huge was their shock when the vicious little weapon rattled off comparatively silently – that wasn't unexpected – rendering the perpetrator's spear into matchwood in milliseconds (that was!). The spearman started retreating, Bell tackling the powerful tribesman and holding him with difficulty until his men swarmed the native. The other Karamojong started to seep back, incensed at their pal's capture, but the Mauser spoke again, peppering the ground at their feet like a B-grade Western until a good 500 yards separated them from Bell's party.

Bell demanded ten goats and sheep for the man's release, and he didn't have to wait long; the conniving traders' plan to have the Karamojong scare off or kill Bell had backfired. He was now hugely respected – it was not lost on the tribesmen that Bell could easily have killed them all, given what the phenomenal little gun had done to the spear – but the Mauser, somewhat understandably, was treated with something akin to naked terror. It became most respectfully famed as 'Bom-Bom', and when Bell would venture out to hunt, throngs followed, merely on the chance of watching the little gun in action. Pitching camp late one night in an area hotly disputed between the Bukora and Jiwé tribes, Bell had an odd experience which made him shake his head afterward; there was always something happening, but even in this pastime which was anything but boring, occasionally something occurred that was extraordinary.

Some lions were spotted leaving the rocky area for the plains and despite the growing dark, Bell managed to anchor two of them quite close to camp. He had just gotten back to his tent and settled himself beside his fire when shouts and a commotion were heard from the direction of the dead lions, and his men who were skinning them. Rushing back rifle in hand, Bell saw one lion skinned already, but the other had returned to life when half-flayed! The men's shock can be imagined - not to mention that of the poor lion! It appeared that Bell's shot had paralysed it, the head still active and angry, while the body was *hors de combat*, and had already had much of its epidermis removed!

One of the skinners had been sitting on the beast when it suddenly growled, and his recount of the event back in camp kept the men entertained for some time. I'll bet; strange sense of humour, those tough porters seem to have had! Bell loved those days in the dry season; no mosquitoes around, full stomachs, ample excitement in sitting up for elephant or lion, hearty companionship; he recalled them fondly. He even introduced his men to football, after rugby produced too many injuries. Despite lugging full loads all day, the men played until dark halted proceedings, anthills and thorns notwithstanding!

*   *   *

In 1910, Bell found himself in the fabled Lado Enclave, where he drank huge quantities of hard liquor with the motley crew of counts, paupers and dukes, while awaiting his hunting license. Once it arrived, he was to reap no fewer than 210 elephant. Although they only averaged 27lbs a tusk, the sheer number still meant more than five tons of ivory. Already by now known as 'Karamojo' Bell, the Scot next hunted Liberia in 1911, which was unusual in that here, the black man ruled the white. Bell maintained his politeness and received same in kind. From there, it was on to French Equatorial Africa at a place called Bangui. As the entire area was a giant river basin, access was difficult, leaving an elephant-rich haven, if one could only get to it...so Bell did; he ordered a steam boat from England which arrived in sections and had to be assembled. When finished, the 35-foot (11,5m) craft was ideal, burning wood for fuel and possessed of a flat, shallow draft. This made traversing the Ubangi River and its myriad islands no chore at all.

Hunting from it was hugely successful and profitable, but tapered off with the rains, the animals always dispersing when no longer beholden to permanent water. Bell – who noted such things with some accuracy – considered at this point in his life that he'd covered over 60 thousand miles (nearly 100 thousand kilometres) traipsing after jumbos, all on foot, and excluding mechanical or mounted transport! Bell headed toward the Chari-Chad watershed (between what is now Chad and the Central African Republic), adding to his bag almost daily from the luxury of the steamer. One day a letter arrived, wherein it was announced that the world had been plunged into the Great War; Bell immediately went back to Bangui, sold everything and made for London, which he reached via Bordeaux. You see, he'd always harboured dreams of joining the Royal Flying Corps...care to bet against him, despite his being, at 34, probably a decade beyond such perilous pastimes?

You guessed right; despite the dodgy entrance process (upon learning that he could ride a bicycle, Bell was granted a shot at becoming a fighter pilot!), the Scot earned his wings. To his great joy, Bell – who had expected to be posted to France – was sent to serve under Smuts in the East African campaign, his airfield standing at the foot of Mt Kilimanjaro! His joyous spirit immediately landed him in the soup, however; chosen to test the newly-assembled and tricky early fighters (the squadron was equipped with B.E.2.Cs and Henri Farman machines), Bell performed such lurid loops, turns and flips that he landed to an apoplectic squadron commander, who awarded Bell the dubious distinction of being the first pilot grounded in the East African campaign, on either side; the Germans never brought combat aircraft to Africa.

Bell was furious, as can well be imagined; a dream lay in tatters, so close to fruition. He applied to join ground intelligence, who were thrilled to get someone with his bushcraft and knowledge of local languages. For some time, Bell was a scout behind enemy lines, even meeting Smuts's chief scout, another legendary bushmaster, P.J. Pretorius. Bell's war sorties were many and varied, and he won the Military Cross twice. He was also mentioned five time in dispatches, a great honour. We are well aware of Bell's courage and abilities, but wartime propaganda publications being what they are, famous names are often mentioned – and created – in these papers. Honour or no, I place rather more value on the promotions and medals. As Peter Capstick wrote, what is beyond dispute is Bell's terrific physical conditioning and phenomenal marksmanship.

These combine to render Bell the greatest ivory hunter of all time. His detractors mention his small-bore fixation as a weak point, but none ever question his prowess. Consider the small-bore factor; in a time when ammunition was unreliable, rifles occasionally too, surely once or twice in a career of any length, even for a naturally-lucky man – and we all know someone who seems to enjoy a Midas touch – one might miss a small, moving, elusive target like an elephant's brain by millimetres, but Bell never did. The fact that so many Bell-inspired hunters subsequently paid the ultimate price when flattened by an irate member of the Big 5 that they had wounded with a light rifle, just makes Bell's own achievements that much more mind-blowing. Add in the fact that walking 60 thousand miles is humbling in itself, but doing so through that terrain and in that danger is another level altogether.

After the Great War had ended, Bell revealed that he was human after all: he needed recovery time. Years of malarial and other effects had taken their toll, and the strain of fighting one's way through a world war wouldn't have helped. Bell had married (to Katie, the daughter of Sir Ernest and the Lady Soares), but his soul yearned for the ivory trail; he returned to Africa, this time (fittingly!) to the Ivory Coast, hunting the Niger and Benue Rivers by canoe with his retinue and old war colleague, Wynne Eyton. They covered some eight thousand miles (12,800km) up the Bahr Aouck and back, collecting great gobs of ivory for most of the way. Bell did mention tremendous numbers of lions, most of immense body size, but the males being poorly-maned. This would be the subspecies *Senegalensis*, the West African lion, and males are indeed huge in body, but sport unremarkable manes.

Bell then returned home to his wife and this time it was to be for several years, the legendary hunter seemingly content at last with his towering achievements. He did eventually get back to Africa, but it was with American friends on an automobile safari. The world had changed. Bell had actually planned one last ivory hunt in 1939, but the Second World War intervened. That motorised safari turned out to be the great man's last really large excursion. He bought an estate in the Scottish Highlands, nestled near Garve in Ross-shire, and named it Corriemoilie. He wrote more; several of the articles he'd penned for the Country Life magazine had been published as a book in 1923, and which has rightly become part of hunting folklore: *The Wanderings of an Elephant Hunter*. Over twenty years later, *Karamojo Safari* came out (published by Harcourt Brace of New York in 1949), which centred more on Bell's fun and games in that legendary region.

After his death, Neville Spearman and the Holland Press published *Bell of Africa*, which had been assembled by Whelan, in 1960. It was essentially Bell's life story and included much of the material from his first book. In his later years, Bell and Katie spent much time sailing and racing their superb yacht *Trenchemere*, the first steel-hulled racing yacht. It displaced 37 tons and was commissioned in 1934. The vessel was requisitioned for government war service in 1939, but was never used and whiled away the war safely in the Caledonian Canal. She was returned to Bell in 1946 and he continued to use her extensively, until failing health forced him to sell her in 1950. Bell had suffered a mild heart-attack in 1947 yet continued sailing, as well as hunting deer and rabbits near his estate with a .220 Swift; he remained a devotee of high-velocity small-bores to the end. A larger heart-attack on 30 June 1954 finally claimed the life of the great Walter Dalrymple Maitland 'Karamojo' Bell; but it couldn't take away the legend.

10.   James Sutherland

Scotland has been the source of a disproportionate number of the great explorers and ivory hunters of legend; they stack up like a Who's Who of fabled African adventurers: Livingstone, Gordon-Cumming, Lyell, James Grant, 'Karamojo' Bell, John Hunter and the subject of this chapter, James Sutherland. Sutherland was born in 1872, and unlike most of the great ivory hunters, he actually hunted almost uninterrupted from 1899 to 1932, when he died. Given the dangers and constant exposure to death in most inventive ways, Sutherland did well to die by some means other than elephant. He was to succumb to poisoning, but was in the field, so to speak, so largely fulfilled his hope that he would die on the trail of an old tusker. Because of this lengthy, largely-unbroken tenure, Sutherland was the elder statesman among the great ivory hunters.

His career can broadly be divided into two parts, the first lasting until 1912, when his legendary work *The Adventures of an Elephant Hunter* (MacMillan & Co. of London) was published; the latter part stretching from then until his death. Despite prodding and his own intentions – he kept his diary and notes up to date – he never published again, which is a great pity: his writing was of a very high standard indeed. The missing latter two-thirds of his career (from a literary perspective) were covered to some extent by Andy Anderson and George Rushby, two legendary ivory hunters themselves, who were both friends of Sutherland. Aged just 24 – and that said, older than many of the other ivory hunters had been upon setting out – the times actually convey to us that Sutherland was a late starter. The elephant populations were already in serious decline by the late 1890s. Sutherland's tenacious tenure would emblazon his name in history.

The young man reached Cape Town with £500 Sterling lining his pockets, a fortune at the time. One suspects that all manner of lout befriended the young Scot, great wealth attracting heaps of 'friends' then, as it always has. He lost all his money to what he termed 'bad investments' and actually spent time in hospital with a gunshot wound…interesting times. This led the dapper little Scot into prize fighting, at the time a ragged and disreputable practice even at its best. Size and weight categories were largely ignored, so a smallish man like Sutherland (175cm or 5ft 9in and weighing just 69kg or 152 lbs) was obviously most accomplished to flourish in these circles. And flourish he did; after a few bouts in Johannesburg – hairy, hoary, gold-rush Johannesburg, probably almost as rough a place as it is today – Sutherland set off for Beira in Portuguese East Africa (now Mozambique).

Obviously short on cash, he was entered into a bout with a large man who had been India's heavyweight champion. That fellow displaced 180lbs (over 80kg) and topped six feet, but the 200-Pound prize went to the gutsy little Scot when the champ was knocked senseless in Round 9. That Sutherland was living a raucous life is evidenced by the fact that shortly after, the Portuguese police sent a cop to arrest the Scot for a 'minor infraction', but that infraction quickly became major when Sutherland put the good constable in hospital. He clearly didn't want to be arrested! Jim got going while the going was good, catching a British steamer headed for British Central Africa (now Malawi). Given this hectic start to his life in Africa, it's little wonder Jim Sutherland chose to 'go legit' and become an ivory hunter (as one does!). It places some perspective on how rough his life had been up until that point!

After serving a year as an apprentice, Jim worked his way up to the north of the country. He actually recounted the loss of a dog as tipping the scales and finally driving him to gather ivory. The dog was Brandy, a bull-terrier which was his first dog in Africa. It survived a going-over by a leopard before eventually succumbing to the eternal tsetse fly. Burying his beloved pet beneath the floor of his trading store, Jim could no longer stand the place and burnt it down, stock and all. He then left on the ivory trail, never to return. Everything was just peachy until 1902, when the Portuguese authorities got wind of the Scot's illicit ivory gathering (read: poaching). They sent a patrol up north to arrest him, but had forgotten the locals, to whom a regular provider of mountains of protein is a veritable demigod. They warned *Bwana Sutherlandi*, and that resourceful gentleman merely hopped over the Rovuma River (now known as the Ruvuma) into German East Africa (now Tanzania).

There he stayed until 1914, but was astute enough to do everything by the letter, applying for licenses and gaining mutual respect from the Germans. Sutherland wrote of an inborn wanderlust from very young, his father having spent much of his own early adulthood gold prospecting in New Zealand and Australia. He also counted his love of the challenge to hold a greater attraction than the fiscal gain. Like Neumann before him, Sutherland totally adjusted to his life of relative solitude in the remote, wild places, finding it immensely difficult to adjust back to 'civilised' city life. He recounted waking to the birds' morning song, maybe some chattering primates or a snort from a buffalo. Sutherland would down a cup of cocoa before exercising with dumbbells every day, followed by a cold bath and rub-down. Tea and biscuits sufficed to break his fast, then onto the trail for elephant spoor.

One eventful morning – around 4am – Sutherland was awoken by Simba, his head tracker. The man was highly excited. 'Bwana, dembo!' he exclaimed (Master, elephant!). Sutherland sat bolt-upright at the magic word. 'Wappe?' he enquired, 'Where?' Nearby, came the answer, and as if in verification, a branch was snapped not far off. It was, however, 4am and pitch-dark, so quelling his excitement, the Scot rolled over, pulled his blanket close about him and re-entered his alpha-trance! The whole of the previous day, the hunter and his party had tracked four big bull elephants, but each time they closed with the pachyderms, the fickle wind would shift, and the bulls would instantly put lots of space between them and the following humans. It was a most-disappointing day, made worse by the fact that the remainder of the safari – those with the food supplies – hadn't caught the advance party up by nightfall. Sleep refreshed the men, but thirst and hunger were maddening.

The men were up as the dawn streaked the sky. Jim sent his two batmen to the Mbemcuru River to slake their thirst, then meet the kitchen party, while the hunter took Simba (carrying the .318 axite light rifle; axite was a new type of propellant powder at the time) and second tracker Chingondo (lugging the huge .577 double). The idea was to get to the elephants which had been heard in the small hours, hopefully collecting one or two before noon, then head back toward the river. The tracks showed that these were the same four bulls that had led the men a merry dance the day before! They were headed for thick bush in which to while away the hottest hours and had some three hours' start on the men, but were feeding as they go. The men figured on closing before the bulls reached their haven.

Around 10am the men closed, but true to the script, the wind again swung and the bulls shot away! This was enough for Chingondo, who'd been carrying the double rifle. He collapsed exhausted, refusing to continue. Sutherland pointed him to the river and took the heavy rifle himself. For four hours the thirsty pursuers were led a merry waltz across some of the worst countryside imaginable: thorn scrub – the default Tanzanian fare, known as the *nyika* (from whence the name by which the country was known before Tanzania, Tanganyika), then elephant grass 4-5 metres high (13-16 feet), then dense thickets, often the haven of lions by day. Crawling after the bulls through some interminably-thick scrub, a crashing sound was heard as the huge animals decamped in haste. They'd winded the men again! Disappointment, fatigue and anger surged through the men, and they collapsed, momentarily beaten.

Close to dozing off, Jim was wakened by Simba offering his snuff-box. Although snuff wasn't his habit, Sutherland was instantly revived, energised and able to think clearly. As it was late afternoon by now, the men figured the 'phunts would make for water, and set off on the trail at a slow jog. After an hour they just managed to spot the tail of the mini-herd as it entered some long grass. With darkness not far off, the men drew on the last reserves of their energies in the cool air, adrenalin coursing through their veins. Their mad dash continued until breaking bamboo alerted them to the bulls' proximity. Espying the bulls from an anthill, the men crept nearer, the wind for once no longer fickle. At length, and at just 30 yards, the biggest bull slowly turned, offering a perfect shot. Jim Sutherland took it, the bull dropping as if poleaxed.

The others rushed to his side, a second falling to a side brain shot. One of the remaining two dashed off, the last standing confusedly by. A heart shot followed by one into his neck vertebrae did for him, the three lying together as if stacked there. With about half an hour of daylight remaining, Jim determined to at least make an attempt on the fourth, so hared off in pursuit. In short order, crashing bamboo *behind* them indicated that the last elephant had circled round, but in doing so, he caught their scent and clattered off again. This resulted in some very difficult trailing through a maze of bamboo. With the light fading fast, Jim thought they'd do better by seeing the lie of the land ahead. Some 100 yards (90 metres) to their left was a tree of suitable height, so Simba made for it, intending to climb it and suss out the scene. He'd only just left when a terrific scream reached Jim's ears, followed by the reappearance of a fleeing Simba!

Behind him was an elephant in full cry. Sutherland yelled at his tracker to break left, hastily firing and hitting the bull in the side of his head. The animal staggered, then came on, unperturbed! Just 30 yards (27 metres) now separated a wide-eyed Simba from being minced. A horror-movie sequence then played out as Simba fell headlong, but adrenalin had him up and at full speed again as if he'd never fallen (somewhat understandably!). In his panic, Simba dashed straight on toward his boss, costing Sutherland precious firing time. Dashing right to open the angle, Jim swatted the bull in the forehead again, the 750-grain surprise rocking the huge animal back onto his haunches. He wasn't down, though, and returned to the long grass from whence both he and Simba had just emerged.

Grabbing the .318 from Simba, Jim put a bullet into the vicinity of the 'phunt's heart, which improved its temper not a bit; instead, the bull swung about-face, with that shrill, elephantine scream of fury. If you've never heard it, I assure you that once you do, you won't forget it. At 40 yards in fading light (36 metres), Jim shot him in the face, but it had no effect at all. Neither did a second, similarly-placed round. The elephant ate up the distance between them, blood streaming down its forehead. Working the bolt, Jim Sutherland realised that his rifle's magazine was empty! "That's you, old son!" he thought to himself, flinging the rifle in the bull's face in one final, impotent act of defiance before diving left off the path. As he did so, a loud report sounded; Simba had managed to drop a cartridge into the heavy double, and just in time perforated the bull through the trunk, the bullet passing through that organ and entering the elephant's mouth.

The elephant swung right, smashing a large tree over and exploding through the fallen branches, to career on for another 50 yards (45 metres) before stopping. Sutherland fed two more rounds into the double and sent one of those into the great beast's heart. It was over. There was time at this juncture for some melancholy reflection by Sutherland, to dilute the elation. The moment seemed surreal, and he wished he could better describe the light, sights, sounds and smells. Trudging wearily over to where Simba stood, Jim gave his tracker's hand a hearty shake before both collapsed, exhausted. They lay for a long while, neither speaking. No words were needed. After a rest, their thirst – which you'll recall, was severe to start with – returned with a vengeance. Simba even made for the dead elephant, lapping up some of the creature's blood.

Sutherland, almost insane with thirst, grabbed a handful of the nearest tree's leaves, hoping that chewing them would yield at least some moisture. Just in time Simba stopped him; the tree was poisonous. Simba tottered into the woods in search of roots while Jim collapsed again. In only a few minutes Simba returned triumphant; he'd found some *ntamba* stems (a water-bearing creeper). The men sucked the juice for what seemed like an eternity, the killing thirst seemingly impossible to slake. Eventually however, some semblance of normality was attained. Next need was for food, and some roasted elephant heart was just the ticket. After washing it down with more *ntamba*-creeper water, the men stretched out beside their fire and were dead to the world in no time.

The next morning, the pair made it to the Mbemcuru River and the main party. A hot bath and good meal did wonders, and they all returned to the bulls for photographs, and to gather the precious ivory. The exertions of this hunt laid Sutherland low with a bout of malaria, but rest, tea, quinine and whisky healed him in short order.

* * *

Sutherland had a notable experience in 1905, his first excursion into combat. This was to help put down the Maji-Maji Rebellion in German East Africa. It was basically an uprising against colonial rule, the Germans being rather more heavy-handed in administering their colonies than were Britain. German levels of efficiency were always going to be nigh-impossible in Africa, and force was readily used in the attempt. The conflict largely lasted until 1908 and raged between Bagamoyo on the east coast (a bit north of Dar-es-Salaam), as far west as Kalenga and everything south of that to the border with Portuguese East Africa, an area which encompassed what was effectively the southern half of the country.

Maji is water in Swahili. The theory – especially when fortified by consuming and/or smoking dubious substances, and assured by witchdoctors of the veracity of the facts – was that the bullets of the authorities would turn to water upon striking the bodies of the 'freedom fighters'. Many of the rebels would later attest to the fact that it did feel like that, but the liquid that trickled down tended to be red and was accompanied by a searing agony. At least, those that lived to recount the experience did…Sutherland's bushcraft and knowledge of the terrain were invaluable to the German authorities and after acquitting himself with honour and distinction – he was even wounded by a spear – he became one of very few Britons in history to be awarded the Iron Cross!

The hair-raising encounter with the four bulls as previously recounted notwithstanding, Sutherland considered his most exciting elephant adventure to be one which befell him in 1908. It was near the village of Sultan Leanduka, which was beside the River Luwegu. The party was trailing a small herd comprised of five huge bulls. All day, they'd been led through dense thorn scrub, interspersed with the thick, razor-sharp reeds which line the rivers in that part of the world, broken only by short trips into the dried-up tributary rivers to the Luwegu. Most people have walked in sand, and doing so in cooking heat, weighed down by heavy firearms while being permanently on edge, won't score highly on any fun charts. At length, with evening looming, the men closed with the herd in a patch of flattened grass, the clear visibility allowing Sutherland to drop four of the five as fast as you read this.

But the fifth…as the great beast dashed across a clearing, away from a fire the men had just started, Jim potted it in the region of its heart. Its reaction was concerning, to say the least. The giant bull spun about and came for Sutherland in a full-on, all-out charge. The speed was terrifying as the enraged creature ate up the distance, but Jim knew he needed to be calm and steady; his next shot needed to count. When the bull got to within 20 paces, Sutherland loosed off the second barrel. It should have been a palpable hit, entering the bull's eye and actually exiting his skull as well, yet he hardly flinched! Jim knew this was it, watching astonished as the huge beast hit him, a tusk slamming him into his tracker, Simba, a few paces to Jim's right. Before he could move, he was picked up by his shirt and rocketed into the air.

During his impromptu flight, Sutherland was convinced that the last meal he'd ever have was his previous one, and was pondering this when he landed on the elephant's back. He needn't have been too concerned about so precarious a perch, because he wasn't long in falling off. The downside was the considerable distance from which to fall upon one's face. Jim was then in that curious state in which people often find themselves during times of mortal danger; there is no fear at all, but all senses and faculties are fully functional. It's likely the sense of deadening shock which serves to anaesthetise one. I wrote of this in my previous book, *No Covenant*. It appears to be the same that seems to numb some herbivores while they are being eaten alive; cheerful thought. Jim wrote (some four years on in *Adventures*) that at the time, he hoped the end would be fast at least, be that by tusk or trampling.

He was contemplating these possibilities, even inexplicably looking to see where his bullet had hit, when he was seized by a shoulder and flung 40 feet (13 metres or 14 yards) away into a tree. This impact knocked him out, and he came to not long after, with Simba shaking him. Some 30 yards away (27 metres), their quarry stood testing the air, looking for *his* quarry! Jim tried to stand, but rather unsurprisingly, couldn't. Having dropped the .577 in the fracas, Jim grabbed the .318, sitting painfully while using Simba's shoulder as a gun rest. He just couldn't keep the rifle steady (again, understandably), and his shot - meant for that vital spot between ear and eye which means a brain shot - harmlessly slapped into the top right of the elephantine noggin. The result was predictable: the elephant was able to locate his tormentor, and came on with renewed fury.

Simba held the barrel steady and as the bull closed to 14 or 15 paces, Sutherland put his next shot right between the bull's eyes. The bull dropped to his knees and another bullet ended his tenure on planet earth. This great beast did feature a strange curiosity in that his tail was totally hairless. Sutherland kept it to show all-comers. The next morning saw the usual photos taken, then Sutherland made the trip 'home' to his base-camp, which was reached by evening. Sutherland wrote that the camp was a glorious sight, waxing lyrical about the tents and the homely sounds of people cooking and chatting around fires. That is indeed a welcoming, wonderful picture, but there's nothing like a near-death experience to help one appreciate the mundane and the commonplace!

Soon the party was surrounded by chattering people, all trying to discern what had happened and why *Bwana Sutherlandi* was machilla-borne (A machilla is basically a blanket attached to two poles, bearing a prostrate and usually-wounded man between the poles). Sutherland was partial to his rub-downs to keep his musculature in prime condition, and never was one more necessary than then; an olive oil and whisky salve served to soon have him feeling almost human again, but the bush telegraph had already advertised otherwise, far and wide. The speed with which news travels on the bush African grapevine can be mystifying and truly phenomenal, and when Sutherland took his impromptu flight into the tree – propelled thence by the elephant – some messengers set off then to spread the news of his untimely demise!

Over a little time, he was luckily restored to the land of the here-and-now. Sutherland laughed to himself at the distorted way the incident was reported a month or so later in the *Deutsch-Ostafrikanische-Gazette* (German East-African Gazette) of 3 October, 1908. He was reported as having picked an opportune moment to leap from the elephant's back before slaying it! The news doesn't always tell the actual story, which doesn't seem to have changed much over time...

*   *   *

Another notable Sutherland sortie involved a huge, murderous elephant named Kom-Kom (the Mighty One). It was in a particularly wild place, between the Lehombero and Luwegu Rivers in what is now Tanzania. Sutherland pitched camp near the village of one Jumbe Iperie, in some particularly thick bush. Between this village and the *kraal* of Nagoromenia, some 30 miles (48km) distant, the vicious bull elephant ran his haunt, raiding *shambas* and even killing people. The women of Iperie's village were even frightened to draw water from the nearby stream; it was against the backdrop of this pathetic scenario that a delegation from the village approached Jim to save them, by hopefully killing the beast. The locals believed the elephant to be the reincarnated spirit of one of their great chiefs from days gone, who had been murdered.

Sutherland was in the business of gathering ivory, and since this bull sported some, saw this as a happy side-effect to his performing a public service. This huge bull was rumoured to while away the daylight hours in the Lerongie jungle, where few humans went at the best of times, and almost none frequented since Kom-Kom had taken up residence there. At night he'd emerge to gorge on the local produce, terrorising the populace and exterminating anyone foolish enough to cross him. Sutherland agreed to assist the villagers and at first light the next day, headed for Nagoromenia's *kraal*. In short order the men were dew-soaked and chilled, the rising sun a welcome comfort. In the late morning, a herd's spoor was found and a short, exciting chase ensued. Two bulls fell to Sutherland's guns but the accompanying villagers assured Jim that Kom-Kom was neither of these.

Heading for the Lerongie jungle, the party passed through the *kraal*, but its crops had been hard-hit the previous evening. The *shamba* owners begged Jim to stay the night in the hope of catching a returning Mighty One in the act. The night however, was filled with stillness, a fact the natives explained away as Kom-Kom being warned in a dream that he would be hunted, and should best stay away. Since he didn't appear, who's to say that didn't actually happen? The party set off again at daybreak and around 8am came across the bull's tracks. A thrill ran through the men: the usual hunting excitement, with the added effect of this huge animal's dangerous reputation. By noon they had neared, the droppings fresher and the broken foliage fresh. The elephant could be heard ahead, but the bush was too dense to see him. Jim waved Simba behind him as was his custom when nearing the quarry.

Suddenly, there came the loud sounds of an elephant crashing through the bracken, and after determining with some relief that the creature was fleeing away from them, the men set off in hot pursuit. The great creature led them a merry dance through the broiling heat, and through the buffalo bean which grew between the stalks of long grass. This plant gives off hairs that coated the men on contact, producing a maddening itch. The only remedy for this back then was to rub the affected area with wood ash, but that was slightly impossible at the time! In more modern times, someone discovered that coconut oil works wonders for countering buffalo bean hairs. At length, Kom-Kom entered a thick patch of vegetation and started to double back on his spoor. He was used to being hunted, and this was a bad sign; the murderous and experienced elephant was tired of being chased.

The men accordingly came on more carefully, nerves and senses on edge. They frequently stopped to listen intently, but no sound emanated from the bush except the wind in the leaves...then followed a moment which would have been funny, had it not instantly placed the men in mortal danger: Simba tried, but failed, to supress a huge sneeze. The result was an instant scream of rage from *behind* the men as Kom-Kom charged the party! The trackers scattered like leaves before the wind and Jim just had time to raise the .577, desperately loosing off both barrels into the Mighty One's face. The huge beast veered away and came to a standstill some 15 yards off. Simba coolly handed Jim the loaded 10.75mm, knowing the double was now empty. All that could be seen of Kom-Kom was the tip of his trunk, testing the air.

When he turned toward the men, Sutherland estimated where his head would be and pressed the trigger. The result was hardly ideal; the Mighty One charged! Frantically working the Mauser-style bolt to chamber another round, Sutherland whacked the bull in the face as his lowered head burst through the shrubbery, the bullet striking some inches above his right eye. Next instant the huge animal hit, and Jim remembers being slammed to the ground slightly to the left, under a pile of vegetation. Kom-Kom's impetus luckily took him several yards beyond Sutherland and he stood sniffing the air, seeking out the hated man-scent. Jim was thrilled to find his rifle undamaged beside him, and chambered the last cartridge. At the same time, Simba and Ntawasie yelled at the elephant to draw his attention away from the white man.

The move worked, and gave Sutherland the time to plaster Kom-Kom in the lungs, which made him instantly forget his new-found target of the two trackers. The bull burst through the bush for some 70 yards to Sutherland's left. Jim knew he needed to extricate himself from the vegetable morass which had half-shielded and half-crushed him. He was beaten and bleeding but given the adrenalin rush, hardly noticed these afflictions; they would hurt plenty later. Meantime he swapped the magazine rifle for the now-reloaded double, and set off after the Mighty One again. The men knew the canny bull would double back again and wait for them, so set off at a detour rather than spoor him. They got to within 12 yards (11m), when a shifting eddy of wind allowed him to scent the men. He circled around to a spot where he expected the men to appear but they had double-guessed him. Through the foliage they stood watching the magnificent beast, tall and proud as he waited to kill his pursuers.

A gap in the bush allowed Jim to brain the animal and he did so, the huge elephant collapsing with his tusks entangled in vines. *Socolai! Socolai!* Sutherland intoned; it is finished! The men took up the cry. Kom-Kom, the Mighty One, was no more. The men spent the night near the huge carcase, and next morning considerable numbers of villagers swamped the area, overjoyed at the demise of the killer bull; they covered the party in food, honey and *pombe*, native beer. All except one; an ancient witchdoctor appeared, highly annoyed that Sutherland had accounted for what he considered a bearer of great fortune. He changed his tune however, when some of the meat appeased his spiritual reservations!

Kom-Kom had reasonably-small ivory, for all his huge bulk; his tusks weighed just 65 and 67lbs. His carcase also yielded an astonishing number of bullets, placed there by numerous hunters: seventeen. But his most notable feature was a tail, the like of which Jim Sutherland never saw before or after: all the hairs on it were white. He kept it as a memento and to show people for its sheer novelty value. Sutherland recounted a full chapter dedicated to his exploits in combating man-eating lions; he did mention that most of these degenerate cats were old and incapable of hunting their usual fare. As time has proven, that is an old colonial view; man-eating lions come from all walks and can be any age and in any state of health, and are more often than not in superb condition. Regardless, Sutherland had some hair-raising encounters with them and won't have slept any easier as a result.

Once, near the Lukumbuli stream, one of Jim's men – Njerembo – was to marry a local beauty named Asalie. A few days before the big day, Asalie and her parents ventured to the neighbouring village to purchase some fowls for the feast; the poor girl was likely lost in romantic daydreams, but whatever the reason, at one stage during the return trip, she lagged a bit behind her parents, a full basket on her head. A loud scream was heard, and whirling around, her parents were just in time to see a huge elephant thunder out of the scrub, fling Asalie down and trample her into an unrecognisable heap almost immediately. To add to Sutherland's regret was the fact that when this occurred, he was away hunting; upon his return two days later, the animal's tracks were covered by multiple elephant tracks. Although Jim considered most Africans to soon forget loss, Njerembo was greatly affected and sadly never had another sweetheart.

Once near the Chiparaerie stream, a tributary of the Mbemkuru River, Sutherland had to deal with an elephant that showed a distinct predilection for tobacco leaves. He raided *shambas* for this crop so often that he gained the nickname Tombacco. Understandably, some people took exception and confronted Tombacco. Most that did perished, horribly. Just two months before Jim encountered him, Tombacco destroyed a native woman and her baby, tied to her back in the traditional way via a blanket. He drove a tusk through the woman's body before kneeling on the pair, crushing them into oblivion. When hunted, the bull would make for the dry arid regions, where he knew men couldn't follow for long. One day Jim tracked him rapidly from a tobacco *shamba* and shot the vicious bull. The reward in addition to public safety was fiscally considerable: Tombacco's tusks weighed 113 and 104lbs.

Sutherland had a couple of interesting instances whereby he came upon sleeping elephants. On both occasions they were members of a group, the remainder of which were awake and standing; on both occasions he shot the prostrate animal first, then potted the others. Neither knew what hit them. Sutherland considered elephant the most dangerous of the Big 5, and if anyone in history was qualified to make such an assertion, it was he. He considered the buffalo and lion tied for second place, with the leopard, interestingly enough, placing third. He believed the rhino trailed the others.

* * *

In January 1929, the Azande tribe in the area in which Sutherland was camped decided to take revenge for the wrongs perpetrated by the French, perceived or actual. They poisoned Jim's tea with *bhanga*, a local paralysis-inducing poison, with the assistance of his cook; the poison is tasteless and kills in around six hours. Only the prompt administration of the antidote – *bakalanga* – will save one's life. As Jim noticed the first effects – legs numbing – he stuck his fingers down his throat and vomited most of the tea up. The French authorities descended on the tribe and Sutherland was the only victim. Even so, he never recovered fully, one leg partially paralysed forever after and with almost no vision in his right eye. Sutherland refused to stop hunting, adapting and riding a mule. In June 1932 he suffered a relapse and was taken to Yubo, where he died despite the care of Dr Warburton of the Sudan Defence Force medical services.

As an interesting aside, the great Tony Sánchez-Ariño came upon Sutherland's tomb in March 1961, near Yubo in south western Sudan, after a lengthy search. The bronze plate erected by his friends was in the process of being prised off by locals who wished to melt the metal down for pipe mouthpieces! A furious Tony offered them money and took the plate, which he had mounted into his fireplace back in Spain, until a suitable time and occasion can be found to restore it to its rightful place. It was the least that the legend that was Jim Sutherland's memory deserves.

11.   George Rushby

Picture courtesy of Tony Sánchez-Ariño

The late, great George Rushby was a most noteworthy individual. Despite a tough childhood, and for most of his adult life, an equally-tough adulthood, George Rushby remained a gentleman. I wonder what a modern man would do under similar circumstances, and strongly suspect that he'd lack the gumption to even remotely approach what George did. Even if they were that rare a being as George Rushby was, it's unlikely they'd emerge from such a tumultuous life while retaining their decency and any gentlemanly traits. As his wife Eleanor was an absolute lady, George was a product of his time. I remember my grandparents well, and although George was almost a full generation older, have heard enough about my great-grandparents to know the stock.

In addition, I tracked down George's son (George junior, but better known as Mike), himself from a wonderful older generation. Speaking with him about his parents just underlined how people are nowhere near as steadfast nowadays as they were in days gone, and all that while maintaining respect and decency that are sadly lacking in current times. More on Mike later. George Rushby's life was a remarkable one, and unlike many of the great ivory hunters and adventurers, his story has been captured in two outstanding works: *The Hunter is Death* (Nelson, 1962), the phenomenal biography by South African writer T.V. Bulpin, and Rushby's own *No More the Tusker* (published by WH Allen of London in 1965), which borrows much of the material from Bulpin's book, as agreed to by the two men. I was honoured in that the copy that I read of George's version was none other than his personally-signed copy to his son, Mike.

In addition, Peter Capstick wrote of Rushby in his *Maneaters* (Safari Press, 1981) – although that focused on Rushby's hunt for the Njombe lions – and the great Tony Sánchez-Ariño dedicated an entire chapter to George in his brilliant *Elephant Hunters, men of Legend* (Safari Press, 2005). George Rushby's African career could broadly be split into two parts: his ivory-hunting days, featuring tales of fantastic profits and poaching; and his subsequent time as a game ranger in Tanganyika (now Tanzania), wherein he famously dealt with the most lethal single pride of man-eating lions in recorded history, the Njombe cats referred to previously. My previous literary venture (*No Covenant*) covers this latter period in George's life. This work will centre on George the ivory hunter.

George Rushby was born on 28 February 1900. Soon after, the family moved to Eastwood, but the first huge event in his life befell George when he was just 18 months old: his father died. His mother soon remarried, but George hated his stepfather, a drunken bully. Rushby told Bulpin that the best thing he ever saw of his stepfather was the last of him. A group of gypsies (Romany people) used to camp on the family's land and in many respects, George was raised by them. The women would carry him on their backs when selling clothes pegs in the villages – doubtless currying favour and sympathy – while the men taught him to box as he grew older. It was no token gesture either; one of George's fellow students was one of the gypsies' own sons, Joe Beckett. He became an accomplished professional in the early twentieth century.

These same men taught George to hunt and poach nearly every Sunday morning, weather permitting. Throw in the books on African hunting which George's father had left him, and an adventurer was birthed who would become a legend. George's family moved to a village named Riddings in the East-Midlands, where he started his schooling. Riddings is a small village in Derbyshire; the 2011 census counted fewer than six thousand residents, and that was a century on. George loved the countryside around Riddings and honed his shooting skills with an air-gun to the point where the local birds and rabbits would have frightened their young into good behaviour at the very mention of the name George Rushby. Years later, lions and elephants may have had the same general feeling...

Then the family moved to Jacksdale in Nottinghamshire, an even smaller village (the same 2011 census counted just over three thousand souls). The now-13-year-old George attended Worksop College near Clumber Woods, while his mother again remarried, this time to a man of some means named Simpson: George's hated previous stepfather had drunk himself to death some time previously. Clumber Woods bordered on the Duke of Portland's game preserves, and the resourceful rogue George (usually with two friends in tow) poached the game and trout for years, eating like kings while easily leading the gamekeepers a merry dance. These same skills would stand him in good stead in years to come, although the targets were to be somewhat larger!

The boys were never caught, and upon leaving school, George went to learn electrical engineering with Oakes & Company at Pie Bridge station (on the Midland Railway in Derbyshire). He'd also frequent the boxing booths, all the while saving any money possible to go to Africa. At length, George set sail aboard the SS Gaika on a £25 Sterling steerage ticket from Tilbury Docks, and landed at East London, South Africa in June 1920. He got a job and played some rugby, but soon packed up and headed for Durban. He was penniless and homeless by the time he turned 21, sleeping on Durban's beaches. He recalled counting himself fortunate to be homeless in a tropical place, where there was no cold of note. Times were tough, and George was lucky enough that a pleasant waitress at the 'Model Dairy' café would slip him the spare cakes left over by others, when he'd go there for a cup of coffee.

Otherwise, George would go to the Salvation Army to be fed, often with a fellow-homeless named Green. Eventually George lucked out for work; he was passing the garage of Irvin, Maule & Mansergh just as they were erecting a sign advertising a role for an electrical mechanic, paying £17 a month. George walked in and was working within minutes. He could hardly believe his luck, the peace of mind that work brings changing his entire outlook. He could rent lodgings, choose his own food; a humbling and valuable lesson in appreciating things, even for the reader. He could take the kindly waitress to a cinema now and then, or a restaurant. Suddenly he had a future. Some two months later, George saw an advertisement in the newspaper for a power-house attendant job in Lourenço Marques with the Delagoa Bay Development Corporation. The pull of the life of hunting and adventure was drawing George up Africa's east coast.

George shot off an application and used his last savings to pay the fare on a British India Line vessel to LM, arriving there just three days after seeing the newspaper advertisement! Upon landing, George went straight to the job address, where the manager was highly amused at his brashness. He got the job though! The work was pleasant and the pay fair. The company ran the trams and supplied the town with electricity. LM back then was a vivacious, lively place, with a vibrant social culture. There was a large British contingent, and I recall my grandparents loving it as a holiday destination. They were equally gutted at the ruin that befell it when colonial rule ended, which has only worsened over time. There was boating, fishing, swimming, social gatherings; but in short order, George Rushby grew bored. He felt one could easily get bogged down by commitments, relationships and routine.

People spoke of marriage, pensions and settling down, normal in so pleasant a place; but a horrifying, constraining web to an adventurous young man! At the end of July 1921, George gave notice – somewhat regrettably – and headed for Beira, the next major port up the coast. He remembered leaving LM with more regret than when he'd left Durban, the time in the South African city tainted by his being homeless there. He did however harbour an inner feeling that his adventurous life would start in Beira. In August 1921, that town however was a backwater, beset by mosquitoes. George looked back at the ship with a tinge of regret as several potential porters literally brawled for the right to carry his single suitcase, which he'd far rather have carried himself. Not much has changed since; this still occurs across Africa and has happened several times to me, to my embarrassment: I am far larger than most of the men trying to carry my bag.

George overnighted at the Queen's Hotel, then took the train up the line to Dondo, and north beyond toward Nyasaland (now Malawi). Where the railhead was reached, he then walked a further ten miles (16km) up the proposed way to the advance parties. He was shown to a large, overbearing Italian, who immediately put George in charge of a gang of African labourers building embankments and cutting drains. That night in camp, George met two men who would facilitate the next major jump in his life: they were hunters, supplying meat to the railway labourers. George questioned them at some length and after a few days bought an old .303 rifle from someone in camp, in exchange for cash and some old clothes. After ten days, George could stand the Italian no longer, and by threats squeezed what was owing him out of the man.

Taking a few labourers with him who too had decided to leave, George headed into the bush. To his good fortune, his new charges were locals, knew the bush well and best of all, they had worked for hunters before. On the first night out in the bush, George was to learn a few social norms about Africa; although he'd grown up humbly, with the gypsies, and harboured no superior airs and graces, he soon saw that the men built him his own fire and tent, apart from their own. When he sauntered over to join them at their fire, he realised that his presence curtailed their conversation, exacerbated by the fact that he didn't know the language. Back at his own fire, he listened to the men talk and laugh while absorbing the sounds of the African night. He felt a deep, inner contentment; he was a hunter in Africa!

The next day, George felled his first African game, a reedbuck. His account had been opened! After several successful months, the rail construction ended, but George then continued in similar vein, supplying meat for the labourers of the British-owned Senna Sugar Estate. By now he'd replaced the rickety .303 with a fine battery, comprised of a 9,3mm Mauser repeater and a .470 Rigby double express rifle. Then one day, close to the banks of the Zambezi, George saw his first elephants. As they stood fanning themselves with their giant ears, George was in no doubt that he was in the presence of Africa's real monarchs. I have always said that the lion may be the king of beasts, but the elephant is the government. If any proof were needed, watch a pride of lion scatter when an irate pachyderm bears down on them! Size counts.

George was fascinated, hypnotised; and this first sighting cemented the idea that these huge beasts would define his life from here on in. There was just one young bull in the heard, no great shakes in terms of ivory, but sporting great quantities of meat! George watched the .470 round raise a dust cloud where his shot struck the bull in the heart, the report surprisingly loud and scattering the herd. He gave the departing bull the second barrel as well, and after a 50-yard chase (some 45 metres), they came upon their quarry, dead as tax relief. The men cut off the tail and presented it to George, who had never felt more content; his first runs were on the board! After four months in similar vein, George's senses were becoming bush-honed, and those senses likely saved his life. One night while asleep, he sensed danger and awoke, silently taking up his rifle.

Silhouetted against the stars was a man with raised spear, entering his canvas shelter! The man's approach was the last move he ever made as George fired. He lit a lamp as his men rushed in, the intruder now merely a dead heap on the ground. The men dragged the body outside and went back to bed. George reloaded and lay awake, wondering if the man had acted alone, but his men's snoring showed they'd not been that bothered by events at all! The next morning, they buried the body and George sought the local Senna estate manager about what he should do. That man suggested that George make himself scarce for a while; the

Portuguese authorities would likely jail him for months while investigating – a languid process – which would be bad enough for someone who was actually guilty of a crime! He advised George to catch the next river boat, which was due that very afternoon, and disappear into Nyasaland (now Malawi) for a while.

George did as advised while the estate manager paid off his men, or found them jobs on the estate where he could. George was dismayed but understood that he had no real alternative. At least the accommodation on the boat was good: he had his own cabin. After four days they berthed, then after a 60-mile (96km) train ride to Port Herald, George was safely out of Portuguese territory. The mental relaxation immediately had George feeling more positive about the new country than he'd felt about the wet, low-lying malaria hotbed that is now Mozambique. There were rolling hills, indicative of cooler climes. From the tiny town of Limbe, a hamlet settled in 1909 (its first bank branch only opened in 1970!), George visited the capital, Blantyre, where he happily learned that elephants were an over-populated menace in the north of the country, and that these required thinning out.

George pointed his nose north, via road and lake steamer reaching Fort Johnson. Then there was a pleasant and scenic five-day voyage to Karonga; Lake Nyasa (now Lake Malawi) has always been noted for its beautiful scenery. Upon landing, George headed for the district commissioner, a man named Abrahams. He was relieved to see the hunter, relaying to George the nuisance the elephants had become, especially around Vua village. They raided crops constantly, killing any people that dared cross them. The locals' attempts to shoot them with myriad small arms usually only resulted in wounded – and further-annoyed – elephants, as well as more dead people. George made for Vua, where the friendly chief was immensely relieved to see the white man. He provided George with guides, and after a day's tracking, the men closed with a herd.

In all, George would shoot 20 animals, but the yield in ivory was pathetic and he was thoroughly unimpressed. He had at least rid the area of some very dangerous animals, not least of which were some *tondos* – tuskless elephants which are hyper-aggressive – but he needed ivory to subsist. George made for Mwaya, a port on the northern end of the lake, and in Tanganyika (now Tanzania). An interesting point of note is that at that northern tip of Lake Nyasa, the lake narrows, providing an interesting opportunity to view the eastern and western shores simultaneously. The eastern side was beautiful, great precipices running down into the water (or more accurately, pushing up from the water to form cliffs), while the western side featured pleasant sand- and pebble beaches. From Mwaya, George headed to the administrative post, a place called Tukuyu.

This is a small town known as Neu Langenburg (New Langenburg) during German colonial rule, some 40 miles (64km) south of Mbeya. George started traversing the cold, wet volcanic mountains, after colobus monkey pelts – which were paying well then – as well as ivory. The ivory wasn't plentiful but was of excellent quality. The monkeys however proliferated, and George did well for several months. Then the market crashed and the demand disappeared; George mulled staying in Tanganyika over in his mind, but the quota there was just three jumbos a year, meaning that poaching would be necessary if one were to survive on ivory hunting alone. He decided to try the Congo, while understanding that the grass always looks greener; but in a quandary, he had little choice. The trackers told George that elephants around Lake Rukwa were both plentiful and toothy, so he determined to go via that way *en route* to the Congo.

The entire journey was through very scenic country; Lake Rukwa was the result of several small rivers draining the Great Western Rift Valley, and teemed with fish, hippos and crocodiles. Elephants were indeed plentiful but the terrain was a nightmare: the notorious *matete* reed interspersed with elephant grass that reached four to five metres tall (12-15 feet), as it does throughout many regions of sub-Saharan Africa. This makes for exciting but dangerous hunting. One morning, George had only two light rifles in tow (a .303 and a .318); after three hours on the spoor of a lone elephant, the party came up behind the animal. The great beast sauntered on unperturbed, even when the men imitated an elephant's rumblings. The bull may have been deaf, or at least hard of hearing, as no human can hope to reach the low frequencies of an elephant rumble.

Eventually the path the bull was making through the vegetable sea was crossed by another, which then swerved almost parallel to the first. The men dashed up it, to get ahead of the bull, and at length waited at a small, trampled-down clearing. When the elephant was alongside the men, a small gap in the *matete* could be discerned – the thick reed grass would easily deflect a bullet, especially a light one – and George fired off a perfect heart shot. The reaction was a shocking one; at speed so great neither man had a chance to react, the huge beast descended upon them, crushing the tracker to pulp in a flash before dashing on for a further 40 yards or so (36 metres). He then crashed noisily to earth, dead. His ivory was considerable but George was heartsick at the loss of the tracker. It appeared that the elephant had no idea where the men were or what had happened to him.

After burying the dead man, George compensated his dependants most generously, but knew no fiscal amount could ever make up for the loss. He also made a mental note not to use a light rifle from such proximity ever again, perfectly-lethal shooting notwithstanding. The great beasts can cause too much damage and death after receiving a fatal shot, in the few yards and seconds it takes them to die. Gutted, George left the area the very next day, onward to the Congo. He headed west, eventually reaching the British administrative settlement at Chiengi on Lake Mweru, a freshwater lake on the Congo River's longest arm. Chiengi is pronounced Chee-yengi and the area sported a famous, very pale-coloured man-eating lion some time before George's arrival, known as Chiengi Chali (the latter word pronounced Charlie). There were many elephant around, but licenses were that tough here in Northern Rhodesia (now Zambia) that George was still drawn to the Congo, where a hunter was permitted four elephant in each province, and where officials could easily be bribed as well...

George hired a dozen porters and made for Pweto, a Belgian administrative post. From there he hired new porters and headed down the Luvua River, hunting on the way. When he reached the next administrative post – Kiambi – he had shot his quota of four elephants, and was well-compensated for the ivory. He instantly took out a new license and canoed down the widening Luvua, shooting along the banks as he went. The river flowed into the Lualaba at a place called Ankoro; from there, George was advised to head inland after reaching Kabinda (with a new license), and hunt westward to the Kasai River, selling ivory and getting a new license at each admin post encountered. This he did, and prospered; so much so that upon reaching Basongo, he had 20 tusks instead of the permitted eight...

George was now really in a fix, the trader he'd sold the ivory to telling him that he should've bribed the admin officer during questioning. It was now too late; George was fined a thousand francs, the surplus tusks were confiscated and worst of all, his rifles were taken away. He resolved then and there, that he would not get caught again. His old poaching skills were about to be called upon again. George took a week-long river-boat trip to Kinshasa (later Leopoldville, then back to Kinshasa with *Uhuru* independence). He was highly annoyed at the Congo and pored over a map to discern where he might head to next. He landed in the port of Boma, a miserable collection of flotsam and jetsam from all corners, and took a job as a barman. Before starting though, he shot a letter off to his erstwhile partner when trading in colobus skins, asking whether the market had recovered sufficiently to warrant his return to Tanganyika.

After three months of near-constant bar fights, news reached him from his partner that a mutual friend had found gold on the Lupa goldfields, and that George should come at once. He took a Belgian ship to Antwerp the very next week, from there popping in to see his family in Jacksdale, England for the first time in three years, then took the SS Norman via the Suez Canal, reaching Dar es Salaam in May 1923. He was still just 23 years old, and back in East Africa! At Kilosa, a whistle stop on the central line, George met Bill Brearley, who was also headed for the Lupa; what's more, he was actually a cousin of George's partner in the colobus fur trade, a man named Lumb. The two walked for three weeks, which was pleasant; it was scenic and the men shot for the pot. But at the Lupa, George went down with malaria, and it was a heavy dose. The doctor advised he leave the area to fully recover, and he returned to Tukuyu, considering farming.

In Tukuyu George learned that the government was issuing 'Governor's Licenses' to crop the near-pestilential elephant numbers. All tusks had to be between 50 and 70lbs in weight (23 and 32kg), and one handed in for every one retained. George applied for a license, and was immensely excited when it was granted. On the Kihanzi River – a tributary of the famous Kilombero – he met the chief of the Mbunga, a man named Makuwa. He ritually blessed George's rifles, to George's amusement; he supposed however that it could do no harm. His amusement turned to wide-eyed surprise as inside a month, he'd collected the 25 animals on the quota, all in the permitted limits, and all of excellent quality! He sold his portion for a good return and promptly received another license. George was exhilarated while the Mbunga were thrilled with the meat windfall, so much so that they inducted George into their own special hunters' guild.

By the time he eventually returned to Kilosa, George had accounted for 53 elephants, none with tusks under 50lbs, his largest being just shy of 90lbs. The two Governor's Licenses had been great for him but the authorities saw the continued farce and stopped this method of elephant control; clearly, the populations would suffer with only the best tuskers being removed from the population. Once again, George had been stalled in his pursuit of an ivory-hunting career. Sitting philosophically pondering his latest stumping in the pub at Kalageris' Hotel, George mused that every time he got going as an ivory hunter, something happened to thwart his endeavours. The only solution seemed to be to turn to poaching; but this would be risky and dangerous. Not being caught was the obvious imperative, should he pursue this option.

George recalled the mass of elephants around Lake Mweru on the Congo's border with Northern Rhodesia (now Zambia). He headed that way, dropping by the Lupa goldfields *en route*. He enjoyed a rowdy, whisky-saturated evening with old friends, then swapped his claim for a .577 double express rifle with ammunition, which was a solid move when after elephant, especially when poaching, and needing to kill quickly. He also seems to have acquired a .450 around this time, but its acquisition isn't recounted in Bulpin's book. George hired porters then set out for Kituta. From there the party canoed some 60 miles (96km) across the south-west of the lake to the Belgian port of Molira (again, a scenic trip), where he took out the four-elephant license for that part of the Congo. George then went to see the traders, making no secret of his intention to poach.

Seeing that the market and demand were there, George was advised by the traders to establish his base on high ground on the border, and overlooking the marsh; from there he'd be able to spot elephants far and wide, while approaching trouble – the authorities! – could likewise be spotted with plenty notice. This base was a few miles north-west of the village of one Tambala, a petty chief who had been a tough for one of the legendary slave- and ivory traders, the vaunted Tippu Tib. Tambala regaled George over a pot of beer with a tale to tempt any adventurous spirit: years before, when the British approached Tib's fort base to destroy it, Tib had his men remove his legendary stockpile of ivory and bury it in a secret cave; then he had anyone privy to its whereabouts killed. Tambala swore the story was accurate but had no idea where the cave was.

This sparked George to spend three months searching all over for the buried treasure; and who wouldn't in his place? At length he returned to Tambala empty-handed and cursing himself for wasting unproductive time. The fat old chief was sympathetic and contrite, reiterating that his story was true, and feeling bad for costing George the time, offered to bless his guns. This time George didn't laugh, remembering the time the Mbunga had done likewise, which resulted in George enjoying the most fantastic good fortune. When he left the hut where the ritual was performed, his trackers were waiting; again, it was to be quite a day. George stood on the vantage point above the marsh, looking down on a sea of elephant grass, *matete* and dried mud. As far as the eye could see, there were elephants moving slowly about, egrets betraying the presence of those momentarily lost to sight in the sea of vegetation. The watching men were spellbound.

George had designed a light ladder in order to see over the grass, and from which to shoot. The men approached two bulls, one far larger than the other. Climbing the ladder and using his .450, George brained the larger bull. The recoil blew him off the ladder, to fall safely into the thick grass, his men holding the ladder likewise sent sprawling. Ascending again to see the effects of his handiwork, George was pleased to see no discernible reaction to the shot, bar the large bull dropping from view. The younger bull was fervently trying to help the older one to its feet, when suddenly the larger animal's eyes flickered open; his brain had merely been creased! He immediately attacked the younger elephant, clearly believing the pain in his head to have been caused by his friend.

He knocked the younger bull over, who was clearly mystified at this ingratitude, and tusked him to death, tearing his stomach open in a savage attack. Blood and entrails were all over the ground when the larger bull at last stood upright, gore from his own wound coating him along with that from his victim. George shot him through the brain and he dropped dead over his victim. Climbing the ladder again, George saw that no other elephant had so much as moved; he looked at his trackers. 'Let's see how much headway can be made by sundown', he said. When evening came, George's tally was 18 elephants killed for a total (back then) of some £2,000 worth of ivory, a huge sum; one bull carried tusks of 80lbs a side, one cow with 30lbs a side was the largest cow George ever shot. All but the first one and the last three were shot with the .318, which had good penetration for the brain shot, but which didn't blow George off the ladder!

The last three were fine bulls around a waterhole just before sunset; two carried excellent ivory, but the last was a *budi*, or tuskless elephant, known as a *tondo* further south. As mentioned before, they tend to be vicious. George killed the tuskers in the blink of an eye, but the budi was infuriated. He stared at George across the water with such hate that if looks could spit, George would have been surfing! The man hoped the animal would run off, but it was furious, its eyes ablaze with hatred and vocalising the most hair-raising screams of sheer rage. Such a creature would be a holy terror to any person it ventured across, so perhaps it was fortunate that it charged into the water, and George blew a hole in its head. It crashed down with a huge splash and never rose again. The blood spread out, merging with the red sunset glow on the water. It had been a halcyon day.

*   *   *

Removing all the ivory took five days, and they were anxious times for George: volplaning vultures advertised the activities far and wide, but no authorities arrived. The ivory was superb, as good as could be imagined; it was cream coloured, finely grained and easily worked, and would fetch far higher prices than the thin, brittle, forest elephant yield. George saw the sense in not being greedy in future; short, quick raids for manageable quantities would raise the least attention. He organised his staff accordingly, returning to Mweru Wantipa to build his base on high ground just over the Congo border as he'd been advised to do. Then he returned to his vantage point, just to see if such numbers of elephant were still about. He took one tracker with him, and upon reaching the point, the two men nearly fell over in shock at the sight before them.

Spread out before them was a sea of elephants some five miles long (8km) and two miles wide (3km), all purposefully walking in a specific direction through the marsh, not even feeding! A massive bull led the centre group of the procession, and George had never before seen his like. He dwarfed even his four enormous lieutenants that followed. Only once again in his entire life was George able to witness a similar spectacle: in the Ulanga Valley of the Mahenge District of Tanganyika (the Ulanga is another name by which the Kilombero River is known). Elephant abound there to this day. Other hunters and adventurers recounted this sight, Bulpin himself covering the phenomenon in The Ivory Trail (first published by Howard Timmins in 1954). Overwhelmed, George and the tracker merely sat watching.

The next day, the marsh was back to normal, its elephant paradise looking sparse against the previous day's incredible sight. George's first day in the Mweru marsh had yielded him 18 elephants, which was to remain his single-day record. He had a day when he shot ten, and on two other occasions shot nine each, but he never again reached that staggering tally. Soon, George's spies notified him that the District Commissioner of Chiengi, one Wickens, was after him. Thus commenced a merry dance through the marsh, with George leading. Poor Wickens had no real chance and was tormented and toyed with at George's whim. After a couple of months of this fruitless exercise, Wickens summoned a second District Commissioner, Norton from Mporokoso. He too would add to a glowing collection of reed cuts, leeches and exhaustion for no reward. The master poacher even left sarcastic, humorous and teasing notes for his pursuers, which would have alleviated their hardship not at all!

George watched the authorities wearily leaving the marsh; he had over £5,000 – a prodigious sum then – in his bank account in Dar, his poaching venture proving most profitable. The British government sent a note to the Belgians, complaining of the poacher, allowed to operate with impunity from the Congo and wrecking Northern Rhodesia's elephant population. The Belgian administrative officer at Molira was apologetic in delivering the news to George, suggesting that he perhaps holiday at the coast. George grinned; that did actually sound good after seven months out in the 'blue'. He had shipped three tons of ivory from Molira, 75 bull elephants providing it. Even though the Brits had no idea who the poacher was – merely referring to him by the name used by the Africans, *iNyathi* (the buffalo), because he was dangerous in the long grass – perhaps it was time to take a prudent break.

George paid off his men and rewarded them with a large bonus to boot; then he took the lake steamer *Vengeur* to Albertville (now Kalemie), booking into Spiro's Hotel du Lac. Spiro – a Greek who was canny and street-savvy – became George's agent when the latter took out his usual 4-elephant licence for the Albertville province. In the hotel, George met two old cronies from the Lupa, Bird and Woollard. The latter made for the Lualaba River, while Bird and George set up camp near each other in the Kamba hills, some 100 miles (160km) north-west of Albertville. It was excellent elephant country and renowned for bulls. One morning, George and his men set off late for no particular reason, and around 11am cut the spoor of a huge, solitary bull. The tracks were unfortunately some three days old or so, but they followed anyway, and were rewarded when this same bull's spoor crossed his own, this time far fresher!

It was now around 4.30pm; excitedly they spoored on. With evening threatening, George had the porters set up camp around a waterhole, taking one tracker to try squeeze out the last vestiges of daylight. With the light fading fast, they heard rather than saw, then closed with, an elephant. Finally, at no more than ten yards, George chanced a shot at what looked like a vital area. In the dark the flame from the rifle was as startling as the noise in the dense forest. The beast crashed off, then stood silently listening. George and his tracker prudently returned to camp, it now being that dark, that even finding the men was some chore. As soon as dawn lit the forest, the men were back at the spot, a blood trail evident. The elephant was dragging a front leg and travelling slowly; it was evidently hard-hit. Warning the porters in the rear to wait, George tracked on, all senses on edge.

After a tense half-hour, a slight movement ahead alerted them still further; then the shrill scream of a furious elephant announced the biggest set of tusks George had ever seen in the head of a huge bull, weaving its way irresistibly through the huge rubber vines which hung from even bigger forest giants. It fell to a frontal head shot, but was merely stunned, and was up again in a second, its fast-disappearing stern facing George. The man desperately leaped to the side to open some angle, his second round still only boring its path into the animal's hindquarters. The massive bull tore through the shrubbery, George after him at full tilt. After 100 yards or so (90 metres), the tracker caught up with him, shouting for George to stop, and conveying that their quarry was now behind them, back where George had fired at it, and was now standing immobile by a tree.

George was confused; he'd been sure the bull was just ahead, but the tracker was a good one and knew elephants. Returning with the man, a huge bull indeed stood crippled by a tree; a brain shot did for him. He sported some superb ivory (some 125lbs a side), but it turned out that he was the one they'd spoored and shot in the gathering dark the day before. The monster that had charged George was another bull! Leaving most of his men at the dead elephant, George raced off after the dream jumbo. The men followed the trail until sundown, then made a fire and spent the night in the forest; but the bull didn't stop and was obviously only lightly wounded. With no food, and staring at a trail already ten hours old, the men had no alternative but to give best. It was maddening, to come that close; although the bull he'd shot would yield a fortune, George was sure this 'one that got away' would've at least challenged the world record tusks (the 226lb and 214lb behemoths from the Kilimanjaro bull).

The men endured a cold, wet, hungry night on the way back, to ever more dream of that giant bull. Some three weeks later, George was on the trail of another large bull, the spoor perhaps a day old. Late the following day, the men closed with it, feeding in a bog, tall razor grass rendering the area decidedly unpleasant for people. In the fading light, the thick foliage obscured George's view, but he closed to within 15 yards and aimed for the heart before firing. The scream of rage that announced the bull's imminent arrival was almost a continuation of the rifle's report, and although he still couldn't properly see the rapidly-closing elephant, George decided it prudent to loose off the second barrel at the mass. The elephant staggered, but came on. Rushby reached back for his second rifle, but its bearer had fled! Cursing, George worked the ejectors, diving out of the way as the enraged bull arrived.

He was micro-seconds too late; the great trunk removed layers of skin from his face and chest in a glancing blow which would have settled George's mortal account, had it landed on his dome. The great beast snatched him up by a leg, and instead of the default elephantine fare of dashing him to earth before tusking him, kneeling on him and generally smashing him into the ground, it chose to throw him backwards while running at full lick, the man bouncing off the great back and into the swamp; this felt blissfully good by contrast. Staring down his rifle's still-open barrels, George was pleased to note them as being free of mud. The problem was, all the ammunition he'd carried on his person had fallen out during his impromptu visit to the swamp via an elephant's back. Frantically, he clawed through the bracken after ammunition, joyfully spying three clean rounds in a bush.

Loading, George Rushby dashed after his quarry, seeing the bull facing him not 30 yards off on a small raised bit of ground. George was about to let fly when he realised the elephant was actually dead. It had turned to face its nemesis and had collapsed on its stomach, the small rise creating the illusion that it was still on its feet. The heart was shot through, further testimony – if any were needed – as to the toughness of Africa's Big 5 in general, and of elephants in particular. George called his trackers, not least because his own wounds could now be assessed and treated. Even though George was in a world of pain, which would increase in the coming week or so, his injuries were remarkably slight on reflection: three cracked ribs and a swollen ankle. George Rushby was clearly a hard individual…

Bird moved his camp over to nurse George, who was laid up for several days. George told him of the giant bull that may carry the best-ever ivory. Bird thought it most likely that the animal had left the district, bull elephants of that size in particular being no fools, and attaining that size by being prudent. George thought him likely correct. After three weeks, George was again ambulatory and accompanied the Mboti Pygmies on an elephant hunt. He was to be nauseated by the cruel mass-slaughter as the little hunters encircled a herd in a ring of fire and burnt almost all to a hideous death. The few that made it through were burnt and blinded, and the warriors had no trouble spearing them to death with impunity. George put as many as he could out of their misery with a bullet before returning to his own camp. But on the way, he crossed the track of an enormous bull, headed for the Kamba hills. Could this be his lost giant?

It was plain the beast was old and experienced. The two full days spent spooring the great animal taught George a lot; his travelling into the wind was clever, but most hunted game did that. What most fascinated George was his method of guarding against being followed. Periodically, he'd dawdle for a time with the wind on his flank, then suddenly dash downwind and hole up in a thicket. Any pursuer would betray himself upon reaching the place where the bull suddenly headed downwind. As elephants do, the bull would while away the hottest hours, fanning himself with his ears in a standing doze or even lying prostrate. Cow elephants don't seem to do this often but bulls do so, and regularly. Supreme confidence and security, one suspects; what would be foolish enough to beard a bull elephant? Clearly, it was shades of 'mad dogs and Englishmen', when it came to the ivory hunters…

The imprint left where the bull had lain clearly indicated ivory sufficient to spur the men on, and by the third day the freshness of dung and spoor showed they were near. As they were nearing the twin summits of the Kamba hills, George actually left the spoor and headed for the points. The view and vantage point would help in glassing the area and spotting the big bull. Less than halfway there, however, a tracker stopped George. He'd spotted the bull, in tall grass. He wasn't that bull of George's dreams but a *Ntonda* – a single-tusker. The tusk, however, was the biggest George had ever seen. He crept to within 15 yards and the giant bull never knew what hit him, falling to a perfect brain shot. The prize tusk weighed 165lbs (75kg), bigger than a man and as heavy. The other had only recently broken off, and George wondered initially if it was indeed his mystery bull; this one however had no previous wounds.

After this red-letter day, George had his porters head for Albertville. He paid them, allowing them to return to their families for a few months, while he pondered a holiday in Dar es Salaam. It was time for another break.

* * *

George was soon bored in Dar es Salaam; there were only so many Greek-run sleazy hotels, and the interest they offered was soon exhausted. As intended in Albertville, he'd paid off his porters, sold his ivory and headed for Kigoma via overnight steamer across Lake Tanganyika. It was late February 1926, and it dawned on George that he could take out the annual three-elephant licence. What was more, it would expire on 31 March, with a replacement taken out on 1 April. Twelve tusks glowed in his mind's eye, and those were just the legal ones! George headed for the scene of his first hunt, the upper Kilombero, where the Mbunga people had inducted him into their hunting guild. He accompanied them on a hippo hunt, conducted with harpoons from canoes, very similar in nature to the way early whaling was carried out. This is co-incidental, as recent studies show hippos to be most closely-related to whales. The Mbunga greatly prized hippos as the animal is fat-rich, and sports several tons of meat anyway.

When the hippo hunt was over, George collected his six elephants, leaving the carcases to his friends, then sold the ivory in Kilosa. From there he had taken a train to Dar, where he sat in the hotel bar, feeling blue. A man sat down not two stools away from him; George recognised him at once. It was Bill Buckley, the elephant hunter who'd given George advice when he was first on the boat to Africa in 1920. The meeting helped George to reflect that he'd landed with £25 in his pocket and now had £4,000. He'd had adventure to boot, and done well out of it, very well in fact. George spent two weeks travelling to Mombasa and back in company with Buckley, and returned feeling far better. The chance meeting rejuvenated him. He then determined to head for French Equatorial Africa, to meet Jim Sutherland and have another go at gathering white gold. From his talks with Buckley, that seemed the only place where legal profit could still be earned from ivory. The days of the ivory hunters were nearing their end.

From Kigoma, George took the *Baron Dhanis* across Lake Tanganyika to Albertville. He'd intended just passing through but in the Hotel du Lac, Spiro mentioned that Woollard was gathering good ivory near the Lualaba River. George headed to an area south of the Kignoa railway station, halfway between Albertville and Kabala on the Lualaba. It was here that he had his second real encounter with African magic (the first being his uncanny good luck each time his rifles had been ritually blessed). I recalled the occasion in *No Covenant*; in succinct form, George was in camp – stone-cold sober, of perfect eyesight and with no trick of the light possible – watching a man some 50 feet away (16-17 yards or 15 metres) pray before a wooden idol. As George watched, the idol moved its head to the left three times, each time moving it back. As the man left, George asked to see the idol, which was made of solid wood and couldn't possibly have moved its head. George was shaken, but he'd go on to encounter far more chilling magic, and to a far greater degree. Ah, Africa…

The next day, George started to hunt. After accounting for seven bulls - the ivory noticeably smaller than it had been previously - he headed north toward Woollard. George found him on the Lukuga River, settled with an African wife, raising a family, all living in an entire collection of grass huts; but on the way he met a Greek hunter whom he later saw after an elephant had tusked the man through the chest. Death at least would have been mercifully instant. Times were changing, and Woollard wanted to stay settled, happy to cease hunting lest he end up like the Greek; but George was still too young to contemplate settling down, and headed north to the French areas. He never saw Woollard again; that fellow died of fever a few years later.

George went via train and river steamer across the Congo to Coquilhatville (now Mbandaka), in the far north-west. Stanley had founded it in 1883; the place is famous nowadays for the wrong reasons: hundreds of Hutu refugees were massacred there in 1997, during the First Congo War. From there George took a paddle-wheeler up the Ubangi River as far as it went, to the French administrative post of Bangui, arriving on 20 November 1926. Scarcely able to contain himself, he paid £90 for an unlimited elephant licence, his first ever. He then got a lift with an eccentric American missionary (sounds like a movie!), delivering a Model T Ford to Fort Crampel (now called Kaga-Bandoro), which took three days; it was a journey of 250 miles (some 400km), on 'roads', and neither man had ever driven before! Each night after exercising, the American would give himself a colonic irrigation – or enema – and George was relieved to reach Fort Crampel, and be free of the man. Incidentally, the Yank went fully mad some months later, and was shipped back to the US for treatment.

The fort was a small place (even now only numbering 30 thousand souls). George got the lay of the land, then reconnoitred as far north as the Auk River, the country desolate, unpopulated by people and thus clearly excellent elephant country. Buffalo, bongo and eland were also numerous, as were chimpanzees, which seems like a fantasy to us in the early 21st Century. George soon came across local Kresh hunters, and learned that in addition to Sutherland, 'Andy' Anderson, Aurelio Rossi and others were in the area. The area was however very large, covering some 40 thousand square miles (100 thousand square km). Then something happened which illustrated two things: 1) further proof (as if any were still required!) of the danger inherent in hunting elephants; and 2) the staggering hardiness and powers of recovery of the bush African.

George was trailing a small herd of six elephants; with him were his two gunbearers and one other man. The country was quite open, grass reaching to shoulder- or head-height, and well-trampled with elephant paths. Concealment was thus sufficient without being obstructive, and the men closed easily enough with the group. George killed the best tusker with his first shot. As usual, the rest bolted in a clump, and George hared after them. Most fleeing groups stop after going some 200 yards or so and look back at what happened to them. But after some 50 yards, the group came racing back the way they'd come, and George had to shoot fast. He did so, two elephants falling to perfectly-placed brain shots. The remaining three veered off, and George watched to see if they'd stop. They didn't, but one paused at a gully before going down it, up the other side and away.

The three fallen elephants were all stone-dead and all three carried excellent ivory. Then one bearer noticed that the third man was missing. Calling for him, they heard a faint reply from where George had seen the elephant cross the gully...George had that sinking feeling as they ran toward the man. He was lying on the ground, covered in blood and dirt, and was using both hands to hold his entrails in. Those wayward innards were protruding from a large gash in his stomach. When the men had run from the suddenly-returning herd, he'd simply chosen what turned out to be the wrong way. It transpired that the elephant pausing at the gully had paused to do this. George sent a tracker back to the following porters to hurry them along, and when they arrived, he grabbed the medical kit. He cleaned the entrails as best he could, put them back and started stitching, using all the surgical thread and finishing the job with ordinary cotton.

George placed a pad over the wound, bandaged it as best he could and held it all in place with a normal buckled belt. Everyone feared for the man's survival, but not the man himself: when George visited him by the fire a couple of hours after sundown, he was tucking into a large piece of grilled elephant meat, and as cheerful as you please. Giving him two days to recover, the party then made a stretcher from poles and bark rope, bearing him along as they travelled and hunted. After a mere three weeks he was almost fully-recovered, a slight bulge where the wound had been his only apparent memento of an experience which would kill most people, certainly most Europeans. George sold his ivory at Rafai, where the resident *hetman* (sultan) of the Azande tribe hosted a trade fair, then the party made for Zemio, for many years the farthest outpost of the French Foreign Legion. Zemio still exists, in what is now the Haut-Mbomou prefecture in the south-east of the Central African Republic.

The Rushby party arrived in Zemio just in time for the Bastille Day celebrations. The feast was a large one and George retired to his slumbers when the party became too raucous. The next destination was the last French outpost, Obo; there George met the fabled Jim Sutherland. The great man told him that there were several other hunters about and that there was enough for all. Sutherland mentioned only Marcus Daly as one to avoid, being aggressive and way too free with other people's food, liquor and women. After a good chat – the two would remain firm friends – George set up his permanent camp on high ground between Obo and the Mbomou River. Just across the Sudanese border was Yubo, a British sleeping-sickness post, where upon Sutherland's advice, George had his personal mail routed.

George's first foray across the Congo border was to prove highly profitable. Having established excellent relations with the Azande tribe on the French side of the border, he was happy when the chief suggested they bless his rifles. Immediately on crossing the border they hit fresh spoor. Following expectantly and nervously, the men heard a strange crooning sound ahead, but it turned out to be a wild man of the forest, excavating a yam with his back to them. Fearing that he'd run if they called to him – he looked that wild – and thus frighten the elephants ahead, the party rushed and grabbed the man, but in panic, his wild strength was prodigious. He was just shrugging the trackers off when George intervened, knocking the man out with a punch to the head. When the man came around, he'd been securely bound and since he understood none of the languages tried on him, the party took him along with them.

Soon they closed with two bull elephants, and George killed both in the blink of an eye. The wild man watched closely as the men grilled meat on sticks and George set up his mosquito net; it was clear he'd never seen any of it before. Then George brought him some meat and Africa's traditional gesture of goodwill, a handful of salt. The man visibly relaxed, relieved. George had him untied and they grinned at each other across the fire as they ate, two creatures as different, yet as similar, as you can imagine. At length they found that the man was able to understand a few words of Ngala, a language spoken around Stanleyville (now Kisangani, capital of the Orientale Province in the Democratic Republic of Congo). Stanleyville was some 400 miles (640km) to the south. When George had made sure the man understood that he was free to leave, his new friend indicated a desire to stay.

George named him Kinanda, and he would become George's finest-ever tracker, totally fearless even under a bull elephant's charge. He eventually became aware of his nakedness, donning some old shorts. The bounty of ivory that was to be directly attributable to his tracking was enormous. Once again, the ritual rifle-blessing had yielded uncannily-good results.

* * *

George hunted from his Obo base for some two and a half years, for excellent returns. The elephant supply was seemingly inexhaustible, especially in the wet season as the new elephants came in from the south, trying to escape the constant dripping, the biting flies and the murderous *siafu* army ants. They seemed to prefer the hot reception from the hunters to those torments. The rivalry between the men was friendly, everyone thriving and comparing tallies of ivory gathered. The great Sutherland – approaching sixty – still managed to top the list every year except 1928, when George beat him. 1927 was George's best year in terms of quantity gathered, but it was obviously a bumper year for everyone: Sutherland pipped him that year. For Christmas of 1927, George hosted the area's hunters at his camp. He'd often harboured thoughts of doing so.

When the French would one day stop issuing the limitless licences, this legendary breed of men would die out. Some would linger on to poach, or become game rangers occasionally engaged in cropping duties; but those would be mere shadows of the halcyon days. The party lasted four days, and George's camp resembled a trade fair for the duration. Of note – apart from the huge calabashes of local beer – was a most curious character: his name was Bakuyu, and he'd simply wandered into George's camp one day. In tow was a strange, lute-like instrument made from a calabash, a flat piece of wood, and four or five attached strings. The instrument made a most pleasant sound, and Bakuyu was a remarkably-talented player. He accompanied the men when they'd hunt, and in the evening would compose verses recounting the day's activities.

The Robin Hood-like scene must have been surreal to witness; his songs were great fun, witty, gave praise where warranted, and helped pass what would otherwise have been boring evenings. At the Xmas party, Bakuyu was in his element; he played his full repertoire, and for all four evenings was the star performer. As usual, and as could be expected, the hunters' talk always reverted to rifles and ammunition. George shared Sutherland's view that the best rifle for elephant hunting was the potent .577 nitro express. As Sutherland reasoned, their trade was to kill elephants, and to do so as fast and as efficiently as possible was essential. He decried the small-bore fraternity, which was noteworthy, as he was a slightly-built, albeit wiry, man. It makes more sense, the 'use enough gun' element leaving far fewer mangled hunters after the fact; but it again shows just how phenomenal Bell was, for instance. Or how lucky…

Sutherland recounted losing a jumbo after using a .318, the *coup-de-grace* shot even administered from a mere foot away as the beast lay groaning on its side. When the men returned to take the tail, the bull had recovered and left! Simpson mentioned that anyone using less than a .577 was too lazy to carry it, and he recalled only Bell as disagreeing with that take. He did make an interesting point, however, remarking that in French Equatorial Africa, Bell hadn't fared all that well (at least by Bell's admittedly-staggering standards). This is perhaps the only negative account I've ever read of Bell (aside from opinions; most of the old ivory hunters preferred using heavier rifles). George recounted his bull that he'd shot through the heart in the gathering dark with a .303; when they found him the following morning, he moved off again. Then they came across him, dead; he'd lived over twelve hours and walked a mile, shot through the heart. Testimony to the elephant, no doubt; but placing question marks over light rifles too.

George did concede that in open country, a .318 was handy, but a heavy rifle imperative in dense bush. Everyone present agreed. A hunter named Christinger asked the master how he'd prefer to die; Sutherland's response was immediate: following an elephant, not before him; i.e., on the trail, not smashed by a pachyderm! Simpson mentioned that he intended hunting for a further two seasons, then would pack it in. The party drank hearty toasts before parting the next day. When George next saw Simpson, it was only his corpse when he was brought to Obo for burial. An elephant had broken his neck with a single, savage blow from its trunk. By that time, the authorities had arrested Marcus Daly, and run him out of French Equatorial Africa. The end of 1928 saw George beat Jim Sutherland's total by a few pounds, and he was thrilled. His sense of achievement was diluted upon remembering that, at age 27, he was at his physical peak, while Sutherland was nearly sixty…

In late January 1929, George was on the trail of an elephant when a messenger brought him a letter from Sutherland; he'd been poisoned. As recounted at the end of the previous chapter, some Azande porters he'd recently hired had differences with the French, and by association as a white man, Jim had *bhanga* – a tasteless poison from the tips of the flame tree – put in his tea. When he'd realised why his legs were suddenly suffering from paralysis, Sutherland made himself vomit. He thus removed most of the poison, but enough had entered his system to cause serious damage. Rushby abandoned his hunt, finding Sutherland in shock and partially paralysed. Jim's loyal assistants had arrested the four men responsible and secured the antidote – *bakalanga* – which saved his life. It was however doubtful if he'd ever recover the use of his legs.

With his camp mules, George managed to get Sutherland to Obo, where one of the missions ran a small clinic, the only medical relief anywhere for miles around. The four prisoners were tried, admitting to having nothing at all against Sutherland; he was merely the first on their list of 'foreigners' – read: whites – to be exterminated. They were only remorseful that he'd survived. That news made the French authorities descend on the tribe, and no other white man in the area had been poisoned; the four received lengthy jail terms, although as Bulpin noted, that didn't help Sutherland much. I like to think it did; at least the (known) guilty men were behind bars; men like that at large would likely have tried again, and Sutherland was hardly able to defend himself. This dapper, energetic and forceful hunter was reduced to a wreck, never again fully recovering the use of his right leg.

Sutherland resumed hunting, but largely as an invalid, from the backs of mules. He had to learn to shoot from the other side, as his right eye, too, had been greatly affected. He could easily afford to retire, fiscally; but he balked at George's suggestion of a vacation to Europe. He knew of nothing but the bush, totally repulsed by large, civilised cities. George went alone, in the second half of 1929. He now had £15,000 to his name and felt a visit to his mother was in order. This announcement caused consternation amongst his men, who now numbered as many as a village, families all counted. George left them financially comfortable, then had three weeks to kill in Bangui waiting for the next paddle-wheeler. In the guesthouse there he met a young giant, John Molteno (the Cape Colony's first Prime Minister had been one Sir John Molteno, and the town of Molteno in the East Cape is named for the family; it now harbours some 12,000 people).

John was recovering from a dust-up at the hands – or horns – of a buffalo. His men left him for dead, so he crawled to a village, from there making his way to a Belgian post on the river. He and George decided to look the Middle Congo over before George headed back to Europe, to see whether it was worthwhile returning to. The Middle Congo's administrative centre was named Impfondo (which is still there, now home to some 20,000 people). This lay some 250 miles (400 km) downriver from Bangui. The start of their journey to the interior was from a small post called Bétou, which is now incidentally home to some 60,000 refugees from the conflicts of the 1990s; the area around Bétou was miserable, nothing but swamp and dank forest. There were precious few elephants and what there were, harboured trifling ivory. There were still many gorillas about, which seems alien now; and the pair met many Pygmies, smaller than those around Kamba at only some four and a half feet tall.

Eventually canoeing downriver, George – who'd split from Molteno when they got back to Bangui – landed at Mongumba on the French side of the river. The countryside was worse than their recent surrounds, even wetter and drearier; but at least there were some elephant about. When George shot the first, he made instant friends of the local Pygmy and Negro tribes, the latter confirmed cannibals. They even gave George a piece of human flesh in thanks for the elephant meat he'd provided. Although gorillas and chimps abounded, the racks were clearly full of human flesh being smoked. George accepted a choice bit, later quietly burying it. Feeling poorly and somewhat lethargic, George returned to Mongumba after only a few weeks, paid off his regretful porters – who'd never had life so good – then headed for an American mission station with a small clinic on the Belgian side of the river.

There, the good missionary – named Wallen – treated him, giving the hunter the available injections but suggesting he make for Brazzaville in case it was sleeping sickness. At length George reached the English mission station of Bolobo on the river's left bank (Bolobo is still there, now a town of 30,000 inhabitants). George was tested by the missionary there, one Daws; he confirmed from blood smears taken from George's neck glands that it was not sleeping sickness, to George's intense relief, but was rather a culmination of malaria doses, an unbalanced diet and constant consumption of quinine. When George eventually made Brazzaville, he was shocked upon selling his ivory: the price had fallen to a paltry eleven shillings to the pound-weight; this made ivory hunting a break-even business at best. With the Great Depression around the corner, the days of the great ivory hunters were over.

Before he left for Europe, George received one last letter from Jim Sutherland, who was doing poorly. He was racked by dysentery, and Marcus Daly had elbowed into his territory unchecked, even raiding the master's camp in his absence. Then the French and the Sudan Government threw Daly out, and he ended up in Kenya. Fitzwilliams called in on Sutherland when he left for England in 1932; he found that Sutherland had a scratch on one of his legs – be that from a thorn or sharp bit of metal – and the poison combined with rampant bacteria killed Sutherland while Fitzwilliams was present. They carried him to Yubo where he was buried on 26 June 1932. As I mentioned in the previous chapter, Tony Sánchez-Ariño luckily found Sutherland's grave after months of searching, coming upon some men removing the commemorative plaque as he discovered the grave. Incensed, he paid the grave robbers instead and took the plate home, where it remains built into his fireplace in Valencia, until a better place can one day be found.

George left Africa and docked in Brussels; he spent some time there before heading to Paris. Both cities were clean, and great fun to holiday in; they would certainly have been in wild contrast to tropical Africa…from there George headed to London to have his broken nose fixed (it had always rankled with him, a memento of his barman days in Boma). When he reached Jacksdale to visit his family, he went down with a severe dose of blackwater fever. For five days he swirled through a feverish, unconscious nightmare. But when at length he eventually emerged, he found convalescing in England terribly tedious; he needed to return to Africa.

*　*　*

And that is where the story of George Rushby, ivory hunter, effectively ends. His adventurous life was however by no means over; indeed, the subsequent chapters would make him world-famous, in game-ranging circles at least. But his last great ivory-gathering days were now behind him. As an ivory hunter, he'd shot some 400 elephants, accounting for another 1,400 while on duty as a cropping officer. For these latter, he'd used the ubiquitous .375H&H and .416 Rigby repeater rifles, but that was mere slaughter; the first 400 had been hunted, at great personal danger. The story of how George hunted down the Njombe man-eating lions is so absurd, so incredible, so noteworthy and so downright chilling that I covered it in some detail in *No Covenant*, my first book – which centres on the phenomenon of lions consuming people – but as previously mentioned, the Bulpin work *The Hunter is Death* (Nelson, 1962) is the definitive story, told to Bulpin by Rushby himself.

To boot, the two men returned to every place George had been. My first edition of the Bulpin book occupies a special place in my library and in my heart, as it is one of the works that inspired me to join the literary circles on the subject, however humbly. To try and précis the first half of a life as full as that led by George Rushby has been a chore in itself, but a few points should nonetheless be made on his latter career. When he returned to Africa, George met his future wife, Eleanor, in Cape Town. After a whirlwind romance – they were married 48 hours after meeting – they moved to Tanganyika to grow coffee. They had 6 children (the eldest son George, but better known as Mike, was contacted by me via the internet in 2003, and when we moved to Australia, we met up in 2008). George senior battled a bit farming coffee, trying that and other odd jobs until joining the Game Department in 1938.

In the years immediately after World War 2, George hunted down the Njombe pride, who'd been operating over several generations since about 1932, accounting for some 1,500 (and possibly as many as 2,000+) people! Rushby proposed the Gombe Stream National Park (later made world-famous by Jane Goodall and the local chimpanzees), and in 1949 proposed the Ruaha National Park. In 1956 he retired to his farm in Lupembe, moving in 1960 to the Cape in South Africa, where he died at Simonstown in 1969. Truly, he was a man who was larger than life, and aside from the remarkable Tony Sánchez-Ariño – who continued to hunt well into his 80s – was one of the very last of the fabled breed of ivory hunters, those greatest of adventurers.

12. Wally Johnson

Picture courtesy of Hunt Forever

The 1988 comedy film *Dirty Rotten Scoundrels*, directed by Frank Oz and featuring two not inconsiderable stars in the lead roles – Michael Caine and Steve Martin – features several profound quotes by Caine's character, a man of culture, learning and experience. Both men play con artists, Martin's character playing at cheap, minor levels like scoring free meals while Caine's character makes large sums from corrupt, gullible and hugely-wealthy widows. One of the gems is the reaction of Caine's character to a report in the newspaper that a capable and dangerous con artist is making their way across Europe, taking people for money at every hook and turn: he asks the chief of police in the French Riviera town – a man who is on the take and a part of the advanced con schemes, and who reads the report – that if this con artist is so good, why are they in the papers?

That may seem a long-winded path to my point, but bear with me; ideally, a con artist, thief or poacher would never be caught, and carry out their heists, thefts, cons and other mayhem without anyone ever being the wiser, much less catching them. A case in point would be George Rushby and his two chums during their school days, leading what game keepers were about on a merry goose-chase, and documented in the previous chapter. In later years, Rushby led the District Commissioners on similar goose chases through the marshes, but understandably, gathering ivory would be a tad more conspicuous to conceal, and thus evasion would become of far greater importance than going totally unnoticed. Most if not all of the great ivory hunters have poached at some stage in their careers, some of them for their entire careers. The vast majority were unknown; many died in this pursuit of white gold, forever forgotten in the winds of Africa.

As alluded to in the previous chapter, it is as well that people such as Tom Bulpin documented the life of George Rushby; otherwise, it is quite possible, indeed likely, that no one would ever even have heard of his sorties, in particular those regarding the man-eating Njombe lions. When I was in East Africa, I researched those events extensively, but African record-keeping being what it is, found not much *in situ*, bar municipal records. There will have been a great number of ivory hunters whose stories are forever lost, and that is a great pity, given the phenomenal exploits of those we do know about. Most of them would likely prefer it that way, many having been drifters, people on the run from the law or merely rogues. Men such as Tony Sánchez-Ariño have documented the lives of many of the great ivory hunters (remarkably-many of whom he knew), and others have done similar.

But they can't possibly have known anything more than a small portion of the men engaged in this most hazardous of occupations. Bulpin himself covered the life of another legendary ivory hunter in his book *The Ivory Trail* (Howard Timmins, 1954), who was a notorious poacher: Cecil Barnard, known by his Shangaan (now Tsonga) moniker, *Bvekenya*. The name means "he who swaggers when he walks", a telling and fitting label. Again, without this brilliant biography, it is unlikely whether the pimpernel poacher would ever have been heard of, and certainly not to the extent he is known today. Incidentally, his grandson – Willem – operates a safari business today, in Botswana. It gets yet more complex: it is difficult enough trying to document and record the white ivory hunters; imagine all the black African poachers? Out of pure necessity, millions of black Africans have poached for millennia. The book *The Adventures of Shadrek* by Ron Thomson (Long Beach, 2001) covers this legendary poacher's exploits in what is now Zimbabwe, during the 1960s and 70s. But most of the men in this field remain unknown.

Despite operating in Mozambique for over half a century, Walter Walker (Wally) Johnson was unknown, even to Sánchez-Ariño; Tony has a phenomenal memory, has carried out years of research and has hunted for over 60 years, knowing many of the most legendary ivory hunters personally. This all just serves to illustrate my point; only a chance meeting on a Zambian safari in 1985 allowed Peter Hathaway Capstick, the foremost hunting author of the time, to document Wally's remarkable story. His work *The Last Ivory Hunter* (St Martin's Press, 1988) was written in conjunction with Wally and is instantly wonderful for its uniqueness, authenticity and for those of us who hail from Southern Africa, its nostalgia, despite evoking some unpleasant memories too. Wally was a tough old bush-hardened man, and among his many noteworthy achievements was surviving a full bite from a large adult Gaboon Adder (*Bitis gabonica*), more-commonly known to Americans and Europeans as the Gaboon Viper.

Snakes fascinate many, my younger brother and I among this number. We pored over information on them, handled them when and where possible and generally enthused about them, as do many African boys. I have kept two as pets, albeit of a non-venomous persuasion. The oldest types are the pythons and boas, which even today retain tiny remnants of hind legs; the animal advanced to smaller, faster and venomous varieties such as cobras and mambas; and the most-advanced, most-evolved snake forms are today thought to be the viperids, which we always found a mite strange. Thick, slow-moving, ponderous snakes were surely less-evolved than creatures such as the lightning-quick mamba, with its no-nonsense demeanour and phenomenally-potent venom? But nature has obviously decreed that concealment is the way to go for serpents, the mamba – though a master of concealment itself – probably too conspicuous due to its aggression and thus likely to be cleared out of areas by frightened people.

This is the same reason tigers and lions, for instance, are cleared out of human areas way before hyenas and leopards are; they are too bold, conspicuous and obviously dangerous. They can't hide like a leopard, although not many things can. Many people coming to Africa on safari are paranoid about the myriad snakes that they envision as being in every bed, boot or on every path. The stories – and there are many – have planted this panic there, but the reality is that most snakes that can't avoid people have learned over time to keep still, their excellent camouflage usually keeping them safe, sometimes at astonishingly-close quarters. So, the adders (and other viperids across the globe) thrive because they blend in well, have huge fangs to deliver potent toxins – all viper species are venomous – and large heads to facilitate fast and easy swallowing of their favourite prey, usually rodents.

The Gaboon adder grows to two metres in length, and at this size is astonishingly thick and heavy; indeed, it is the heaviest viperid, carries the highest venom yield of any snake on the planet, and has the largest fangs of any snake, up to five cm (two inches). To give you an idea, a specimen 180cm (five feet, nine inches) long caught in 1973 weighed over 11kg (25lb) with an empty stomach. A bite from those huge hypodermics is reportedly excruciating, and I believe the sufferers, having no desire to test-drive their statements. I have watched footage on Gaboons swallowing rats, and it is fascinating, more proof of the advanced evolutionary state of viperids: it takes hardly any time at all due to the size of the massive head, whereas a python, for example, can take literally hours to swallow its (admittedly far-larger) meal. When Peter

Capstick and Wally were compiling his story – between 1985 and 1987 – they went to some length to research previous survivors of this incredible snake's bite, and found only one other adult human who had gotten a full dose from an adult Gaboon who didn't join the choir invisible.

The camouflage of the Gaboon is mind-blowing, their colours undeniably beautiful, even to people with snake phobias. In many snake park enclosures, one has to look long and hard to spot it among the leaf litter, and can often only do so when it moves or flickers a tongue. Reading Capstick's book, one gets some sense that, even though Wally survived the bite, he went through hell on earth before emerging at the other side. The devilry of the venom would remain in Wally's system for some time and it was many months before he could walk properly again. Some peculiarities of the Gaboon bear mentioning here; the species is extremely passive by venomous snake standards, and some have handled it with no bite forthcoming. They also seem to keep venom for when it is needed, by choice not always injecting venom (as indeed can many venomous snakes; the Gaboon seems not to, more often though).

But when they do bite and inject venom, you have a problem; the Gaboon will often not release as would a Puff Adder, for instance, and thus pours great gobs of cytotoxic poison through those massive fangs. The venom isn't specifically toxic compared to mamba venom, which has a propensity toward fast absorption and is fast-acting, and is nowhere near as potent as the venom of most of the Australian venomous varieties; but as mentioned, the snake hangs on when it does bite, and pumps in huge amounts. All this should clearly illustrate to you that when this thing *does* bite, elsewhere is an excellent place to be. So, when Wally copped his dose, he looked down to see the snake attached to his leg. Kicking it off, his ordeal began. The first problem – and people who haven't lived in Africa can't possibly understand – is that his men wanted nothing to do with the affair. Seeing the species, the men decreed that their boss was going to die, simple as that. Even his lifelong tracker, Luis, felt this way.

The only thing stronger than the fatalism of bush Africans is their superstition; cases have been known where a man hexed or cursed by the witchdoctor literally lies down that night and dies. A snake is the seed of the very devil himself to many Africans. They can't stand even looking at them for fear of invoking a curse. There was a further complication: if Wally were indeed to die, his men would have a problem, the authorities likely suspecting them of killing and robbing him, regardless how contrite they were. Wally was determined to live, and swore long, loudly and repeatedly until his men got him to where he could receive treatment. Wally came from a place and time foreign to most modern people, and the stream of epithets delivered to his men was impressive in its variety and creativeness. By the time he was treated his leg had swollen to cartoon size and the pain was such as he'd never envisaged possible.

Wally had an ancient antivenin kit and had to inject four ampoules into himself; of course, two were out of date. First, he had to cut a gash over the fang marks in his leg, then inject the strange, milky gunk into the wound; but the lancet for the purpose had been stolen long since. Desperate, Wally implored the men to find him any sharp knife instead. At length, one of the rural chaps produced a rusty razor blade from his hair. As Wally noted, it was many things, but sterile wasn't one of them! Wally duly cut the X-gash and while one of his men sucked the venom and blood out, spitting it out, Wally started penning a letter to his wife, telling her a Gaboon had bitten him and that his men were innocent of anything the authorities may accuse them of. He then needed to get to proper medical treatment or die, but his men didn't want to know. Finally, a rugged bush-type agreed to go with Wally; he'd been hanging around camp, helping cut up meat and so forth. The fact that he'd never even been in a vehicle before was of secondary importance!

The man carried Wally to the driver's seat, from whence he drove as best he could; his companion at least spoke Shangaan and passable Portuguese. The old Toyota Land Cruiser was a vehicular nightmare with a propensity for stalling, but they made it to a distant sawmill, the lights of which were shining in the dark, before Wally passed out. When he came to, the men were feeding him whisky and their supervisor, a German, was away. After more screaming, swearing and threats from Wally, the sawmill staff finally sent him to hospital with a driver. Wally kept drinking water the whole way, interspersed with sessions of vomiting up great gouts of black blood. They reached the hospital at 2am; after painkillers, more antivenin and a tetanus shot – the last-mentioned of which may have been a tad irrelevant – Wally got word to his wife, who duly arrived with the intention of getting Wally across the border, to the Umtali Hospital in Rhodesia (now Zimbabwe).

This was accomplished, Wally's whole side by that time darkening from a superb shade of blue to an intimidating black. For several weeks Wally lay there in great pain, his leg twice the size of the other one. Once out of danger though, he and his wife headed home, where it took a further three months of rest until he could get about with the help of a cane. The better part of a year would pass before Wally could walk properly and hunt again.

*   *   *

Wally was an absolute entrepreneur; at a young age he'd already dabbled in (and often made huge sums from) such diverse pursuits as diamond prospecting, banana plantations, gold mining – by which I mean actually owning entire mines – saving villages from man-eating lions and even working as a shipping clerk! The key to his success was diversifying, never ceasing to keep an eye out for opportunity, and always being self-sufficient. One needed ingenuity in adverse circumstances, and Wally had that in spades. It was those two traits – self-sufficiency and ingenuity – without which ivory hunting would have been impossible. It is actually a strange harking-back to a time when man was rapidly becoming the dominant species over some huge and volatile creatures; the adaptability and mental fortitude to overcome a massive physical disadvantage. Wally recalled often going three days with no sign of a spoor, nothing at all.

For equal lengths of time, one often had nothing to drink; that alone was sufficient to drive men to lengths they would never usually so much as contemplate. The only water was often in old filthy pools, churned to mud by elephants; or in footprints in the rainy season, which the elephants had urinated in. Wally recalled baking under the sun by day, being frozen at night, and more often than not, starving or thirsty to the point of near-death. As Capstick wrote, one needs to be cognisant of the conditions under which the ivory hunters operated, to fully grasp the implications of the profession. Few other occupations have had so small a margin for error. The critical fruits of one's self-sufficiency and ingenuity were mobility in the field, and the ability to get home, back to any modicum of civilisation. Otherwise, one's bones would feed something in the food chain; usually hyenas, if the lions left any; or the elephant that assisted one into the next world actually left enough matter intact, so as to be identifiable as bones…

It was 1933, at the height of the dry season; Wally was some 80 miles (130km) from LM (Lourenço Marques, now Maputo) when his vehicle decided that the connecting rod would look aesthetically-pleasing if it were to spear its way through the crankcase. That repaired, Wally noticed the engine was in desperate need of some gaskets, so he stalked a nearby waterbuck bull, shot it, and using a flattened tin and the still-fresh waterbuck hide beneath it as a seal, had the car functioning again as well as any new gasket could have done.

Wally also had a small safari trailer which often sheared its axles; one evening during the Second World War, it happened again. With Wally was his long-time tracker and hunting companion, Luis. The men had just made a fire as night fell like a blanket, which an African night so often does. Luis voiced his concern at the developing situation, and Wally looked up from his axle repair: surrounding the campfire was a pride of lions, and closely! Being wartime, ammunition stocks were low, but the lions were that bold and that close that Wally felt he should make a statement, shooting the nearest big cat. The others hardly reacted; the men threw firebrands at them, actually hitting them, but the only reaction was a snarl, and a jump backwards. Then the recipient would immediately return.

Those lions were almost certainly man-eaters, as Wally recounted; the area is renowned for them, as I extensively documented in *No Covenant*. One also gets a gut-feel, and people often seem to just *know* when the cats are intent on eating you; I covered that little nicety too. Wally had that much experience with lions that he knew man-eaters from the garden variety. The lions sat watching the men, looking for an opening, and Wally had to use another bullet or two in keeping them at bay. As the light improved with the approaching dawn, the men towed the trailer away, broken axle or not.

Wally's .318 had a rusted barrel, and when fired, it would expand the brass case into the breech craters; this meant that ejecting the empty case resulted in the extractor tearing the case in half. As one might imagine, this allowed Wally only one or two shots before the rifle was jammed thus, and when hunting elephant, this could result in a squashed hunter. 'Jammed' was certainly the operative…so Wally sought to address the problem, and his ingenuity again came to the fore. Realising that the .318 would likely be the cause of his demise soon, and with .375 ammunition rarer than hens' teeth, Wally heard of a fire at a gun shop in Umtali, where most of the stock had been consumed. He hastened thither, looking for a new barrel. He scratched about in the gun shop debris and found a perfect 9.3mm barrel with the stock completely burned away. The barrel was still in excellent condition, the rifle likely having been brand new.

For a couple of Pounds, Wally acquired the Mauser piece, and it fitted the .318's action as if made for it. Wally fitted it and it still required some machining, but he had plenty of 9.3mm ammunition, so was determined to make the effort. First try, the sights were dead-on! The rifle was tremendous, a hard-hitting calibre for its weight that European hunters swear by, and many professional hunters today favour. Although it lacked the clout of the .375H&H – which remained Wally's favourite 'good-for-all' rifle – the Mauser was almost as good, and most crucially, ammunition was no problem. In Wally's words, it was a real mamba of a rifle, so it obviously had some bite!

* * *

Once, Wally was out with a young man who had the first Land-Rover in Mozambique, a vehicle with a special place in my heart as I owned one, and in the hearts of many famous hunters and game rangers. Paul Grobler (featured in a following chapter) and his family swore by them. The Savé River (pronounced Sah-Vay) was in flood, and rising further. The men realised that if they didn't cross it, they would likely be marooned for weeks, possibly months. At length, an enterprising tribesman made a canoe by stripping a huge bark sheet from a tree, then sealing the ends. The men then disassembled the referred-to Land-Rover, crossing the rising river in stages, each time with as many parts as the craft could manage; once everything was on the other side, they reassembled the Landy and drove home, a full five days later! The modular nature of the vehicle, the tribesman, his excellent boat and sheer luck had made it all possible.

Wally recounted his elephant-hunting years as the toughest of his life, a horror of thirst, hunger and fatigue. In 1937 the Portuguese Government opened unlimited elephant hunting in Mozambique. Wally was then 25 years old, and conducted his last safari aged 72, which amounts to nearly a half-century in this most perilous of occupations. His tally at the end of it all was some 1,300 bull elephants and around 60 cows taken in self-defence. This actually places him above Bell in the list of bulls taken, if not in the overall pantheon of legendary ivory gatherers; but as Peter Capstick wrote, who would ever have heard of Bell, had he himself not written? It was a great service Peter provided to Wally, elevating him into people's consciousness. As mentioned earlier, Wally was unbeknownst even to Tony Sánchez-Ariño, who hunted Africa for over 60 years.

Wally - recounting his story to Peter on the banks of the Mupamadzi - remembered when the unlimited hunting started in 1937, his very first recollection being the death of one De Waal. He had shot a pachyderm in the leg to immobilise it, approaching to take a photograph. For some reason, he approached the bull from the front, even insanely touching the tip of its trunk with his rifle muzzle, to see if it was still alive! Given that up to that point he'd only administered a leg-shot, and somewhat unsurprisingly, it was. The bull launched forward and De Waal's last chance was up when he fell over a log. The elephant stamped him into what Wally described as chunky peanut-butter and jelly. Next cab off the rank was one Juan Domingues; he and his son approached two bulls at a waterhole. Armed with a .470 Nitro Express double, Juan had his son return to camp.

The son dutifully obeyed, as did sons of the time; but the next he saw of his father was when they brought his body in. Juan had approached the second bull from the rear, and saw that he couldn't get in a shot unless the elephant turned around. When this happened, the man fired for the brain, but only got one shot off. The rifle was later found, intact and in working order, with no explanation as to why he'd not fired the second barrel. Perhaps a lack of time, which seems possible if unlikely. Regardless, it was academic for Domingues: the elephant tusked him through the head, killing him instantly. He was buried near the camp. Wally's next recollection was of a German who ran a sisal plantation. One day he set off after ivory and when he was later found, it was clear that he'd made contact with an elephant. He was described as completely smashed; his own workers couldn't recognise him. The body had been literally torn to pieces.

Into this picture, Wally started taking his son out elephant hunting with him, Walter Jnr killing a few, starting at age 8! One day, Wally took a friend with him who fervently wanted to take an elephant. It was his friend's 22nd birthday. The two young men went to an area near the Savé River and started enquiring at the native villages after elephantine crop-raiders. At this point, Wally reminded readers that Mozambique in 1937 was rather different from the perception today; people then were literally dying of hunger by the hundreds because of elephants consuming their crops. Wally was there to see it, and it was heart-rending to witness. Elephants had been protected and were completely stripping full cultivated fields. This was the reason the authorities had recognised the problem and allowed unlimited hunting of elephants. Wally walked his friend right up to a very good bull, maybe some 15 yards away, and his friend killed it with one shot in the brain.

The pair moved on toward the Savé, the rains having just started. They realised their petrol stocks would never suffice, so as he'd done before, Wally bought up the entire stock of palm wine from a nearby village, distilling it five times to use as propellant fuel! It worked a treat. He still recalled the name of the village: Machaze. The town still exists, a principal of the district of the same name. The party was then joined by a German who ran a nearby sawmill; they neared a herd of 30 or 40 jumbos. As the men zeroed in on a good bull, they had no idea that some of the herd had moved in behind them. They were sandwiched, and the first they knew of it was when they heard a slight noise, turning to see a large cow bearing down on them in full flight! The German snap-shot her, but she didn't fall, and the German took both tusks through the back. He was then pummelled to mush and died instantly. Wally was really saddened by this event as the German was a good man.

Next Wally had an interesting experience; the local tribesmen would direct them to any elephant in the area, and one day near the Savé, seven bulls were found. Luis stayed with the quarry while the tribesman returned to tell Wally. It was baking hot when Wally came up to the bulls, around noon. He could only see the tusks of some, maybe 40-pounders, but he hoped that those he couldn't see might sport heavier ivory. As they do in brutal heat, the bulls stood flapping their ears, to cool the blood in the network of thick veins. At length, Wally saw two good bulls and dropped one; the elephants milled all around him, and he next shot a sixty-pounder, which was hard-hit but made off. Following, Wally came into open country, and there well ahead was the injured bull, badly hit and walking slowly. He needed to close with it before it reached the forest ahead, but it was some distance and Wally raced on in the crushing heat, more exhausted with each step.

Wally made it to within 50 yards but could get no closer; soon he had to run again and closed to 30 yards. He was hoping the jumbo would turn its head to look behind it, sufficient for a brain shot, but it never did so to the extent necessary. Wally was lining up on its spine when suddenly the great rump started growing larger! The bull was charging backwards, and when it got to within ten yards it spun about like lightning. Wally dropped it with a frontal brain shot, but felt this amply illustrated how intelligent elephants are, and how aware of proximity to a following enemy. Once, when Wally was at a place called Chinzine (Chin-zee-neh), he stopped in at the *Chefe de Poste*, which was not only a prudent and customary courtesy, but was required by the law. This was because the locals would report any dubious stranger as likely being a poacher.

This *Chefe* was known to Wally anyhow, and in chatting, the man mentioned two crop-raiding bull elephants that were terrorising the area. They'd hole up in deep cover by day, the locals too afraid to track them there, and emerge by night to consume great quantities of crops. At least one was said to sport arrowheads shot into him by desperate locals (I'll bet that improved his demeanour no end), and the pair had recently been confronted in the early evening by a woman beating a tin with a stick. She died, horribly. The *Chefe* had seen her corpse, and most thoroughly dead, she was. The man implored Wally to shoot the bulls. He recommended a shooting platform which his men had erected for just this purpose, at a central waterhole the bulls always frequented. So far it had been too dark to kill the bulls, and any random firing in their general direction would, again, have thrilled them to bits, I'm sure.

Wally had his son, Walter Jnr, along for the ride; when they saw the rickety structure, they preferred the devil they knew, remaining on the ground and exposed to hyenas and lions (which gives some idea of what the 'platform' looked like...). Night fell and it got really dark after 7pm; soon, the unmistakable sounds of elephants splashing and drinking were audible, and Wally readied his rifle, then whispered to his son to switch the torch on. There illuminated in the beam were the two bulls, not 15 yards away! Wally dropped one with the side brain shot, the other making himself scarce. Before he could ghost away though, Wally put a bullet into his heart area. A great crash soon after indicated that the shot had been a good one. As Walter Jnr switched the torch off, Wally asked if he'd noticed anything strange on the ground.

The younger Johnson hadn't, but Wally had; "Turn the bloody thing on again!" he blurted out. Before them, a mere yard from their blankets, was a mass of scorpions. Wally was convinced it must have been a migration of some form. Not merely hundreds or thousands; *millions* of scorpions! Their combined movements created a strange humming sound, pink pincers and stingers everywhere. As can well be appreciated, the pair scarpered to the other side of the lake, far less concerned about anything else they may encounter in the pitch dark! I wondered if Wally still thought the ground to be better than the platform after that, but at least they could run away. Scorpions can climb, and if they'd encountered the swarm several metres up, the men would surely have sustained some injury when descending, at the very least.

A few years later, while on safari with a client, Wally recalled similar. The client had just shot a good kudu, and Wally was about to leave the vehicle to join him. Again, the entire ground was awash in small pink scorpions! They were so numerous that Wally had to drive around to the client; for some hours, the men couldn't even approach the kudu. No-one could ever explain this phenomenon to Wally; where they all went, he had no idea, considering holes in the ground to be their most-probable destination. As Wally recalled, it was like a horror movie, only real!

*　*　*

When he started gathering ivory, Wally thought night-hunting would be the answer; it would attract less attention and he'd avoid Mozambique's crippling heat that way. Soon, however, he realised that following up animals in the dark was nigh-impossible, not to mention immensely dangerous. It was surviving the wilting conditions or standing a high chance of not surviving at all; so, daylight was reverted to! Early in the piece Wally had a very fruitful month, collecting 43 elephants. The biggest carried 85lbs a side. He saw one sporting over 100lbs a side, but had no clear shot and had to watch the prize escape. On another very profitable trip, Wally shot 30 elephants at a place near Zumbo (Mozambique's most-western town, of some 30,000-35,000 people). The animals were robust and the ivory plentiful, and of good quality.

The men dried heaps of meat on that trip, which was literally all the payment most of the men wanted; 'meat for meat', they called it. Wally did however have a cautionary note for employers the world over; human nature being what it is, he needed to remain vigilant. One day he just happened to glance in the rear-view mirror as a large pile of dried elephant-biltong sticks – tied together in a bundle – flew off the side of the vehicle as they neared home. Clearly, the men were stealing meat and intending to fetch it later. He stopped the car, loudly and roundly berating them, and in so doing kept a lid on such happenings. When Wally started ivory hunting, he was often accompanied by Harry Manners, a man who was later to become a legend of the entire region. They were to spend years together after ivory. Wally was then lightly-armed with a .30-06, Harry even more so, with a .256 Mannlicher.

As had the great Bell, they sawed an elephant skull in half to see exactly where the grey matter resided! Strangely, Wally recalled losing several bulls to the shot into the angle between eye and ear, preferring the heart shot. I say strangely, as many – Capstick included, who also noted Wally's comments as strange – swore by that shot as invariably lethal. Still, to each his own! One noon on the Savé River, it was (as usual) cripplingly hot. Having established via the locals the most-likely spots for bulls to roam, the party neared seven bulls, fanning themselves in the shade. Wally could only see two, and knew that if the wind changed, he'd soon see none! Finally, he saw a sixty-pounder, dropping it with an ear shot. Running on, he felled another three. It was physically lambasting, but worthwhile: the bulls felled averaged 55lbs a tusk.

Then a nearby chief provided information that Wally was to head to a certain nearby mountain. He found some twenty bulls, felling eight after some hard running. The best yielded 50lbs a side, the smallest, 35lbs a side, not a bad haul. Wally left the meat (a huge mountain of flesh) to the tribe as payment. The best tusks Wally ever gathered were 160lbs a side, which is huge by any standards; but he wounded one carrying over 200lbs a side. The massive beast crossed into the Kruger National Park, and that was that. Wally believes the animal died there, but there was no way to follow: the Kruger wardens employed a policy to shoot poachers on sight. In addition, they closely monitored all giant tuskers within their boundaries, even assigning rangers and wardens to monitor them full-time while within the Park.

Over time, Wally came to realise that the ivory dealers in Lourenço Marques were in contact to manipulate and manage market prices. The hunters were sold the same story: that they'd been off in the 'blue' for so long, the price had fallen on the world markets. Each successive dealer told the same story, the price varying by only a few pennies from that of the previous dealer. Meanwhile, the hunter would cart his heavy ivory with him, eventually having no option but to accept the best offer, however meagre. Wally reckoned that he'd been duped out of many thousands of Pounds over the years; and there was nothing he could have done. The dealers had a captive market, and exploited it to the full. At one stage following a banana crop disaster, Wally had no alternative but to try make a go out of ivory-gathering. He managed to buy an International truck, so he gathered up his .30-06 and ventured forth.

Later, Wally acquired a Brenneke 11.2 x 72mm, an odd and uncommon calibre for Mozambique. Ammunition was rare, so he had to be really sparing and prudent. When it ran out, he was totally at a loss otherwise. Wally recounted elephant hunting as being immensely tough; the sheer logistics involved mean that even hard men can wilt, or die. After walking all day, over rough terrain and in blazing heat, the hunter finally closes with an elephant. At the crucial moment, the fickle wind turns, the great beast scents the man and disappears, three sails to the wind. Sometimes one would follow, for two or three days. No extra water or food is carried; these are too heavy. Soon the supplies one can cart, run out. As Wally said, get thirsty enough and you'll drink any liquid you can find in the bush. I'll leave that to your imagination, but already in this book I've recounted desperate men drinking the blood of a felled victim; or the muddy, elephant urine-befouled water in wallows or footprints. Just when you'd finally close with the herd, they'd scent you again! Right back to square number one…

Abandoning the chase, which was sometimes inevitable, meant another two- or three-days' travel back to camp, again with no food or water. Wally painted a mental picture for Peter Capstick there on the Mupamadzi, describing a typical crop raid by elephants, and the subsequent following up by an ivory hunter. There is little doubt that an elephant is a highly-intelligent creature; they would descend on a village, usually at night, and principally in search of maize (corn). Any other fresh produce would disappear into their vast insides as well. Then they'd scram, travelling hard for some 10-12 miles (16-19km). Around midday they'd seek shade to rest out the crushing heat. Obviously, Wally would look for the best tusks. Wherever the herd found themselves in the late afternoon, they'd make for the local villages. Wally would get up close behind them, then scream at the herd. This would buy him some seconds of confusion as they turned to look at the trailing human; in those moments he could shoot the good bull or two that may be present.

The best and biggest bulls never associate with cow elephants. These bachelor herds – usually a giant old bull or two, accompanied by a few younger *shikaris* – were used to being hunted, and were accordingly more aggressive. The scream tactic was risky when in herds of 30-40 animals, though; the hunter would then invariably be charged. The cows were almost always the main protagonists. Once early in his career, Wally saw two bulls together and dropped one; unbeknown to him, he was actually in the middle of a herd. As his awareness of the situation hit home, he felt his rifle oddly light. The recoil of his shot had popped the magazine's baseplate open, all the unfired cartridges bedecking the ground! Luckily for Wally, the herd all gravitated toward the stricken bull, five females on each side actually managing to lift him, rather than erasing Walter Walker Johnson from the annals of African ivory-hunting folklore before he'd really gotten going.

Off the entire party of pachyderms set, crushing a path *en route*. After his heartbeat had reverted to some semblance of normality, Wally followed. Some 15 minutes later, he came upon the dead bull, all the other elephants gone. For some odd reason known only to them, the other elephants had urinated on the dead bull; Capstick recalled having seen this phenomenon too. Wally felt the intelligence and social structure of elephants to be really moving, but the herds had to be thinned out. He considered the level of humanity appalling in Mozambique back then; in a cutting message for most of us in this twenty-first century – and especially in comparatively-affluent, first-world countries – Wally remembered seeing human beings starve to death, which takes on further significance when one's own actions can a) provide them with plentiful meat, and b) remove the source of their famine with its night-time crop depredations. Raising funds and watching documentaries on countries suffering from famine just aren't quite the same thing...

The elephant problem was so severe then, that the *Chefes de Postes* began to issue the local populace with rifles. As Wally recalled, the incompetence of many so armed resulted in a countryside awash with wounded elephants. He considered there to have been at least as many people killed in the act of the shooting, or by wounded pachyderms afterward. As usual, human greed (or was that opportunism?) would rear its ugly head; Wally sardonically recounted where all the ivory would end up: with the rifle-providing *Chefes*...the bottom line – and I'm firmly in agreement – is that a child's life is worth more than that of an elephant. I can hear the rabid green fringe loudly disputing this; but then, they've never grown up in a developing country...

The distances covered on foot by the ivory hunters beggar belief; Wally took his old International truck to an area called Panda. With no four-wheel drive back then, the vehicle would have to be left somewhere, and 60-70 miles (96-112km) covered on foot in two days! Any given trip after elephant could mean a two-hundred-mile round trip (320km). Wally camped near a large lagoon, the locals delighted to learn that Wally had come to shoot elephants. They'd not seen white men in years, and the crop damage caused by elephants was extensive. Meat-starved, they were largely subsisting on fish for protein. Early next dawn, Luis and Wally were shown two huge sets of tracks, but the bulls were moving fast and the men couldn't close with them. The locals directed the party to a nearby pan, noting that the bulls were headed to a dry area and would have to return to the pan to drink. As usual, the locals were spot-on; Wally was ready when both bulls returned and soon after, was the owner of four fine tusks, averaging 80lbs each.

As they went from village to village, Luis translated the people's complaints to Wally: the crop depredations by elephants had gotten totally out of hand. It was so pathetic, that many people had already died of starvation; those who hadn't were reed-thin and digging in the bush for root and bulbs. When they found them, they'd eat them on the spot, so a stronger person couldn't steal them away. It was that bad that Wally postponed his hunt to visit the local *Chefe de Poste* and ask what was being done to remedy the situation. That hero unconcernedly responded that he had written to Lourenço Marques for maize meal, but hadn't yet received any. Wally left, infuriated at the man's apathy and determined to do something. He shot a few elephants for meat; but – and people who have lived in Africa will understand and relate – the locals wanted maize meal as well!

Wally gave all he had, two 50kg sacks (totalling around 220lbs), which didn't go far among the hundreds of starving wretches. Wally gave the most meal to the worst-affected, but the people were still too weak to farm for themselves afterward. All the while, the pachyderms were ruining the crops, so Wally shot nine more, then went upriver and killed another nine. He felt these twenty-odd elephants would surely have helped, but then he drove the 200 miles (320km) back home – and as he said, not 200 miles of American highways either – returning with the last eight bags of meal that he had. The round trip took eight days, and spent petrol he could barely spare, but after that, Wally felt sure he'd saved some lives.

* * *

Wally had a friend who was a mad-keen photographer. One day, with dusk looming, the pair were following a very large elephant track. Just a few steps away, beyond a small clearing, stood the elephant, facing away from them. Wally's friend filmed for a few minutes, Wally drawing a bead on the animal all the while. Suddenly the elephant whirled about and came for the men! Wally dropped it to a brain shot at eight measured feet! The giant pus-filled hole under its eye, a tusk wound from a fight with another bull, explained its venomous demeanour. Elephant were open game in

Mozambique then, except in two areas: Pafuri, beside the Kruger Park, and Maputo Reserve in the south. Around that time, Wally bought a plane and learned to fly, showing Walter Jnr the Maputo Reserve from the air. The plains supported huge elephant herds, among them one day a giant bull, with easily 150lbs a side. Wally cut the motor to glide down for a better look, but the engine refused to reignite!

This is it, thought Wally; killed, and my son too, into a herd of elephant…but at the last moment the engine fired, and they soared skyward. Clean shorts were however likely necessary for both…in the Savé River's Massengena area, Wally killed a bull with 160lbs a side, but that region was soon shot out: the storekeepers started supplying the locals with firearms. Wally's favourite time to hunt elephant was in the rainy season; spooring was easy and the hunter could easily find standing water. The foliage was green, quiet to travel through and plentiful, so elephants could eat without having to traverse huge distances. After the heart-rending episode with all the starving people in the Panda area, Wally returned to the Savé, and a village where the elephants had killed a young man just three days before. As Wally said, to echo what I alluded to in the introduction, the people would go out in the dark to save their *shambas*, walk right up to the elephants, with the outcome starkly predictable. As Wally mused, even the best forensic surgeon couldn't have reassembled the pieces…

Wally felt that as a hunter, one could never really relax, never let your guard down. A local told Luis and Wally that he knew where the elephants were that had recently accounted for the young man; they went along with him and after only two hours, came upon the herd, right in the open. There were two decent bulls among them and Wally dropped both, right next to each other. A third bull ran past and Wally raced in pursuit, but couldn't close sufficiently and had to give best. When he got back, the two felled bulls were gone. Obviously, both had merely been stunned; the spoor showed they had actually gotten up against each other, then staggered off, each supporting his companion! Wally had been convinced that both were dead. It was as well that he hadn't propped his rifle against one and smoked a pipe; as he mentioned, if he had, that would most likely have been his last pipe…

Wally tried for days to find the wounded bulls but they had vanished. Later that same trip, Wally and his crew came upon another bunch of elephant. Walter Jnr was in tow on this occasion. This was to be a day to remember, but not for the right reasons.

The only good bull among the group was in the middle, surrounded by cows. The men couldn't even see enough of him to gauge his ivory. Wally had the .375H&H with only three cartridges, while Walter Jnr's .318 had eight rounds. After waiting for half an hour with still no view of the bull's tusks, Wally decided to shoot the cow screening him. He really should have killed it, given the ammunition situation, but for some reason he didn't. Things happened fast; the cow charged immediately, Walter Jnr dropping it stone-dead with a frontal shot. Like lightning, a second cow replaced the first, Walter Jnr performing an action replay and sending her the way of the previous one.

A third popped into the second one's just-vacated space; she went the same way as the other two (Walter Jnr's eye at least seemed to be most definitively in that day, and fortunate that was, too). At last, the bull was visible: a *tondo*, or tuskless male! He was massive. Another cow charged and Wally dropped this one, but had to feed it two shots. No more .375 ammo, only five rounds of .318 standing between the men and perdition in its surest form. Walter Jnr swatted yet another cow, but this one didn't fall; instead, she bore down on the hunters, screaming fit to chill the blood. Wally grabbed the .318 from his son as the men scattered like leaves before the wind. As he tried to shoot the rapidly-closing cow elephant, the .318 only ejected half the previous fired cartridge. Nothing Wally could do would fix the jam.

Jam was rapidly becoming the men's likely next state; Wally's far younger, fleeter son was by now well ahead and Wally was convinced he was a dead man. He could even feel the earth shudder as the massive animal closed with him. Then suddenly - remarkably, mercifully - the noise and vibrations behind him ceased; the cow had at last succumbed to its wound! Wally thanked his lucky stars; the tracks showed the reaching trunk had been no more than three feet (one metre) behind him when the cow fell. Wally never used a .318 again. As Capstick noted, that was the calibre which had caused the great Bell problems, too. The phenomenal achievements of Bell notwithstanding, most people would agree that a .318 is way too light for work on jumbo…

Wally continued on toward the Savé, accounting for twelve good bulls over the following fortnight. The elephant were all savage, due to the locals' *penchant* for cable snares. An elephant being the size it is, and possessed of great strength, most specimens merely pull away from the securing rocks or trees. That means feet and trunks cut deeply, often right through. Wally called the cable snare the great curse of Africa, and right he was; they are the cruel feature of a large, poor and meat-starved populace. My ex-wife's uncle, whom for years ran a large and successful avocado farm and nursery in the Nelspruit area of South Africa's Eastern Transvaal (now Mpumalanga), felt similarly about cable snares, and would regularly clear them off his farm, constantly berating his staff for using them. Yet, the snares always seemed to reappear…

*　*　*

Wally saw some strange genetic aberrations among elephant, as one would, having spent so many years on their trail. Once, he shot a bull with a normal tusk on one side, and three tusks on the other! Another had five on one side; small tusks all, but five, nonetheless! Capstick mentioned the skull and tusks in the Explorers' Club in New York, residing in the corner of the top floor. The Club is on 70th Street; the skull features two tusks on each side. Most theories have revolved around lightning strikes splitting the tusks, but that is most unlikely. The animal would likely not survive, and anyhow, the tusks are normal, each with its own root. There is no sign of splitting. It is likely merely a genetic curiosity, as can be found among all species.

Wally's next destination was the mythical Simbiri Forest, a huge wooded area on Mount Mabu. It was all but lost in later years, named the "Google forest" as it was literally rediscovered by Dr Julian Bayliss, using Google Earth! In recent times it has unfortunately been subjected to heavy logging, but back in Wally's day, it was immensely dense and wooded. Wally was hunting with a friend, each with his own tracker; when they'd find two sets of tracks, they'd split, each following a set. The bush was that thick, that one day when this split happened, Wally hadn't gone ten yards before Luis signalled the presence of elephant. Wally lined up on the bull he could see; but the bush was that thick, he failed to notice an even bigger one, mere feet away. Luis saw it, and thinking Wally blind, mad or both, hightailed it away!

Before he could fire, both bulls charged at once; Wally potted the closer of the two, with three shots before ducking behind a small tree. The bull was reaching for Wally when in desperation he fed it a fourth and final dose, right under the chin and up into the brain! It had been that close. Wally dashed after the other bull, which was screaming horribly and bearing down on Luis. The bull suddenly knelt down and Wally thought Luis was a goner; elephants usually kneel on people to start the festivities, before the main course of trampling and tusking, even though that often isn't required. Wally shot the beast in the hip and as it slowly rose, he noticed with relief that Luis was some way ahead, running like the wind. It was then that Wally noticed this second elephant was a huge tusker, going well over 100lbs a side. Reloading one shot at a time as he ran and fired, Wally fed it five solids as the bull headed for a large flood plain.

Eventually darkness won out, and back in camp, Wally's friend – who'd also shot a bull – had the nerve to ask that he be allowed to find and kill the wounded giant. For some reason, Wally relented. Early the next day, the men set off in different directions. Wally killed a bull and was back in camp by ten a.m. To his surprise, his friend was already there! Wally assumed the man had quickly gotten the giant, but he hadn't; he'd obviously closed with the great beast and been given a thorough scare. He told Wally the area was wild, so he intended going back the following day! Wally was furious, telling him the bull would be lost. He ranted so long and so hard that the man retired to his tent. The bull was indeed lost, unnecessarily suffering, likely dying somewhere near and providing those windfall tusks to some lucky passer-by to boot.

A few days later, two bulls were fighting right in the water at a large *pan* (flood plain). As Wally watched from the bushes, two more large bulls emerged behind him. He crept as yet unseen around the side of the *pan*, but then the bulls winded him. All four left in a hurry, Wally dropping a 70-pounder in the rush. All day the men trailed the remaining three on the run, not once stopping; but the bulls were trotting too, and eventually the men had to give best. The following day, a curious thing happened; the men were trailing a big bull, some 50 yards (45 metres) behind him. It was blast-furnace hot. Suddenly the lead tracker gave out a piercing shriek. The bull had passed a tree in which was a large beehive. He had either inadvertently bumped the tree or the hive; or, knowing an elephant's intelligence, done so on purpose!

It was largely academic to the men; the entire party was stung half to death, and as Wally mentioned, if you doubt the tales about the savagery of African bees, I dare you to try them sometime! Another odd experience befell Wally when shadowing a large herd one day; there was a strange whistling noise over the herd, which no-one could place. At length, Luis pointed out one animal in the herd that had no trunk! A wire snare had cut it off, right up near the base. The creature was weak from starvation and Wally put it out of its misery. He recalled another sad tale of cruelty; one time while spooring a huge elephant, the tracks revealed that something was amiss with its gait. After Wally closed and shot it, he discovered a heavy spear lodged in the back of its skull from a drop-trap. Wally considered the elephant to have wandered about in this way for a year; the spear had missed the neck vertebrae, the pus and rot in the wound spelling agony.

Wally recounted many other things to Peter Capstick there on the banks of the Mupamadzi, and later at Peter's home in Pretoria, South Africa. He recalled clashes with leopards, many sorties after buffalo (Wally shot some 2,000 over his career, one of which gored him most definitively through the leg), and of course some hair-raising episodes with lions. Mozambique has a history of man-eating lions, as do many other African countries, and Wally had several close encounters. He also recalled some spooky tales of witchcraft and black magic, known as *tagati* in Southern Africa and *mbojo* in East Africa. In Mozambique, it is known as *cuchucuchu* (pronounced *cush-cush* as in cushion, the second and fourth consonants barely breathed out). Some of the tales really make one wonder, but I'll leave them for some other time.

Wally's time in Mozambique was about to end in tragedy, as it did for so many others. In short, Wally's home of 50 years was about to be swept up in a series of horrors that left it a mere playground for Communist revolutionaries. Only now, in the second decade of the 21st century, are some of the reserves – notably Gorongosa – starting to thrive anew. Wally's wife Lilly had died sometime before it all came to a head in 1975, and for this Wally was grateful. She was at least spared the shock and horror, which he believes would have killed her anyway, and this time unpleasantly. Wally was embittered and his voice took on a harder edge as he recounted this part of his life to Peter Capstick. The Winds of Change – or Gales of Chaos? – which brought about the end of colonialist rule in Africa are well-known; the dominoes started in 1957 with Ghana's independence from Britain, gaining momentum and with full support from China, the Soviet Union, East Germany, North Korea and similar Marxist luminaries.

As Wally said, anyone believing that these countries' aim was peace and freedom for Africans just didn't know Africa. To quote Robert Ruark, people believing this have no experience of "Uhuru-ed" Africa. The 'freedom movements' have unquestionably ruined Africa for indigenous Africans and merely brought a new kind of subjugation to its peoples. Many Western countries are actually guilty of collusion, gullibility and ignorance in supporting those movements. But it's now way too late; African nations are the world's poorest and continue to fall exponentially-farther behind global development, with each passing year. Mozambique was not a 'white colonial vs black oppressed' country; it was a remarkably non-racial society, which believed a Mozambique free from Portuguese rule could benefit. The civil war for independence had raged since the 1960s. Then in 1974, there was a coup in Portugal.

Relations with the Soviet Union were restored; emissaries were sent from Portugal to negotiate with the powerful Marxist movement of FRELIMO. Control was lost, and by June 1975, Mozambique became independent. Then the civil war really ramped up as RENAMO countered FRELIMO. It seemed the Marxists were hell-bent on destroying all infrastructure, logistics, everything the Mozambicans had built over decades. Wally headed to the port of Beira, 160 miles (256km) away, to fetch supplies. On the way back, he was fired upon with AK-47 assault rifles and even RPG-7 rocket-launchers. Despite this, he made it through several road blocks manned by heavily-armed FRELIMO militants, by passing himself off as English (any white was assumed to be Portuguese, and thus fair game). Then he reached a road block, at which there were several child soldiers…

In his truck's toolbox they found five ancient, greening .375 H&H cartridges. That was enough; he was an armed spy, out to kill the new President (Samora Machel). The kids beat Wally up with their rifle butts, while the adult soldiers sat by, yawning. At some length, a FRELIMO district administrator happened by and told the kids the cartridges were ancient and likely wouldn't even fire. The child warriors cared not; they literally took Wally's vehicle to pieces in their search for a rifle. Wally was then locked in a hut while all waited for the commandant to return. Wally was eventually taken to headquarters to see this man, and after hours in the blazing sun, was told to pack up, which meant reassemble his entire truck. This he did; then he was surprised and mightily relieved to hear that he could go; the commandant had heard of Wally, and, also a keen hunter, had made the same mistake before of leaving hunting ammunition in his vehicle.

Wally made it home, past several further road blocks, but thankfully, none of these were manned by crazed child soldiers. Wally took all his ivory, arms, ammunition and gold ingots, burying the lot on his property; he would never see his wealth, accumulated over decades, again. Not long after the 1975 independence, Wally had to go to Umtali in Rhodesia (now Zimbabwe) for some mine piping. But he wasn't allowed back into Mozambique; he was merely told that he *used* to live there. The gate was shut, the border officials' argument most convincing: four AK-47s were pointed directly at Wally's chest. Wally returned to friends in Umtali, writing letters to the authorities in what used to be Lourenço Marques (now called Maputo) for the next six months. They eventually even answered him on official government stationery; he was prohibited, and if found in Mozambique would be shot on sight!

By this time, Walter Jnr was working in Botswana as a professional hunter, so Wally joined his son, as he too held a professional license there. He became a Botswana citizen, starting life over again at the age of 63. His married daughter and her family lived in Los Angeles and so Wally started spending part of each year in the US. After some time, a German who had worked for Wally named Herbert confirmed that everything – vehicles, gold, ivory, bank account, guns, ammunition, furnishings, photos and personal documents, absolutely everything – had been taken and reappropriated for the Marxist cause. Herbert himself was arrested for being a war criminal (rich, coming from FRELIMO), until someone pointed out that he was only 5 years old when World War Two ended!

Herbert was deported to West Germany, from whence he'd eventually been able to get in touch with Wally. Already an elderly man when he met Capstick in the mid-1980s, Wally is gone now; he passed away in 1990. His tale is epic, his losses enormous, crippling, crushing. But he is noteworthy as being, with Manners, Nyschens and Sánchez-Ariño, among the very last of a unique breed. One of the protagonists in a following chapter suffered similarly, and he was every bit as much of a legend. These old warriors' spirits remain undefeated.

13. Harry Manners

Picture courtesy of Antiquarian Auctions

It is interesting, how fully the ivory hunters lived; they were intense, powerful individuals in a hyper-dangerous world, and their experiences seem to have been just as accentuated. They often lived wildly, experienced mortal danger with almost monotonous regularity, lived through towering highs and sank to plummeting lows. A case in point was Harry Manners, whose phenomenal success was offset by some crippling heartbreak, and in this, he wasn't alone. Harry was the most famous post-war Mozambican ivory hunter, and due to his skin's propensity to sunburn red, gained the Shangaan (now Tsonga) moniker of *Nwalibungu*, or 'Red One'. This harks back to the nickname of the most famous ivory hunter of them all, Bell, who was known as *Longelly-nyung* ('Red Man' in Karamojan). Of medium height and slightly built when young, Harry started lifting weights while still at school, and was even to become Mozambican weight-lifting champion. He made sure his physical frame could match his mental tenacity; giving up on possible spoor was never his bent.

While never as well-known, or as well-commercialised as East Africa, Mozambique was and still is a special piece of wilderness. Its protagonists loved it dearly, and for extended periods it was as fine a hunting ground as any. The decades of civil war, natural disasters and famine have not erased from history its reputation as a fine hunters' paradise. Harry's career was largely split into two parts: his days as a phenomenally-successful ivory hunter, which lasted from 1937 until 1953; then his time as a safari guide, professional hunter, cropping officer and game ranger, which lasted until his retirement. He recorded his exploits from the first part of his life in his excellent work *Kambaku!* (from the Shangaan word for 'old bull'). The first South African version (1980) omitted some of the original chapters but the Amwell Press version, printed in the

US in 1986, contained the full manuscript. Harry's great friend Tony Sánchez-Ariño wrote the foreword to that 1986 version.

Kambaku! was reprinted by Rowland Ward in 1997, that version (of which I have a copy) featuring a foreword by the late Brian Marsh, another of Harry's friends and a legendary figure from Southern African hunting circles himself. Although Harry alluded to one day telling the story of his safari days, he never got around to penning a memoir of this second phase of his life. It is a pity, as he was a gifted wordsmith, and *Kambaku!* is occasionally touching. Manners obviously harboured a sensitive soul beneath the granite exterior. Fortunately, we have the accounts and records provided by his great friends and fellow hunters, so the exploits of Manners did not go totally unrecorded regarding that second part of his career. Harry Manners' relationship with his father was a tense and fraught one, great fatherly love by modern standards largely not the norm in prior generations. I have instantly felt great sadness for such individuals, as my brothers and I were blessed by having a wonderful father.

*   *   *

Although Manners and his father would clash and disagree – and Harry would shed no tears when the old man was laid to rest – the younger Manners' great love of the outdoors had come from his father. Harry sat listening on the *stoep* (verandah in Afrikaans) of their home, spellbound, as his father would recount his sorties to his friends. The older Manners had spent six years in the (then) German Cameroons on Africa's west coast. Harry was born in Grootfontein, South Africa in 1917, and was just six years of age when the family moved to Lourenço Marques (known to the entire region as LM). Harry's father ran a shipping firm, intending that his son would continue with the business when he retired. Six years working there was however plenty for Harry, for whom the call of the wild was impossible to deny or to ignore. By 1937, he heeded the call. Harry's original discussion with his father over his calling didn't go well; as many budding youngsters will have experienced, the discussion seemed to be a monologue, the fierce old man brooking no disagreement from his son.

Harry was then sixteen, and his response to his father shooting down the idea was determined disagreement! He made up his mind to follow his calling, and being a studious scholar, and a near-constant target for the school bullies, started by building his physical frame into one not to be trifled with. By the time he wrote his final school exams, no-one tried to. Then commenced his time with his father's firm in LM; after a three-month probation period sans pay (!), he began to earn and soon acquired a .30-06 bolt-action Winchester rifle. With a couple of Portuguese friends who owned a hunting car, Harry started to venture out hunting over the weekends. It had begun.

It is interesting to note that Harry's hunting companion on many of his early weekend forays was none other than Wally Johnson, the subject of the previous chapter. It was midnight one chill night deep in the Chibuto district, north of the Limpopo River and some 200 miles (320km) from LM. The dogs in the nearby village started a chorus of barking and wailing, safe behind closed hut doors to prevent them being carried off by leopards. Harry and Wally both sat up from their respective slumbers on opposing sides of a now-dying campfire, their skins prickling and ears straining. What were the village curs barking at? Harry added a log to the fire, the *mopane* wood slowly showing tiny blue flames around its base that turned bright orange-yellow with cracks and pops. Then they heard it: the unmistakable rumbling of an elephant, followed by the sound of a tree being cracked for good measure.

Slowly the dogs quietened as the pachyderms moved off, the hunters musing that the quarry would be far away by dawn; but at least the young men knew the elephants had been there, and could track the huge beasts with the advantage of accurate timing. Soon, Harry heard Wally snoring again, but he lay awake for some time, his senses still aroused. His thoughts drifted back to the genesis of this hunt; it was the pair's first big, long-distance safari. He and Wally had planned it for months, saving up until a trader from Chibuto, Pedro dos Santos, had told them of this fine hunting ground. Wally acquired a 9.3mm Brenneke, Harry a 10.75mm Mauser, both with solid bullets. Harry hadn't even mentioned it to his father, who would've been most displeased...sleep overtook him then.

Dawn found them up and after the elephants, accompanied by three trackers from the village. The tracks were huge; the village trackers confirmed that the group would be bulls only, due to their silence. Cows and calves make far more noise staying in touch, the squealing, grunting infants much like small people in that respect. The trackers thought the group comprised maybe twelve bulls, this news greatly exciting Manners. Early in the piece, the bulls fed along their way, but soon this ceased, and they merely walked. After three hours in ever-increasing heat, the men stopped for half an hour or so. The two white men each had a mouthful of water, the trackers forsaking even that despite the sweat streaking their bodies. One tracker kicked open a piece of elephant dung, pronouncing the bulls still far ahead. The dung was cold, dark-coloured and dry on the outside. Since the countryside was open, he announced that the bulls wouldn't stop until sufficient cover had been found.

At a converging point of several elephant tracks, the two youngsters rested, exhausted. The trackers deciphered which way their quarry had gone from the maze of spoor. After a short time, a branch cracked, all wariness evaporating from the men as if by magic. As Harry wrote, at last, this was it! Even the leaves were still, there being no perceptible breeze. One tracker licked a finger, raising it to feel which side cooled against an almost impossibly-slight wind. It's an old African trackers' trick which we learned while still very young, but it was new and marvellous to Manners then. The tracker motioned that the men circle round to the right. Minutes dragged by until one tracker froze, pointing ahead. The hunters saw nothing in the thick foliage until the great beast moved, and Harry laid eyes on his first African elephant. Trembling in fear and tension, he and Wally waited until a clear view of the head was visible, then fired together.

The great head shuddered, then dropped from view. Then the unmistakable sounds of a herd bearing down on them, inexorably, unstoppable, had the men running for their lives. The trackers raced ahead, shedding backpacks and water bottles, discarding anything to lend wings to one's feet and save your life. After the fastest and most terrifying 100 yards of Harry's life, he glanced behind to see nothing following, so stopped his mad flight and called out to the other men. Wally had just breathlessly asked if the herd had stopped chasing them when an elephant head and chest appeared over a bush at a mere 30 yards! Through the milling dust, several more were discernible beyond it. The first elephant fled, the others following suit in its wake. The two young hunters ran alongside, at 20 yards' distance. Harry remembered the sensation of the ground trembling beneath their feet as the herd decamped.

Among the giants, one bull towered above the rest. His tusks were phone-pole thick, easily extending eight feet beyond the lip. As Harry lined up on his shoulder, a lesser bull filled his sights, taking the 10.75mm slug amidships. Their first bull was as dead as global peace, having collapsed flat onto his stomach. His tusks went 80 lbs a side; not bad for one's first elephant! In the fading light, Harry

– forever the photographer – managed two or three good photos. The party staggered into camp late the next day, filthy, exhausted and triumphant, but above all else, parched to the point of near-madness. Despite their thirst, Harry felt a celebratory beer was in order! I have always marvelled at the old Western movies, when visibly-dehydrated cowboys stagger into some backwater saloon after surviving the desert, only to order a whiskey in a barely-audible croak…modern times have revealed that diuretics such as alcohol, even tea or coffee, are most ill-advised when dehydrated. Ah well, they must have bred them tough back then!

The ivory had to be collected, but the journey was at least far easier this time, the men driving the truck through the open country and going the rest of the way on foot through the wooded area where the herd had been bearded. That was only a mile and a half (some 2,4km). With them were the trackers and some men to chop the tusks out. In the end, many villagers accompanied them to recover what meat could be harvested. The trackers had noticed more vultures gathered nearby; upon inspection, the second elephant – the one Harry had mistakenly shot when lining up on the giant bull – too lay dead. The carcase had decomposed sufficiently for the tusks to be easily drawn out of the skull. This second pair of tusks were perhaps half the size of the first victim's. Wally sat smoking his pipe while the trackers cleaned the tusks to gleaming in the lamp light. He reckoned the ivory would more than cover the cost of the safari, and was very satisfied with how events had unfurled; but like a regretful fisherman, and in stark contrast to his companion, Harry was lost in thoughts of 'the one that got away'; he wondered if he'd see the huge bull, or others of his size, ever again.

* * *

That first ivory hunt affected Harry Manners greatly; he would never be the same again, and his mundane office job now became like a sentence, to be tolerated in sullen silence, since he had no other means of supporting himself. He wondered about some of his Portuguese colleagues in the office and at the wharf, who had already married young and had dependents to show for it; Harry at least was as yet unencumbered, free and young. He bided his time until he could leave the malaise of the office existence. He said nothing to his father, whose views on these dreams of the wild had been made patently clear; now pushing sixty and of failing health, the senior Manners was further removed from his son than ever. Meanwhile, Harry and Wally would go out weekends whenever possible, to the *kwazine* (pronounced kwa-zee-neh) forest around LM. This was an impenetrable mass of ten-metre-high scrub in which elephants whiled away the daylight hours, and offered immensely dangerous hunting.

The wind was flitting and fickle, and more than once the scattering herd, upon winding the hunters, fled almost directly over them. Harry and Wally found that when this happened, they had to shoot the lead animal, almost on top of them, which would allow the remainder of the herd to flow by on either side of them! A sure cure for indigestion, no doubt; eventually, Harry had to concede that Wally's take on the area as a hunting destination – that the danger was not worth the risk – was spot-on. The pair turned to hunting antelope on the open plains, the resultant meat sales offsetting their expenses nicely. One night, a celebratory dinner (it was Wally's birthday) turned into a brawl with a bunch of rowdy sailors, the police arriving and arresting everyone before releasing the innocent.

Wally and Harry were among this latter group, but the damage to the social standing of Harry's father was not inconsiderable, and the senior Manners told his son what he thought of the occasion. He added that he had a good mind to fire his son, but Harry had taken enough; the next day he resigned. Harry set off to become an ivory hunter, soon unearthing a master tracker named Sayela, who was to become Harry's gun-bearer, tracker and foreman. Even among the bush-savvy Shangaans, who were accomplished hunters, Sayela stood out. He knew the high-rainfall hunting paradise between the Limpopo and the Savé Rivers out of his head, able to find waterholes when Harry was totally directionless. He was at his imperious best after elephant through the thick stuff; time was irrelevant to him. Sleeping on the trail meant nothing. The final prize was the imperative.

After a hunt, Harry would leave him at his village, and after selling the ivory in LM, and a few days' break, would collect him again on the way back into the blue. One day when Harry picked him up, Sayela was grim. Harry could instantly see something was wrong. One of Sayela's wives had run away, and complained to the chief, one N'gwenya (crocodile in Shangaan). Sayela had been summoned to the headman's village but he'd thought it better to wait for Harry first. The falling out had started the usual way: a beer-drink, an argument; but then it took a different turn, Sayela's wife clearly possessed of far more venom than the average Shangaan wife. She shattered a clay pot over Sayela's head, which act promptly resulted in the usually-calm Sayela beating her savagely. She fled screaming. Harry was nonplussed; a Shangaan beer-drink normally ended in a free-for-all fight, but this one had ended in the wife reaching the chief.

Harry steered the Ford van to N'gwenya's hamlet, slat-ribbed curs and half-starved hens scattering at their arrival. Some bare-breasted women looked up from their task of pounding the hard, white maize into coarse flour. The chief sat under a shady tree like a fat, khaki-clad spider on his low stool, his rotund-bellied, middle-aged physique a mark of his stature. He was not thrilled that Sayela had at last deigned to show himself, and not come earlier. Both Harry and Sayela approached the chief in the customary manner, lightly clapping their palms in greeting. The sovereign acknowledged Harry, but before Sayela could answer the chief's cutting questions, Harry stepped in. It was he who had delayed Sayela, as it was well known that Harry was his employer. Harry pressed the chief for the fine he would mete out, and that he, Harry, would pay it. It was a clever move, as a fine would require the chief's presence at the District Administrator.

N'gwenya shifted uncomfortably, and said the matter had nothing to do with Harry. He was still Sayela's chief, and had mentioned no fine. Harry made to leave then, with Sayela; the chief's eyes glittered. He assented, and would speak with Sayela upon the hunters' return...if Sayela was still alive. Strange comment, thought Harry; damn the female gender, he thought, as they drove away. Always, the cause of trouble was a woman...he chanced a sideways glance at Sayela, morose and silent beside him in the truck's cab. Chico, the cook, lay sprawled in the back among the supplies and fuel drums. The cursed journey was about to reveal its first fruits. A fortuitous burst tyre allowed the men to discover a near-comatose Chico, almost overcome by petrol fumes from a leaking fuel can.

After reviving the cook, and with him seated in the cab, they continued, but soon snapped a driveshaft in some potholes made by elephant feet the previous rainy season. They weren't far from the village, so taking bare essentials, set out into the blackness of an African night. The news there was bad: no elephants in weeks. Harry was stuck, sending away to LM for a new driveshaft. This entailed bribing the chief with palm wine, the chief's son taking a message some 80 miles (130 km) on his ramshackle bicycle through wild bush country, to Caniçado on the Limpopo River; Harry knew the district officer there. The officer would telegram LM for the driveshaft, all of which would take weeks. Harry hunted to kill time. With two assistant trackers from the village, Harry and Sayela cut the fresh spoor of four bulls on the third day. After four hours of tracking, they heard the bulls swiftly decamping, having scented the men.

A splash of good luck then momentarily ensued: Harry dashed to head them off, shooting the rearmost with a flashy, oblique rear-brain shot. The ivory wasn't huge but was at least a start. Then the chief's son returned, with the new driveshaft, lathered in sweat, after a mere eight days. The repair was fast and the party at least had wheels beneath them again, crossing the bone-dry Sungutana River, and stopping at the small hamlet of Magondene. Of course, they had seen elephants just two days before; (usually, the bush folk would lie unashamedly at the chance of meat) but Harry knew these people well. They were a reliable source of information. Signs of 'phunt did indeed abound, but each time they'd close, the fickle wind would turn, scattering their quarry like quails. One morning a huge, lone bull's tracks were found. When at length they closed with him, in a knobthorn- and sandalwood forest, Harry whispered to Sayela to use the 10.75mm when he fired the .375H&H, so they made sure they dropped the animal.

Harry drew a bead on the great earhole, but as he pressed the trigger, the huge animal rocked back on its heels. Both rifles roared almost together, but the bull turned about in his own length and disappeared behind a closing curtain of foliage, Harry feeding him a raking rib-shot just before he exited stage left, pursued by no bear. The men listened for the sound of a huge crash, indicating a falling elephant; but instead, the sound of breaking branches came from far ahead, indicating an elephant in full and rapidly-disappearing flight. Harry cursed under his breath; none of their shots had taken effect. The elephant was motoring and for several miles the tracks showed this, the prints clearly dug in. A few drops of blood were sometimes found, but never enough to induce hope. Then the three black men froze in mid-step: across one of the tracks lay the freshly-sloughed skin of a black mamba.

To the Shangaans, this was a bad omen. They were convinced that they would not get the bull, but Harry was in no mood for superstition. It was early in the day and the water bottles were full. The men continued and by the afternoon the bull's pace had slackened. Harry looked at the dense bush surrounding them and shuddered; it was zero hour. At length, one of the trackers spotted the top of the great head at 30 paces, the trunk testing the air. The men saw him turn, then he disappeared from view. A great roar welled up, pounding feet meaning he was coming, and fast. He had chosen his time and territory well; the foliage completely hid the great bull from view. Then the bushes parted and Harry dived aside, the huge tusk flashing by as the elephant crashed over where the white man had just been. It clattered on after one of the trackers, screaming and roaring.

Cold fear and adrenalin spurred Harry on, the Magnum ready in his fists. The fleeing tracker shot from side to side, the huge beast matching him as Harry chased it in turn. Each time he'd get close, the animal would shoot off in another zigzag, trumpeting fit to chill the blood. Then the noise ceased, and Harry's consternation increased: the elephant had caught his victim and a thumping, mashing sound emanated from his efforts. Horrified, Harry exploded into view, the rear spinal shot the only one available. He was winded however and the shot failed to have the desired effect; the bull instead screamed and came for Harry! His next shots hit it in the eye, then the throat, the bull lurching away through the bushes. Harry raced to the broken prone form, dirt-covered and with clothing torn to ribbons. It was Sayela; somehow, he was still in one piece.

His eyes were open and his breath rasped through his throat; Harry lifted Sayela and the tracker stiffened, then went limp as he died. A nearby crash indicated the elephant had fallen; Harry raced over to it, and when its red eye spotted the hunter, it battled to rise again. Harry settled its hash with a final brain shot, then returned to Sayela. The other two trackers stood by, dazed. The men covered Sayela's body with thorn branches sufficient to thwart the hyenas until the next day. They would return to bury Sayela properly, and Harry etched an epitaph into an old tree at the spot. Revulsion hit the white man, that this constant reach for ivory had cost him the life of a good man, a faithful servant of five years. Harry had to report the death to the administrator, and when he came across one of N'gwenya's headmen, he told the shocked old man that Sayela was dead. Any scepticism he may have harboured for African black magic evaporated soon afterward: his luck immediately turned for the better.

One day during his travels, reaching ever north, Harry heard of Minengi-wa-Nsuna (Shangaan for 'mosquito legs', clearly a spindly individual), a fabled witchdoctor. Eventually reaching the old man's dwelling, Harry exchanged pleasantries and had a short chat with him. The sage's only counsel for Harry was in his parting words, ever etched on the mind of the hunter thereafter: go well, hunt well, but always carefully. That afternoon the clouds built up considerably and by nightfall, the rain was sheeting down. Morning brought clear skies and with spirits high, the men set off through the fresh, still air and wet-leafed *mopane*. In next to no time, they cut spoor of a solitary bull elephant, easily tracked in the muddy ground. The going was easy, the bull totally unaware he was being followed, signs of near-constant feeding evidencing this. Accompanying Harry was his cook / tracker Jonas, and two local trackers. Beside them, Harry espied a small *mopane* tree, and he shinnied silently up it, hoping for a visual vantage point; but instead, he got something else.

The hunter became aware of a faint buzzing, glancing up to see the hornets' nest he had just disturbed. The occupants saw him too; they immediately zeroed in on his face, neck and arms, stinging relentlessly. Harry's descent was far faster than his ascent, and he almost landed on Jonas, who became a second beneficiary of the hornets' attention. Meanwhile, the two locals were signalling frantically, and within seconds the wall of vegetation opened, revealing the massive head, trunk and tusks of the elephant, who had heard the ruckus, and come to see what was causing it. He raised his head, then lowered it to charge, as Harry's bullet caught him plumb in the forehead. He dropped like a stone, the four men exploding away, more from the hornets than from the elephant! Harry daubed medicinal alcohol on his stings as the men set off to retrieve the meat and ivory, grateful that he wasn't allergic, and hoping to never experience anything even remotely similar, ever again.

Three days later, the men happened upon a huge herd of some fifty bulls; a real opportunity, albeit one fraught with real danger. The tracks gradually led from the scrub *mopane* into a formidable *simbiri* hardwood forest. Harry remembered the challenges of hunting in the *simbiri*, from his initial forays with Wally Johnson. The wind was fickle and the hunting as a result hovered between futile and fatally dangerous. By mid-morning they heard a cracking of trees up ahead, stopping to test the wind; but it was as fickle as could be, flitting first this way, then that, by breezes the men could hardly feel. Harry remembered the witchdoctor's counsel: 'hunt well, hunt carefully'. He thought to himself, the only way to do that in this forest, was to avoid pachyderms altogether…then decided to keep the herd in earshot, perhaps 200 yards distant. The elephants and the men whiled away the hottest afternoon hours,

Harry noticing that - unlike cows and calves - not once did the herd of bulls call or trumpet.

With the shadows lengthening, the elephants were silent, so the men approached where the animals had rested the hottest hours away; the bulls were gone. Harry lit his pipe, the smoke showing the wind to be steadier and more predictable. The game was on. The men crept along; Jonas heard them first. The men trailed the elephants, hoping the forest would soon end, as daylight threatened to do likewise. At last, the territory reverted to scrub *mopane*, the men halting at a huge, red-brown termite hill. They flitted from bush to bush for some 150 yards, waiting until the herd was well out in the open. The elephants tested the air with raised trunks, then the bulls all sauntered forward, satisfied; it was a most impressive sight to behold. As the men reached camp, around ten pm that evening, lions were roaring in the distance. One of the guides carried a stick over his shoulder; attached to it were six elephant tails. Two bulls had been 100-pounders, the other four in the 60-70-pound class. Harry tipped a mental hat to Minengi-wa-Nsuna.

After hunting the Panda region successfully, Harry headed south-east toward the coast. The party left the van at Mazive (pronounced ma-zee-veh), filled with ivory from its Panda excursion. To all sides were lakes, the fresh fish a welcome change to their diets. One morning before sunrise, they hit paydirt: the fresh tracks of three bulls were clearly imprinted. One was absolutely enormous. The air was still, and the men followed fast, coming upon the bulls within an hour. The elephants were in a clump of *tzondzo* trees, resting before heading for thicker cover. The biggest bull's ivory invoked a low whistle from Jonas; the tusks were thick, evenly-shaped and almost reached the ground. Harry used the undergrowth well, approaching to within thirty paces of the giant. The other two were faced in opposite directions. The .375 roared, the huge bull collapsing onto his knees. Harry shot a second bull in the earhole, that one too collapsing. The third was off running, and Harry raced to collect it as well.

At eighty yards, he chanced a head-shot, which in retrospect should have been a shoulder shot. The bull turned and bore down on Harry. When the bull was practically upon him, he shot it through the trunk before flinging himself to the side. The bull thundered on by until he reached his fallen comrades. Harry retrieved the rifle, and with the last shot in the magazine, dropped the third bull too.

The biggest bull's ivory went 130lbs and 127lbs; the other two yielded less than that between them. It had been a good day.

* * *

Manners wrote a captivating chapter entitled 'The Lamp and the Plough', which is filled with the strangeness of Africa. Harry and his men ventured still further afield, and after seven hours' tramping came upon a miserable little hamlet. In the shade sat two elderly women, clad in filthy shifts, watching an equally-filthy child. Harry's party murmured greetings, the youngster soon being sent to summon the village's only man. Questioning the women about game movements would be a waste of breath; the default answer was literally that as women, they knew nothing of such things. The child returned with an old-timer, smoking the eternal *kandudu* cigar, common in that region. It consists of a hand-rolled tobacco or palm leaf, filled with shag tobacco, and most adults – women included – smoke it in that part of the world. The old man was named Malampo – the lamp – and upon being pressed as to the presence of elephant, confirmed that a huge and cunning bull lived not far from there. He eyed the men strangely, Harry trying to discern whether or not the old fellow was off his head.

He knocked his pipe out, told the old man they were rested and ready, and asked that he lead on. Malampo stopped by the women long enough to slake his thirst from a calabash, then set off out of the village, beckoning the men to follow. They followed, and an hour later the terrain had changed to rolling hills, with shoulder-high grass in the dips, dense forests on the rises. Leaving the path, it wasn't long before the signs of a feeding elephant appeared, but nothing was fresh. Upon an apex, the ground sloped toward a lake with forests at each end. Here, Malampo declared, they would find the great bull. Descending in the mid-afternoon, more elephant feeding signs were plainly visible and Harry started thinking the old madman may be sane after all. Near the lake they cut fresh spoor, the old man smiling eerily as if to say, 'I told you so'. The tracks were enormous, Malampo jerking his thumb in the direction they were headed. Over to you youngsters, he cheekily indicated.

The forest had opened and closed behind the great bull and one would never think an elephant could penetrate such dense foliage, if it weren't for the tracks. Malampo confirmed that both forests were the same, all around. Jonas held up his hand, a muted thumping emanating from somewhere deep within the morass – a tusk knocked against a tree, maybe a stamping foot? – sounding out a regular, repeated challenge to come in, if they dared. The entire region was called Vilanculos, the land of jungle drums, and Harry chuckled that even the elephants seemed aware of this moniker. He remembered the words of Minengi-wa-Nsuna: "Hunt carefully". He knew that advice was vital here. So, they waited; the thumping stopped, feeding sounds were audible; still they waited. It became dark and the gnats arrived; Harry quelled the desire for a smoke. Still, they waited. The bull came nearer, and as they caught a glimpse of a massive tusk, something warned him and he turned around. Still, they waited.

Harry motioned the others to stay put behind their blind of bushes, nearing the edge of the forest. He heard a rustling and at last the huge bull appeared; but it was too late. It was pitch dark, and Harry couldn't even see the rifle's sights. In the blackness, the huge bull ghosted right by him, silent as a wraith, and wisely he held his fire. To wound the monster in the coal-black night would have been suicide. Harry felt his way back to the blind and the men; he declared to Malampo that they would try early next morning. The men were at the lakeside before dawn, where it transpired that old Malampo had been a soldier, sent to Macau years before with the Portuguese army, an entire company of black soldiers with white officers. His eyes grew misty as Harry allowed him to carry the old Mauser 10.75mm, while Jonas lugged the heavier rucksack.

The bull had left his haunt and headed north, Harry and Malampo considering that he had seen Harry, raised rifle and all, in the blackness. After six hours they rested and had a drink; Malampo told Harry he had seen the giant four times, and that his tusks met at the tips. This explained how he'd traverse his jungle mass without getting tangled or caught up: the tusks formed a giant plough for him to divide the bushes like a ship's prow. After long tracking they heard a distant rumble, then silence. They saw a puff of dust and Harry motioned the others to stay put, Malampo hoping to back him up as the old soldier revived within him. At twenty paces Harry sent a .375 surprise into the bull's ear and it dropped like a rock, but he then got the fright of his life.

A screaming roar rent the air, followed by crashing and parting bushes. The elephant Harry had shot was a *shikari*, an accomplice. The giant bull was coming! Dazed, Harry saw the massive head, the spread ears, the gleaming eyes, the huge converging tusks…through that daze Malampo shouted "Dubula!" (Shoot!), then Harry was shaken into alertness as the old soldier fired the Mauser. The bull staggered, then turned and bore down on the old man. Harry at last woke up and fired obliquely into the brain as the old man shot from the front. The bull ploughed into the ground, kicking to rise up again as Malampo backpedalled, then fell. Harry killed the elephant as it struggled half up. Through the dust the men rushed to the old man, who had struck his head on a tree root. He had a faint pulse and groaned when he came to. He had seen the slight movement to the right as Harry was about to fell the other elephant, but rather than endanger the white hunter, had rushed instead to assist Harry. Of such stuff are old soldiers made…

* * *

And so, Harry and Jonas headed to the swamps. A day's driving took them to Vila Fontes on the Zambezi, where they crossed on a rail truck, the only available bridge. From Don'Ana on the south bank, they headed east to Marromeu, the headquarters of the Senna Sugar Estates. The administrator pointed Harry toward Gustave Guex, whose tin-roofed white dwelling was twenty miles distant. His hunting camp, however, was a further thirty miles on from that. Game was plentiful, the bush lush and green. Guex greeted Harry with a slight French accent and treated Harry to the luxuries of a hot shower, a drink and a gourmet dinner. Guex lived well, perhaps as well as any remote hunter ever did. He had plenty of labour, a paraffin burning refrigerator and other refinements. He told Harry the buffalo were more plentiful in the area than anywhere else in Africa.

Guex had hunted them for twelve years to feed the sugar workers, accounting in that time for a staggering 7,000 head. Guex had been tossed six times, and as a result had spent lots of time in hospitals. The men headed east, looking for jumbo, but there appeared to be none; everywhere there were buffalo. Harry thought of the American West before the arrival of the white man, wondering if the bison herds there were similar. Guex had lent Harry some potent binoculars, and glassing the swamp, he spotted four bulls just showing above the papyrus, about a mile distant. It was on again, the age-old dance; Harry felt the excitement as they set off.

The men walked along the swamp's edge, then through water to where some harder ground appeared beyond it; they could hear the bulls now, but couldn't see them. There was no tree to climb, and while Harry and Jonas wondered what to do next, the Sennas motioned them into the papyrus, where they actually walked on floating islands of vegetation. It was a relief to finally reach solid ground again, as keeping one's balance was difficult enough, had it been done without a rifle. Lifted onto Jonas's shoulders, Harry could see his targets, the closest bull just 35 yards away; but he could see no tusks. He had no choice but to shoot first and see later; the kick of the big rifle almost blew him off Jonas's shoulders as the bull dropped; the other bulls milled about, confused, and unsure as to their next move. Harry slid down and made for the felled elephant.

Reaching it after pushing through chest-deep ooze, Jonas lifted the white man onto the bull's carcase and Harry scanned for the others. As Jonas appeared beside him, Harry saw them: all three making for the edge of the swamp to escape, but headed straight at the hunters! It was a lucky windfall for the men and the lead elephant took a frontal brain shot at twenty paces, the second following suit, its giant head half-supported on the rump of the first. Then Harry had a misfire as the final bull bore down on him; ejecting the errant cartridge to a crescendo of curses, Harry shot it at closer range than he'd ever shot an elephant before, the eye gleaming evilly at him. The beast rolled with a deep rumble, Harry potting him again. Beaming, Jonas let out a very big breath, which had no doubt had been held since the trio bore down on them. The Sennas made their way to the battlefield. Harry wiped the sweat and swamp water from his face, trembling as the adrenalin came off.

The soaking hot bath back in camp was as wonderful as the sundowner, after the mess of the swamp; to Harry Manners – and doubtless, countless others before and after him – sundown was the best time of the day, especially if the day's hunt had gone well. The day's tasks were completed, tomorrow's problems were for tomorrow, and the sense of general well-being as the heat of the day eased, the friendly chatter of the men, joking and laughing while preparing the evening meal, competed with the birds' song. The campfire and a sundowner after a muscle-soothing bath completed the picture, as insects whirled around the light from the pressure lamp. Two days later, the storms – which had been building – descended with a vengeance. The camp at least had lots of food, as it was impossible to do anything other than batten down and wait the deluge out. When the rain eased to a drizzle, Harry ventured out, before cabin fever drove him crazy.

Harry took Jonas and two Sennas and roamed farther, leaving the rest of the men to repair the damaged camp. One Senna shinnied up a tree for a look-around, then started gabbling excitedly; the others all ascended too, and Harry's skin prickled when he saw the cause of the excitement: a herd of elephant – all bulls – filled the swamp, such as Harry had never seen before. The Sennas opined that the bulk of the herd were on hard ground, the swamp not consistent wetland all the way through. Jonas was concerned that there wasn't even a tree to hide behind, and where Harry just saw ivory, Jonas warned that they may soon head to their graves. The jumbos seemed to be gathering for a migration of sorts, perhaps awaiting nightfall. An added concern was the extra water now flowing into the swamp from the rains. It was time to act; now or never. Leaving excess equipment by the trees, they entered the papyrus, Harry using a makeshift sling to keep his hands unoccupied.

The party moved from vegetation patch to patch, one Senna falling through at one point and needing rescuing. Harry wondered why there appeared to be no crocodiles in the swamp, but then he'd seen no fish there, which might explain it. The chance of getting crushed by pachyderms may have been a factor, too. After an hour they neared the bulls, an even more impressive and intimidating sight from close up. The herd stretched for half a mile (some 800 metres or so), from what they could see. It may have been larger. Harry thought the herd to comprise some three hundred animals. He glanced at the men and unslung his rifle; "Well, here we go..." he whispered to Jonas. The bedraggled group of men made it back to the tree that afternoon, twelve bulls having fallen to the .375's shots. At the first shot, pandemonium broke out as the herd dived into the swamp, flattening papyrus like dried corn stalks.

Harry shot as fast as he could, chest-deep in the filthy water. At one stage they climbed up on a carcase and shot from there. The confusion of the herd resulted in one small pocket bearing down on the men, Jonas firing too until they turned away. At the edge, Harry poured the water out of the Magnum; had they not turned the stampeding group, Jonas's prediction of their watery graves would have been an awful reality. The strain and the wet weather took its toll and by evening Harry needed to medicate himself, the fever and shakes well on top of him. Harry endured a bad night and slept a bit in the dawn hours, when Jonas and the men ventured out to retrieve the ivory. None of the Africans were the worse for wear; as Harry wrote, the rural black African takes some pounding before one gets him down.

By the end of the second day, all the tusks were back in camp. Harry was most regretful that the meat could not be retrieved, but the water had immersed most of the carcases by the time the last tusk was removed. Harry and Guex decided it was indeed time for a break, the rains now making a rest unavoidable. Gradually the trucks made it to more solid roads. Harry headed back toward Don'Ana, then swung south toward Beira. He needed time to ponder his next great odyssey, and the as-yet unexplored lands to the north beckoned…

* * *

Lourenço Marques was booming, changing beyond all recognition. The fulcrum around which Harry's life revolved was about to change forever; he met Carmen, the great love of his life. She would grow to dominate his thoughts, even when – especially when – he was out hunting some remote region. She slotted effortlessly into his life and they were soulmates in the truest sense. But his life-altering relationship would end in tragedy, which befell so many of the ivory hunters. Living life fast, hard, and dangerously has its risks. I won't embellish too much on this relationship, this book being about the elephant-hunting exploits of the hunters, rather than other facets and aspects of their lives. All I can do is point you toward *Kambaku!* It is a brilliant book and Harry was a gifted, sensitive writer. He was understandably devastated by losing Carmen.

* * *

As have many hunters and game-control officers, Harry spent a great deal of time lending a hand to save people from marauding crop-raiders. Elephants in particular cause immense damage all over Africa (and Asia, for that matter) to people's crops. Given the size of their appetites, it is not surprising that a few animals can literally eat a family or hamlet's entire year's supply of corn / cassava / millet / peanuts / other (take your pick) over the course of just one night. In poor regions, this often means starvation for countless people. If you doubt this, go visit the rural wild places in Africa, and question the locals. I have, and have seen it. Regardless of one's religious or moral leanings, no human being can starve while an animal continues with impunity to abet that starvation. Man-eating cats are (somewhat understandably) hunted down and killed with due urgency; the crop depredations amount to the same outcome, if somewhat more benignly.

One dark night, Harry and Jonas were summoned to eliminate a group of bulls that had been devastating a group of smallholding farms. Carmen was along with them, her first foray up close with elephants. The munching of stalks was clearly audible as the party approached. Jonas had them kneel, and silhouetted against the stars, there the giants were. At a signal, Jonas switched on the torch, all feeding abruptly ceasing. Harry aligned on the nearest bull more by instinct than by vision, the torch being poor. He touched off, the huge beast falling with a huge roar. The others fled in the direction of the nearby huts, shouts from startled people adding to the pandemonium. The shot bull rocked in his falling momentum and rose immediately, stern to the hunters. With hair-raising speed, he whirled about, his head and tusks arcing upward, small eyes gleaming. His head dropped for the charge, but Harry had seen all this, a hundred times before and was ready. As the head of the great beast dropped, a .375 H&H surprise entered its forehead just above eye level. The elephant thumped down, conclusively this time.

The district was free for now, the surviving bulls unlikely to return for a while, given their scare. Harry returned to LM. After the rains, the Buzi Plains were impassable, so Harry and Jonas loaded their truck on a steamer at Mambone on the Savé River, docking at Beira to bypass the Plains. After three days' unhurried travel, they reached Tete, then headed ever north, the hilly landscape dotted with *tsondzo* trees. Huge trucks carrying all manner of supplies passed them the other way, on the route between Tete and Blantyre, in British Nyasaland (now Malawi). They drove through Blantyre, then headed east to re-enter Mozambique. The entire area was heavily populated, and both men yearned for quieter places. The further they went, the more scenic the terrain became, distant mountains appearing blue and fertile, well-watered country all around.

Harry thought it would be ideal for tea, and sure enough the foot of each mountain was covered in tea plantations, interspersed with the eternal acacia. Harry had his hunting permit stamped by the administrator (as was required) at Mlanje (Milange in Portuguese); he was impressed with how far they had come. When he learned that Harry was after ivory, he suggested a wild area which the locals said no white man had ever been, beset by the tsetse fly and largely uncharted. Harry was drawn like a moth to a lamp. Hiring six Lomwé porters, he headed for the wild zone. The bush was dense, tangled lianas and tall trees suggesting high rainfall. Signs of game were everywhere, but best of all were some huge elephant tracks. Harry and his men spent two months building roads and bridges, then headed back to Mlanje to write to Carmen and receive news of warm greetings from Gustave Guex! The Bush Telegraph travels far and fast in Southern Africa.

Into Harry's life rode a master tracker, Chisulo Namuli. He would turn out to be a buffalo hunter without equal, fearless and well-versed in the ways of the giant wild cattle. His relaxed demeanour and easy grin spoke of quiet confidence while he had received military training, thus learning how to use a rifle; he also spoke a little Portuguese. The next day the party would venture out, and as Harry pondered the morrow beside the campfire, the men's muted murmur of talk was suddenly silenced by the roar of a lion in the distance. Harry thought about hunter and hunted; the risks, the challenges. Little did he know, the following day would lead to a brush with his own death…the next day saw the men marching through the wet morning, *tsetse* flies biting them though their clothes as they walked. After an hour, a mud-wallow revealed tracks like small bathtubs. Harry smiled and lit a pipe while the grey louries in a nearby tree sounded their raucous "go-away!" cries.

Their path was momentarily blocked by a group of six massive buffalo bulls. As the men started to edge backwards to give them a wide berth, the bulls turned as one and fled through the trees. Then the heavens opened and the men were pelted by heavy falls. Eventually the rains relented and tracking was more difficult, but by-and-by, the party closed with three large bull elephants. Creeping forwards as only experienced and intelligent hunters can, nerves taut to breaking point, a branch broke perhaps forty yards ahead. Thumb on the safety catch, Harry felt that something was wrong, never a good sign. Humans too have advanced warning systems, as I've touched on before (John Taylor especially was tremendously perceptive, and others have also shown incredible sensory ability). The words of the old witchdoctor, reminding him to hunt carefully, replayed in his thoughts. Through a gap in the foliage, a bull's head was visible, Chisulo moving aside as Harry lined up.

The magnum cartridge bored its way into the bull's head, and it sagged, Harry working the bolt to chamber a second round for a go at the next bull; but that second animal, which Harry had glimpsed beyond the first, melted into the bush immediately. Then all hell broke loose; Jonas shouted a warning directly behind Harry as the third bull was almost upon the men. He'd circled back and as Harry's first shot sounded, came for the men with a roar and a thump of huge feet. Harry remembered Chisulo diving away and the grass parting as the huge head appeared almost directly above the men. Harry fired, the bull staggering but not falling. The stagger at least allowed Harry to dive away and get behind a huge tree as the massive beast came on again, ears spread and bellowing. Harry desperately worked the bolt and fired into the upper leg, anywhere to buy him time for another, telling shot. The giant trunk snaked around the tree, reaching for the man while a tusk smashed a shower of bark off.

Harry dashed for a second big tree, strangely remembering feeling no fear at all, just a forlorn desire to not die here, now, in this way. He slipped, half stumbling as he made the second tree, the animal closing the distance. Harry Manners was about to die, and he knew it. Then salvation arrived in the shape of Jonas; two powerful, gnarled black hands grabbed the bull's tail, a loud shout from the black man drowned out as the furious bull bellowed his disapproval. He spun to address this new threat, but Jonas clung fast, lifted off the ground but safe from the reaching trunk. Harry snapped out of his dreamy funk, and as the huge squealing animal swung broadside to him, he sent a .375 round winging its lethal way into the earhole. With a deep rattle the bull fell, the brave Jonas rolling clear. His face was ashen and mud-spattered, and he shakily gabbled that this was a hunt they were sure to remember! Then his knees buckled and he sank down beside the huge carcase. It was then that Harry noticed that Jonas's right leg was lacerated and bleeding.

The huge back foot had scraped Jonas's leg open; Harry knelt beside him, choked with gratitude. Jonas's unarmed act had saved his life. Harry doctored the injured limb with the medical kit. When the tusks were brought to Harry a week later, one had been split by a bullet, undoubtedly the reason the bull had furiously charged at the first shot.

* * *

Harry was planning a trip to Blantyre when Chisulo appeared out of the gathering dark; he breathlessly implored Harry to accompany him the following day. Upstream, in the pass between Murripa and the mountain alongside it, he had seen huge numbers of elephant; as he said, "too many!" He said they were like a river in flood, and had come from the north; Harry was convinced! They set off, wandering through the mists and pre-dawn darkness in the still, cool air. As the first sunrays started to ward off the chill, they found the tracks. Chisulo had not fibbed; the spoor covered half a mile (some 800 metres), but on the debit side, they were at least half a day old. After a short rest the party started on the trail, tracking laughably easy with a highway of elephant spoor to follow. Into the afternoon they trailed, the *tsetses* now seemingly hell-bent on draining their blood supplies. The foliage was dense, luxuriant, green and lush. Leopards and pythons abounded, the monkeys and small antelope which proliferated attracting them in large numbers.

The herd had been feeding as they travelled, never slackening their pace or deviating from their travels. At length the men stopped and camped surrounded by trees and beyond them, by the huge mountains. They all drifted off to sleep, Harry the last to go down. Through his fuddled brain an alarm signal roused him, but he was too late; a snorting, tramping rhino burst into their midst, stamping the fire out! Rhino have often been recorded performing this impromptu fire-brigade service. One porter was struck a glancing blow but no-one was seriously hurt. Dawn found them on the trail again. At the next mountain they closed with smaller, dispersed groups of the migration's rear-guard. The vegetation was dense, the herd noise indicating a family; bulls are nearly silent. A leopard sunning itself melted into the undergrowth. The trees harboured turacos and samango monkeys. Each group they approached, the fickle wind would turn and the elephants scattered. Harry had seen no bulls, no tusks worth gathering. The men turned for home, Harry disgusted with himself for actually being glad at not having disturbed this golden opportunity.

In the gloomy and wet mountain forests, Chisulo's buffalo-hunting skills were on daily display, and Harry recalled them as staggering. The buffalo is difficult to hunt under ideal shooting conditions, where one may have time and open space to relaxedly place several bullets into the vitals; but move into dense vegetation and the game flips totally. The animal often seems to dash on regardless with a heart shot to shreds, sometimes expiring 200 or even 400 yards away. At close quarters, that leaves a bullet-resistant specimen with more than enough time to fundamentally change the appearance of a human, and the remains of people so caught are often difficult to separate from the soil. Regardless of the animal, the danger, the weather or anything else, Chisulo's smile and glint in his eye instilled confidence in Harry, often seemingly-unfounded; but without which, they'd have been dead men, many times over.

When the animal would burst from cover in a final charge – particularly when wounded and nursing revenge in his guts along with the searing pain from the bullet – it needed to be dropped, dead. Chisulo carried Harry's old .375 while the white man used his newer one. Both would immediately fire together, looking for brain or spine shots, which are instantly fatal. At such moments, a slow reaction or a misfire meant death for the hunters. Yet Chisulo was unfazed, although his effectiveness was decidedly limited against elephants. Different strokes, Harry pondered. One time, they followed a huge wounded bull into long grass, the bright red, frothy lung-blood suggesting he'd expire soon. But although one may be alert and do everything right, surprise is often telling, as in combat. Right beside them, a deep grunt announced the bull's arrival as he exploded from the cover, both men's shots failing to anchor him.

In a flash the buffalo hit Harry with his blood-flecked muzzle, the rifle spinning from the man's hands. Flat on his back, Harry desperately shouted for Chisulo as the bull lined him up for a goring. Years later it still made no sense to Harry how his legs weren't destroyed, but next thing he knew he was clinging to the bull's head, arms over the horns and body draped over its head. He knew he had to cling on as the buffalo – heavily wounded, remember – lifted him with its powerful neck as if he were a kitten. Harry's shouts for help became strange-sounding squeaks in the moment of mortal danger. Through the haze Chisulo appeared, firing twice from close range, the second a telling neck shot. Harry rolled clear as the great beast expired. He stood up but weak-kneed, had to sit again immediately. He was cut, bruised and smashed but after gingerly examining his frame, found no broken bones.

*   *   *

Soon after, Harry was to collect his first lion; it was one of two large males feeding on a kill, so intently that they ignored the men's approach. Harry potted the beast in the neck, the other decamping so fast that Harry had not even time to reload in time for a second shot. The dead lion – cautiously approached; remember Capstick's adage that the 'dead' ones get you – was a beauty, luxuriantly maned. Harry felt no elation and although he was an ivory hunter, considering elephant hunting the pinnacle of the sport, he did feel that this was unquestionably a king among beasts. Harry kept the pelt and skull, his men keeping the fat and cartilage, both of which are highly prized. In short order he was to collect two more out on a hunt for elephant, as a buffalo herd in flight revealed a disembowelled calf, and several lions in thick cover. Harry shot two through the gaps in the foliage. Both had full, yellow manes, the second clamping a small bush in his jaws, as lions often do in their death-throes.

* * *

Harry's red-letter, halcyon day came when he hunted the Monarch of Murripa, a legendary and huge old bull elephant that he'd glimpsed and had haunted his dreams ever since. Murripa was a steep mountain with bamboo thickets on its sides; ascending it was thirsty work in the heat, and rests were frequent. At the forest-shrouded rim of the mountain's crown, the men found spoor. The tracks were all huge, but one stood out even among these. Into the dense forest the trail led, darkness overtaking the men and necessitating the decent, which was tricky in the dark. Harry's torch gave up the ghost so Chisulo fashioned cut bamboo slivers into sheaves, which lasted until they reached the ground. Next morning, they returned, and just above half-way up, the spoor showed the elephants had left, startled, in the night. The trackers reckoned the bulls had found the men's spoor and being wise old bulls, knew what the tracks meant.

The men knew they now had a long slog ahead of them, it being Harry Manners' habit to never ignore a possible spoor. In their favour was the fact that it was early, and Harry had taken extra rations in case of just this eventuality. They descended the slippery slope, resting their tortured leg muscles at the foot of the mountain before setting off again. The spoor headed south all day, then veered west, into the setting sun. It was a long, hard slog like many other similar days, but every so often they'd find deep parallel gouges where giant tusks had furrowed the trail. At a mud-wallow they found two holes five feet apart where the bull had buried his tusks into the clay, so he might stand; Harry's pulse quickened when Chisulo knelt in the mud, inserted his arm up to his shoulder and announced he couldn't feel the end of the hole. At the evening campfire, Harry reflected on the day and pondered the one following, while massaging his aching leg muscles. The men were quiet as they ate their evening meal of stiff maize porridge, *nyemba* beans and cassava, washed down with tea; the next day promised more slog.

They were exhausted and needed to deliver similar work the following day, so guard duty was out. Harry silently prayed that no night prowler would choose that night to visit horror upon the party, a dangerous but unavoidable risk to take. Their collective luck held. The men were up before the dawn and back on the trail; the bulls appeared to have relaxed with the coming of darkness, their pace visibly slackened. Here and there they had voided, and stripped foliage to eat. At last, a distant rumble followed by the thump of something solid against a tree trunk electrified the men, fatigue evaporating as if by magic, as adrenalin coursed through their veins. It was then that potential disaster appeared: a small herd of sable antelope, some thirty yards distant, between the men and the elephants. If they were startled, the pachyderms too would disappear like wraiths.

The men froze, a familiar elephant rumble and the cracking of a branch consoling the sable that all was well. They slowly meandered on. The relieved men neared the elephants, Harry feeling a strange connection to ancient times, like cave dwellers approaching mammoths. But there was one telling difference: cradled in his paws was a .375 H&H Magnum rifle; although his confidence seemed to have deserted him, spotting the giant was almost an anti-climax. Through a split in the foliage, suddenly there he was; Harry glanced back at his companions, their expressions too reflecting wonder bordering on fear. Harry neared to thirty yards and decided not to chance a head shot; aiming just behind the shoulder, he touched off. The bull switched ends after recoiling slightly, emitting a roar as Harry sent a second raking shot into his huge lungs. The massive elephant smashed away through the vegetation, trees and bushes snapping like twigs before his rush.

Behind him Harry heard shouts, then a shot and heavy elephantine footfalls, as the other two bulls ran straight through the now-scattering men, and away. They took up the spoor immediately, the giant charging fully 100 yards before slowing to a walk. Blood now stained bushes and grass a bright red; ahead they heard a crash and Chisulo's eyes gleamed as he declared the bull to have fallen. Harry wanted to dash on, but instead exercised the hunter's caution born of long experience. The bull was majestic, surreal and colossal, even in death. Despite all his years as an ivory hunter, and given the company he was in – where emotions are largely taboo while hunting – Harry harboured a huge lump in his throat and felt the tears running down his cheeks, although he managed to prevent himself from weeping openly. Strangely, he noted that he'd not shed a tear at his father's passing, and anger at the thought made him stop forthwith.

The Murripa bull's tusks weighed 187 and 185 pounds, the fourth-largest ever recorded. When Harry collected his mail from Milange, his life changed forever; there was a letter from Carmen, who was enjoying the Durban beaches, and which he read eagerly. But then the postmaster sorted the mail received that day, and gave Harry a letter from Carmen's father; the love of Harry's life was dead, pulled out to sea by a rip and as far as they knew, devoured by a shark. Harry prayed in his agony that she had drowned before any shark ripped into her. In his grief, and as men often do, Harry became reckless, a dangerous leaning while hunting elephants. Throughout his violent madness his men stayed by him, and Harry castigated himself during quiet reflection for endangering them; but each following day when his blood was up, he was the same ruthless, vindictive killer again. Over time he was to heal, but Carmen's death affected him greatly.

After 1953, when ivory hunting was closed in favour of hunting safaris, Harry joined Werner von Alvensleben's Safarilandia, the largest and best-known safari company on the entire Southern African sub-continent. Just before Mozambique became independent (1975), Harry went to South Africa, finding employment with the National Parks Board in Skukuza (Kruger Park's capital), where he imparted his wealth of knowledge onto an entire generation of Kruger rangers and cropping officers. He retired to nearby Nelspruit, where he died in 1997. By then he was rightly acknowledged to be a legend.

14. Paul Grobler

Left photo: Picture courtesy of Richard Harland

Below photo, L to R: the author, Paul Grobler, Marie Grobler, Steve Grobler (Paul and Marie's son), Jenny Grobler (Steve's wife). Picture courtesy of Jason Swemmer

The man featured in this chapter is a towering, larger-than-life, impossibly-competent human being. The length of his tenure in so hazardous a career beggars belief. He has probably shot more jumbo than any man in history, and by some margin. After 45 years in the ivory-gathering,

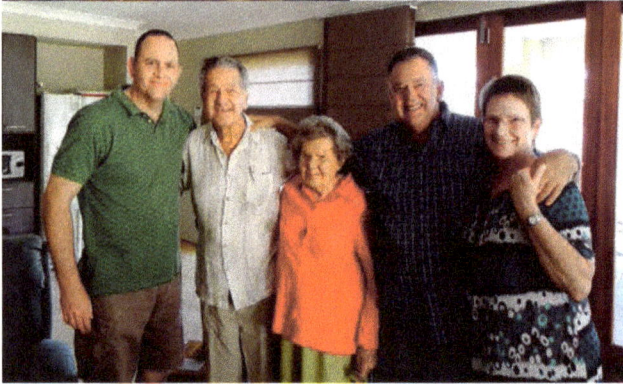

cropping and hunting industries, his has been a life which started in the era of travel by ox wagon, and has run through to see iPhones and iPads. But Paul Grobler holds a special place in my heart, because I have met him, visited with him, heard his story, eaten with him and have the photos to remember the times by.

*   *   *

In late 2014, my then-wife and I drove to a house in Warner, in south-east Queensland, Australia. Inside was a 92-year-old man, his wife, son and daughter-in-law. When I shook his hand, the innate calm and wisdom of years glinted at me as his eyes sparkled with life. Speaking to him in his Afrikaans mother-tongue, I was truly humbled and privileged, and told him so; the wonderful, serene old man's eyes grew quite emotional, visibly moved that I should laud him so. But it was warranted, and indeed, could not possibly even scratch the surface of recognising him enough. By the time he stopped hunting in 1990 – already aged nearly seventy – this man had almost certainly shot more elephant than any person in history. I had just met Paul 'Kambada' Grobler, a living legend. Chance meetings are indeed wonderful for all their random unlikelihood; my ex-wife's then-boss was an ex-Zimbabwean, one of many who had their vast farms invaded, and had to flee for their lives in the turmoil of Mugabe's government, and the land-grabs by 'war veterans' who weren't even born when the bush war finished.

She mentioned this legendary individual to us one night, when my ex-wife mentioned that I was writing of the great ivory hunters, as her husband knew him. Paul Grobler; the name rang a bell, and led to me buying the excellent biography of this phenomenal man's life, *African Epic* by Richard Harland. It is a book which Rowland Ward first published in 2003; Richard, himself a hunter and cropping officer of note in Zimbabwe, is well-known for his 2001 autobiography, *The Hunting Imperative*. I read the book on Paul's life, then re-read it, before getting in touch and going to visit the family. Stephen Grobler met us at the door; Stephen is Paul's only surviving child and only son. He lives with his parents and his wife, Jenny. After likely scanning us and being satisfied that we were ok - and didn't appear to be thieves, con-artists or mad - he granted us access to his home, with a cautionary word. "Remember," he said, "the old man is 92."

Steve need not have been concerned; the man we met was still as sharp as a tack, a beacon of experienced calm that I so admire in the elderly, who have lived hard, good lives. We also met his wife of sixty years, Marie, a diminutive elderly lady with the steadfast look of a born survivor. In his remarkable life, Paul Grobler was many things; he successfully farmed with tobacco and stock animals. Eventually, he became a fine golfer, a linguist and philanthropist. He was involved in the first major culling operations in Southern African game parks, which culminated in his mind-boggling totals of elephants shot; he became a successful safari operator and was ground-breaking in the crocodile farming industry. But his most famous exploits were as an ivory hunter, the rewards from which helped finance his early farming ventures. He survived all of these careers – many of them exceedingly dangerous – and more. He is no less than a testimony to the indestructibility of man.

Perhaps the story of how Paul received his Shona moniker, Kambada (little leopard), will help paint the picture as to why this was no ordinary man, and his life was to be anything but the mundane, average one. The year was 1948 and the District Commissioner for Mtoko in Southern Rhodesia (now Zimbabwe) had summoned the capable young man several times already to save the local people's crops from the depredations of elephant; but this time was different. This time, the trouble was more than mere raiding elephant, which in itself can result in starvation for entire communities. This time, the words 'man-eating leopard' brought a whole new dimension to the problem. As the Ford 1-tonner bumped along the tracks and paths, Paul used the time to discuss the situation with Bennet, his tracker and hunting companion. Bennet hailed from Nyasaland (now Malawi), as did many of the workers Paul employed on his farm, north-west of Salisbury (now Harare).

Bennet, a quiet young man of slight build, agreed that he and Paul gather as much information about the leopard incident before acting, as the vehicle bumped and scraped along, guided by a local on the back who occasionally shouted directions. Three hours after leaving the outpost of Mtoko, they reached a hamlet and the guide tapped on the roof as he called out "*Pano*" (we are here). There were lengthy African-style greetings and beer calabashes offered; Paul was invited to sit on a stool in the shade of a tree while the headman held court. People gathered in silence as Paul quizzed the chief on the score, after all the pleasantries had been dealt with. A girl of 8 had been killed and the people had been too afraid to approach the body. A group of girls had just gathered water in pots from the river and were walking back. Her friends in front heard her screams and the leopard's growls, and had fled. One girl had not returned. Paul bid them take him there.

Two men were detailed with the task, but *en route* they pointed out the home of a *nganga* – a witchdoctor – and refused to go any further. They thought the girl had been killed further along the path, but would await the hunters there. Paul and Bennet soon found the place where the leopard had attacked the child, torn clothes and bits of clay pot scattered about. In some granite boulders just off the path, they found the pitiful remains of the little body. The leopard had consumed most of the child. Both hunters noticed that one of the leopard's prints were strange, with no pads. After the villagers came to remove the child's remains with a blanket, the hunters started to scour the area. Nothing. Only once did they find tracks of the killer, with three paws and a stump. They walked the hills, visiting other kraals, venturing far and fast. On the third morning while glassing the valleys, Paul spotted something white: the tip of a leopard's tail bobbing in the grass as it walked!

The men crouch-walked to a bush some twenty paces ahead of where they thought the cat would appear, and into view a leopard limped. Paul shot it dead right there, a smallish young female with the left front paw amputated at the wrist, likely by a snare. Undoubtedly the culprit; but knowing Africa's propensity for the accursed wire snare, the cat was itself, too, a victim…Bennet hoisted the carcase onto his shoulders, then dumped it upon their return in the village courtyard. Paul spoke quietly, "The three-pawed *mbada* (leopard) is dead; it is finished." The crowd parted to allow an old crone through; she started ranting unintelligibly, shouting unnervingly at Paul, who was not just a little taken aback at this ungrateful display. In Shona, she screeched: "Did you kill this leopard?" Paul answered in the affirmative. The hag declared that the spirit of the animal now lived in Paul; he was now the *mbada,* before ambling off down a path! Shaken, Bennet told Paul that she was the old *nganga*, and they had better appease her with some gifts sometime soon.

Paul returned two days later to collect the hide, having shot five crop-raiding elephant bulls. Unrolling it back at his farm, Paul saw that someone had cut the right front paw off too; did this have something to do with the strange black magic avowed by the old woman? Some weeks later, Paul was back in the area to destroy more marauding elephants, so taking maize meal and salt, he and Bennet dropped by to visit the *nganga*. At the base of the hill was a suspended tin can; Bennet rapped it with a stick, the answering clunk of a wooden gong sounding soon afterward. Up they went and in a clearing was a large hut, the thatched roof overhanging the walls by several feet. A raised mud wall as high as a seat encircled the hut, and perched on a blanket with her back to the men sat the crone. Paul called out the traditional request to enter, "Goh-goh-ee", and was answered by "Pinda" (enter). In the African tradition, both Paul and Bennet respectfully enquired after the weather, noting the good crops, stock, beer and abundant mopane worms.

After a long silence, the hag spoke. "Kambada, why are you here?" She addressed him as the little leopard; Bennet's countenance was impassive when Paul glanced at him. He stammered that he was here to bring a small gift and hunt the crop-destroying elephants for the Commissioner. The witch turned slightly and spoke over her shoulder: "You will shoot many, many elephants, Kambada. The leopard must hunt. Go and hunt." Bennet motioned that they should leave. That night, staring into the campfire, Paul mused that this was his twenty-sixth birthday, and he was immersed in superstition well beyond his understanding. He asked Bennet if he thought the leopard's spirit really *was* inside Paul; the black man said he couldn't be sure, but did note that the witch was no longer angry. Perhaps she felt that this hunter was a good place for a hunter's spirit.

Richard Harland wondered what the old woman would say, if fifty years later she could have met Paul again, who by then had cheated death several times on land, in the air and on water, all while accumulating more elephant-hunting experience than anyone in history. He felt that perhaps, she might be impressed; even proud. But he settled on imagining that she would merely nod, knowing that his life was destined to be this way.

* * *

On 15 February 1922, Paul Grobler was born to Gert and Elisabeth, parents of South African Boer stock, on the family farm near Rusape (Roo-sah-peh), which lay close to Southern Rhodesia's (now Zimbabwe's) eastern border with Portuguese East Africa (now Mozambique). The family had moved there from Louis Trichardt in the northern Transvaal province of South Africa, as prospects were better up north. Paul was one of eleven children, and commenced his schooling at Milton School in Bulawayo, but reverted to farm life when his father developed cement poisoning. The senior Grobler had to change career to save his hands. The adventurous life was idyllic for a boy, and Paul was the ringleader of the farm urchins as they roamed the farm, hunting cane rats. These huge rodents make good eating, and Paul had most of the team herd the rats toward him and a few other good archers.

Paul had just turned nine when his father took the family north, into the Zambezi Valley on a hunting trip. Paul was in heaven; his siblings weren't thrilled, but the adventurous spirit was ecstatic as the family stocked up on biltong, boerewors (spiced farmer's sausage, a fabled and much-loved South African fare) and water. Paul soaked up the sounds of the bush, likely pestering his father for answers as to what made them. When good water supplies were come across, the family would outspan, Gert Grobler going off on horseback to hunt. On one such occasion - and at the ripe old age of nine, remember - a remarkable occurrence showed the direction Paul's life would take. Gert was out hunting while the family was camped at a large pan (small natural lake). The cattle herders ran to the wagons with news of a large bull elephant sporting fine ivory, drinking at the pan a few hundred yards distant.

The men urged Paul to go and shoot it, but the boy replied that his father had expressly forbidden the child to touch any firearm in his absence. This was no idle threat, and no trifling matter: anyone who knows the Afrikaners will be aware of an abiding discipline and a patriarchal society – particularly back then – which brooked no back-chat or disobedience. But this nine-year-old harboured the spirit of one who was to become one of the greatest-ever ivory hunters, and the imploring Africans didn't have much convincing to do, paternal threats be damned! Paul found his father's 7,92mm Mannlicher-Schoenauer, a German weapon on the excellent Mauser action, but probably too light a weapon with which to beard a large bull elephant. To increase the danger, there was only one round in the weapon.

Off the little party set toward the pan, the heavy rifle difficult to carry for what was essentially a little boy; at the edge of the tree line, the men stopped and pointed out the huge bull, its large tusks on full view as it drank. With his bowels working overtime due to advanced apprehension, the boy was led to within 30 yards, using a large termite hill for concealment and to steady the weapon. When the giant animal lifted its head and drank, an irregularly-breathing Paul, only vaguely aware of where to place the side brain shot, pulled the trigger. The recoil sent the child sliding down the side of the termite nest, but when he regained his footing and peered around the mound, he saw the bull collapsed half in the pan, its last breath bubbling through the trunk. The men approached the elephant cautiously, but it was dead.

After his father had returned and had seen to his horse's needs, then washed and changed, one of the staff asked if he'd been successful and gotten an elephant. Upon learning that he had, the man declared that he doubted it could best the one the little *bwana* had collected! Gert had the man summon the boy from his usual place at the men's fire. Placing his broad leather belt beside him, the older Grobler questioned the younger. When the score had been established, the father belted his son for disobedience. Paul accepted his punishment as just, and the two shook hands afterward, as was the Afrikaner way; this is designed to prevent festering resentment. Then they set off to see Paul's elephant, and Gert had to admit, at 60 lbs a side (27kg), it sported far better ivory than his had done! The following morning, the butchering could begin after the massive animal had been dragged from the pan.

Gert and Paul breakfasted on fresh bread baked in a nearby anthill hole, some sausages and impala kidneys; as they were washing it all down with coffee, the elder Grobler announced, cheerfully enough: "So you want to be an elephant hunter, son? Today you come with me." This was unexpected, and Gert rode his horse with Paul and the trackers walking – the boy occasionally running – to keep up. It was an exhausting day, broken only by a short stop to eat some oranges and a longer one to get outside their lunch of cold meat & sandwiches. They travelled far and fast without once spotting elephant tracks, returning to the wagons in the afternoon. Paul was literally all-in, exhausted and scratched, but was exhilarated and happy that he'd kept up. One wonders if the father purposefully wandered aimlessly, the lesson being to show the child that elephant hunting often entailed miles of exhaustion for no reward; but it's at least as likely that the men were indeed looking for spoor, yet found none. The previous chapters of this book have clearly illustrated that this was the nature of the business.

On returning to the farm, Paul was to survive the first of many occasions which may have claimed his life; the oxen used for the hunting trip succumbed to nagana, the disease borne by that scourge of domestic animals (and to many the saviour of Africa's wildlife as a consequence), the tsetse fly. At the same time, Paul went down with malaria, which rapidly morphed into blackwater fever, usually the result of repeated doses of malaria. He was subjected to the treatment of the time, which sounds archaic; but then again, the proof is in the pudding: the boy was placed in a bath of dried kraal manure, hessian bags and warm water, and had to sweat his malady out in the smelly confines. This he duly did, at the cost of much of his skin, which peeled off. Worse, and as is often the case with blackwater fever, Paul suffered a relapse which this time was mercifully less severe. The young man had survived his first brushes with death, an enemy over whom he was to enjoy many often-unlikely victories.

The Great Depression was at its height and people everywhere suffered; some of Paul's older siblings had left to marry or find work, two others had died. With fewer mouths to feed, the family could afford to have Paul attend school again, this time at a boarding school near Beatrice, south of Salisbury (now Harare). Gert however had no car, so Paul would go with neighbours on their trips to town, then hitchhike with one of the large Road Motor Services (Rhodesia Railways) trucks the rest of the way, sometimes having to use this method the entire way. How times have changed; imagine a nine- or ten-year-old child having to be handed over to fate in this way, merely to attend school? In reality, this was hardly ideal even back then, but in the Depression, what was one to do? Also - and people who have lived in Africa will relate - for people in remote places (and for a huge percentage of the indigenous populace), it has always been thus.

Paul had two years of school to make up, cramming extra classes in over weekends and holidays, and managed to get back up to speed by the age of fourteen; but then Gert could no longer afford the school fees and Paul again had to leave school. The headmaster – a Mr Collingwood – was sorry to see him go, and put in a word for the diligent youngster with the nearby Beatrice gold mine. Paul started as a surface worker, then did extra work to progress. Within a year he was on underground shifts, and by age sixteen had his miner's ticket and blasting certificate. Things moved fast for the young man; a South African exploration company was hired by the mine to use their diamond drilling equipment, and Paul soon joined them, easily mastering the equipment. His pay had increased dramatically, and Paul bought a half-ton Ford van, proudly driving it to his family farm and presenting it to them as a gift. Gert sheepishly admitted that he still had not learnt to drive!

The drilling company moved to the Copperbelt in the north of the country, then on to the south of the Belgian Congo; Paul was the hunter for the crew, shooting for the pot, and further north – in the Congo River basin – Paul was interested to learn that the Pygmies used poison blow-darts more than bows and arrows. Come 1939, Paul tried to enlist but was rejected as he was only seventeen. He kept trying until he was accepted as a reserve, spending a fruitless year in Gwelo. With so many men away at the war, Paul found work with the African Explosives & Industries (AE&I); the huge organisation still exists, now known as the AECI (African Explosives and Chemical Industries). It was here that he was to survive another brush with death, and this time it was remarkable that he did.

It being law to dip cattle in arsenical baths, the AE&I had a deal with a mine in the Que district (now Kwekwe) whereby the arsenic-rich ore was sent to the Rodia factory near Salisbury. The arsenic was extracted and the ore returned to the mine. Paul worked on the extraction, but with arsenic usually imported from South Africa, the Rodia management weren't aware of the critical importance of protective clothing and breathing filters. Soon, the team of nine extractors were deadly ill, seven dying and another losing a lung. Paul survived, but only just. Rodia arranged work for him with Rhodesia Breweries, overseeing fermentation tanks while he had to drink six pints of brewer's yeast every day to absorb the poisoning. Slowly, his nails returned from white to pink, his thick black hair returned in place of the white tips and his damaged skin healed. Even so, when I saw him in 2014 and 2015, the damage on his lower legs was still horrifying to see, dark black and purple covering most of the lower limbs.

Some of the best times in Paul's life accompanied the bad; after a couple of years' courting, the well-mannered and athletic young man married Marie van der Merwe, a Salisbury secretary, in January 1945. Rhodesia Breweries' gift was a 40-gallon canister of beer! When a fully-recovered Paul returned to Rodia, the workers had suitable protective clothing and no further arsenic casualties occurred. During this time, Paul's life took an historic turn: his brother-in-law, Phillip Kruger, introduced him to Danie Bredenkamp, who worked on elephant control for the Lands Department. These people thinned out elephant herds that were damaging tribal crops. This may sound flippant today, but if anything, is even more relevant now: as the human population share more space with wildlife in tribal areas, the damage caused by elephants can be catastrophic for poor subsistence farmers.

Paul asked Danie if he might accompany him one day; the big easy-going farmer said he'd welcome the assistance, and maybe Paul would be involved in the longer term. It had started.

*   *   *

Danie was a farmer by trade, but worked freelance on elephant control for the Lands Department (the Southern Rhodesia Game Department was only to come into being a decade later). Danie was impressed when the young man recounted his only previous elephant success, as a kid of nine. As the truck bumped along the dirt road toward the Mtoko district, Paul thought Danie's setup a good one. He had a couple of days' leave from Rodia and had brought his one and only firearm along, a .303 ex-military weapon – likely a Lee-Enfield – with hunting stock, and using the 215 grain Kynoch round-nosed ammunition (the military 174 grain, sharp rounds which worked so well against people were poor performers on large game). Reaching Mtoko took half a day and when fresh damage to sorghum and millet fields was at last located, it was too late in the day to set out after the culprits.

Paul picked Danie's brain on elephant hunting until well into the night, and recalled these as some of the most enjoyable evenings of his life: sipping on after-dinner coffee, the blue tongues of flame licking along the *mopane* logs, the occasional crack and pop of the fire joining the night birds in providing the soundtrack of the bush. Paul was relaxed and truly happy, his soul – as have those of so many people before him and since – soaking up the wonderful, seductive atmosphere of the African wild places. The next morning saw the men on the march, led by the two locals who had spent the night in camp. Reaching a village after an hour, the crop damage caused overnight by elephants was considerable. Tracking was easy, as they followed the path of destruction. The trackers thought the herd would number some thirty cows.

Paul watched the trackers closely, learning their age-old and brilliant craft as they went. By late morning they closed with the herd, the rumbles and feeding sounds adding to the atmosphere and increasing Paul's excited apprehension. Danie had the party approach from downwind and the man directly behind Paul urgently hissed a warning, pointing low to the right. Paul had just bent to look through the vegetable morass when a large cow elephant commenced her charge. As Paul settled the .303 nicely into his shoulder, Danie's .375 boomed beside him and the cow crashed loudly down through the shrubs. "Come," Danie ordered, as they raced after the fleeing herd. In an opening before the men, a group of cows were crossing and the men each got off three rapid shots before the animals disappeared. Reloading, the men froze, listening.

There was the sound of the crashing fall of a large animal, then another, and one more as the beasts went down. Waiting a while for the shot animals to die, the men had a drink, then carefully followed up every blood trail, coming upon five dead elephants. After rechecking and criss-crossing the area, they returned to the carcases. One had two bullet wounds, thus accounting for all six shots fired. There were no wounded elephants left to wander with agony in their bodies and hateful revenge in their hearts. It's no secret that wounded big game animals account for people, and elephants are able of causing frightful damage at the best of times. Paul was satisfied with the performance of his rifle, but Danie cautioned that it was unlikely to be effective when frontal head-shots were required on bull elephants. Next morning the men collected the tusks, then carefully learned the anatomy lessons from the shot placement.

When Paul recounted his experiences to Marie back in Salisbury, she smiled at his excitement, his face lighting up with enthusiasm at the recollections. I enjoyed reading this in Richard Harland's story, as I fully understand the almost childlike excitement. My ex-wife commented in the past on the same reaction in me. Africa's wild places truly do get well under the skin. Paul couldn't wait to get back into the wild, unspoilt places and hoped Danie would soon call upon him again. This duly happened, broadening Paul's experience with each hunt as the men traversed several different districts, building survival skills and bush craft. Within a year, Paul's brother-in-law had bought a second farm, and Paul agreed to run this second farm until he could buy his own. Of course, the opportunity for the odd hunt was a given too, which was Paul's main driver for leaving Rodia.

A couple of months later, Danie called Paul; the crop-raiding elephants had headed to the Zambezi Valley, after visiting havoc on the local people. Over the course of three nights, they'd destroyed corn, melon and pumpkin stocks, and had even torn open grain storage huts raised on stilts. The eight bulls that were the culprits had slaked their thirst at a pan *en route* to the uninhabited areas in the north. The men found them spread out, the noises of breaking branches the only way to discern where each elephant stood. With the wind fickle, the men realised they needed to act fast. Danie brain-shot the first, the far more mobile and nimbler Paul rushing onto high ground to cut off a small group of five. His .303 cracked five times, and all five bulls were down. Danie's trackers were mightily impressed with Paul's rapid successes. As for Paul, he drank from the canvas water sack while marvelling at what a fine invention it was! Nothing like a severe thirst, finally slaked, for developing appreciation!

Paul wondered at this point about the two escapees; elephants' advanced social structures and long-distance infra-sound communications were as yet unknown, and the unanswered questions troubled Paul. Danie was impressed with his quick-fire haul and decided it was time for the Lands Department to hire Paul on elephant control, so he could crop on his own; he did however reiterate his warning about using a .303 on big bulls. Paul's hunting ramped up as the Lands Department, Tsetse Control Department and district commissioners summoned him to assist with crop-destroying elephants. Hunting was part of life in the 1940s for rural Southern Rhodesians, and the "little leopard's" experience grew almost daily.

*   *   *

The dry season of 1946 was a long and severe one; the government had put a £1 open hunting license in place to hunt the Zambezi Valley. This was what later proved to be a hare-brained scheme to control tsetse fly by killing the game; the prevention of crop-raiding was seen as a welcome side effect. Lion, leopard and rhino were off the bill, and thus prohibited as permissible game, but for all other species it was open season. Paul would take the Ford One-tonner and it did yeoman service, which Paul was only able to fully appreciate when he later experienced the stunning abilities of the Land Rover, first made in 1948. Paul acquired one of the first in the country and used them for many years in different guises and wheelbase lengths. As a sidenote, when I visited Paul and Marie in 2014, we spent some time discussing Land Rovers, a common love.

As mentioned, Paul bought one of the very first ones in the country and was a loyal customer ever afterward. I owned a late model Defender, the spartan, utilitarian vehicle that may be sorely lacking in creature comforts – hell, that's why we bought them – but is as close to unstoppable off-road as any commercially-available vehicle has a right to be. The Groblers loaded theirs at times impossibly heavily; a buffalo carcase and several men in the back was no challenge, despite the vehicle looking like it was about to stand on the rear bumper. At length, our discussion headed toward the fact that they aren't the world's most comfortable vehicles, and certainly can't be described as fabulous to drive on the road. It was left to *Tannie* Marie to close the discussion, probably tired of men-chatter; "Remember," she sagely said, in a voice which brooked no argument at all, despite its quiet and calm delivery, "they are called Land Rovers…not Road Rovers!"

Back to the Zambezi Valley; Paul hunted elephant around the Batonka villages. One of the main crops was cannabis (marijuana), and that is still the case today. The authorities traditionally allow the Tonga people to use this drug. The area was infested by tsetse, Paul soon foregoing comfort in the extreme heat by wearing long trousers and even a jacket, in preference to the constant savage stinging bites and thorn of the *jesse* bush. After a fortnight or if lucky, a month, he'd return to farming and to seeing his family, usually filling the Ford with ivory. It was at this time that Paul was to cease using the .303 on elephant. Danie had been proven correct. The first clear hint was when he put fifteen rounds into an elephant which escaped, never to be found again. Paul was sick with regret, and the next sortie drove the point home. Paul was after five bulls, dropping three to brain shots. While his men removed the tails, he followed up the remaining two.

But when he returned, the original three were gone! Paul had to follow them up, killing two before evening, then returning early next morning for the third. He was hugely relieved to gather it by midday, but the lesson had been clear. He initially moved on to the ubiquitous .375 H&H Magnum and the 9,3mm (a preferred European calibre almost as effective), but then graduated to the heavier calibres, sampling the .416 Rigby, a .425, a few .458s, a .465, the potent .460 Weatherby, the .470 and even the giant .600 Nitro Express. Around this time, he made for Mozambique (then still Portuguese East Africa), from whence news emanated of the Senna Sugar Estates paying hunters well to supply their workers with buffalo meat. He could gather one elephant for every forty buffalo supplied. Paul duly cropped some 300 buffalo, but felt an attack of malaria coming on. He returned to civilisation to recover, then went back to collect his licensed elephants.

Paul's trusted tracker, Bennet, had arrived at his farm one day in 1947 looking for work; he had come on foot from Nyasaland (now Malawi), via Portuguese East Africa (now Mozambique), and arrived on the farms of the Southern Rhodesian plateau. He was to become closer than Paul's shadow, a vital constant in a role, the importance of which will already be clear from previous chapters. Bennet's hand-rolled newspaper-and-shag tobacco cigarettes were his eternal companions, and Paul cannot ever remember him being without them. One day, Danie Bredenkamp arrived at Paul's homestead, having tried and failed to raise them via telephone. Elephants had been raiding smallholdings in the Mtoko area, and the locals demanded action. Paul and Bennet headed thence and after viewing the damage, Paul tallied the losses – some twenty bags of grain in total – vowing to shoot an elephant for every ten bags lost. This sadly meant a third animal, as the neighbouring villagers who had suffered no losses, would feel hard done-by, at having received no meat…those who have lived there will relate!

When Paul announced this, there was laughter and the nodding of heads in agreement. This attitude of rural Africans towards wildlife - that they are merely meat - and the rapid habitat loss due to the sky-rocketing human population, are they reasons why wild animals in Africa are endangered. These are also the reasons why they will be extinct in the wild in our lifetimes, unless secure and functioning reserves and well-managed, ethical hunting concessions are prioritised on that continent. As you can see from the example Paul described above, these are facts, not opinions. Hardest of all for Westerners to understand, is that the people are correct; Africa's social problems of rapid population growth mean a massive demand for people to be fed. In rural areas, the keeping of an animal for anything other than consumption would be an absurd idea, and the way pets are treated in the developed world would literally be laughed at in Africa. Paul shot three of the bulls, out of a group of six, and the people were duly fed.

The following month, in another part of the Mtoko district, Paul and Bennet had to find and shoot another three bulls, among them the producer of the largest track Paul ever saw. He had never seen so large a spoor, and he never saw its like again. Paul shook his head as he told Richard Harland, the print was the diameter of a 44-gallon drum; unbelievably huge. I laughed when I questioned the old man about this; "Jis!" he exclaimed in Afrikaans ("jeez!"), and shook his head just as he had to Richard! This was obviously the bull of a lifetime, to have left such an impression on so prolific a hunter, and one with so lengthy a tenure. Paul and Bennet set off following the large tracks, which in short order separated from the remainder of the group. All day the huge bull travelled downwind, generally heading west. Paul considered this behaviour to be the reason the bull had lived so long, but it may have been lucky, or just exceptionally large, age regardless: as bulls age, they often surround themselves with younger bulls, to benefit from the younger animals' sharper senses, because the old-timers' senses weaken with age, as do humans'. Staying alone may be risky as one's senses fail.

By nightfall the bull was still off in front, the men spending an unpleasant night plagued by mosquitoes before being chilled to the bone in the morning cold. They ate their cold *sadza* (a sticky maize porridge) and biltong while thawing beside a small fire. Paul remarked to Bennet that he'd heard distant dogs barking in the night, and that they'd need to drop by the village for food. When they reached the village, they were readily assisted with pork and more *sadza*, the inhabitants well aware that Paul would in all likelihood soon provide a windfall in elephant meat. Back on the spoor, the men found where the huge bull had spent the night, dozing beside a tree on the bank of a stream. When he moved down into the dry riverbed, he left two grooves, some four feet apart, and on either side of the massive footprints…! Paul's heart leapt; these were tusk marks! The men knew they dare not lose this bull now; Paul had an ivory license on him, so could keep the tusks.

The men dug into the sand to fill their water sacks, beside the hole where the elephant had made its own hole to slake its thirst. The bull led the men in a north-westerly direction, ever downwind. When the spoor crossed bare ground in a mopane forest, the toes were dug in; the bull was alarmed and going fast. Paul cursed their luck, knowing they couldn't cut the distance and circle around the wily animal while it used the wind so cleverly, and that it was heading for the steep hills of the Mazoe River valley, along the border with Portuguese East Africa (now Mozambique). Another night came and went, again passed in much discomfort, this time at the base of the hills. The bull crossed the Nyadiri River, which at least allowed the pursuing hunters to replenish their stocks; after hours of hard slogging, they crossed the Mazoe River, the powerful current threatening to sweep the men downriver. Bennet told Paul that if he'd wet his tobacco and matches, he'd have turned back; he was only half-joking, the omen even more foreboding than the actual damage to the cigarette-junkie Bennet.

By mid-afternoon a heap of whitewashed stones piled into a cairn indicated the Portuguese East African border; but there was no way the men were going to turn back now. They decided to plead ignorance if it ever came down to it, claiming to believe the marker to be a mining claim or grave! Effectively poaching, by late afternoon the men came upon the great bull resting in the shade of a tree overlooking the deep Ruya River valley. Paul shot it, his careful stalk with pounding heart over the hillside's stony slope culminating in a single brain shot. The huge tusks, the massive feet; Paul's excitement was diluted by a pang of regret for the fallen giant. Its tusks went 114lbs and 112lbs. Of note, Paul eventually sold them to Arthur Levy, the well-known ivory dealer and owner of Manica Cycle Company of Salisbury (now Harare), who mounted them in the foyer of one of his office buildings, the fittingly-named Ivory House.

Crop-raiding groups of bull elephants were constant; one persistent group numbering a dozen had proved elusive, but kept up their depredations. After some time, Danie managed to shoot one, but the group hadn't gotten the message. Paul caught up with them in the hills one morning, killing 6 in one go. A week passed, then Paul and Bennet were summoned to deal with another small herd below the Zambezi escarpment. For three days, the men tracked the eleven bulls, which would venture to the kraals then return to a range of hills some ten-to-fifteen miles distant (16-24km), but couldn't ever even sight them. Paul determined to catch the bulls red-trunked, in the cultivated fields at night as they raided. The fields featured lookout platforms, flimsy structures just four feet square intended to hold two children, who would be sent to watch over the fields when baboons or birds set upon the crops. They would then be expected to beat tin cans, shout, wave flags or garments, whatever drove the thieves away.

The small platforms were supported by four poles some ten-to-twelve feet tall (3-3,5m), with the bases buried, and reached by a rickety ladder. They were not designed to support two adult men, a heavy rifle and a car battery; but support all of that, the one unwillingly did! Paul won; he'd bet Bennet that the structure would hold, the tracker strongly doubting. Clearly, it was anything other than steady. The darkness sank like a cloak, flitting bats and night insects the only sounds in the stands of ten-foot sorghum. The elephants ghosted into the field right on schedule – just after dark – and Paul pondered the fact that they appeared right by the platform, which he'd chosen as it was downwind from where they normally emanated from. A pumpkin was squashed with an audible wet crunch; Paul indicated to Bennet where to shine the light, and the beam froze the elephant caught in its light.

The .375 boomed, Paul's excellent headshot dropping the pachyderm like a stone. Chaos erupted at the loud report, the remaining bulls rumbling and trumpeting. Momentarily, Bennet panicked, the light flitting first here, then there, each time finding an elephant. Paul hissed at him to hold still, another bull freezing in the beam and falling to Paul's second shot. Then the lookout was bumped, and the men tumbled to earth in a heap of timber, humanity and equipment, but luckily unhurt. Paul grabbed Bennet and made for one of the dead bulls, for some protection from the milling, angry survivors. Dropping down low, to try see silhouettes in the dark, Paul made out what looked like an elephant's back. It was however quite low down; then he remembered the clay pit the people had dug, using the clay to coat their hut walls. In the dip, pumpkins and other gourds had grown; a bull was calmly standing in the pit, eating pumpkins, while bedlam reigned on level ground!

Closing the distance, Paul could barely make out the head and a tusk gleaming whitely in the gloom. With both rifle sights invisible, he judged as best he could, and fired. The bull collapsed, dead. At this last shot, the remaining bulls decamped. Paul was sure they'd now leave the area, and move into a tsetse fly zone, some twenty miles distant (32km). Here the men accounted for six more bulls and a herd of cows, but then had to return to the crops: the remaining eight raiding bulls had resumed their depredations just four days after his previous excursion against them! This was surprising, and unusual; once again, the bulls used the hills for a base. This time, Paul and Bennet waited for them in the *mopane* woods, between hills and crops, looking for their most-used pathways. This was evidenced by the quantity and freshness of the droppings. Paul shot five of the eight. The locals were extremely grateful, thanking Paul profusely; he told them he'd been lucky to intercept them so fast, but the men knew better, proclaiming the real reason to be the fact that Kambada thought like an elephant...

One day, Paul and his men had just returned to camp and were unloading the buffalo they'd shot for camp meat, when the man who'd been sent down to the river to start the pump came running to report that four bull elephants were crossing the Zambezi, from the Northern Rhodesian (now Zambian) side. One, he reported, carried huge ivory. Paul took Bennet along, and some half a mile distant (800m), four bulls were just coming out of the river on their side. Pausing long enough to grab the .416 Rigby and his binoculars, Paul set off at a run along the game path atop the river bank, Bennet in tow. With the sun going down, the men knew time was of the essence, and almost ran slap-bang into the four bulls as they came up the bank. The men froze, by sheer luck downwind. The riverine bush was so thick, that when Paul stealthily followed upon seeing the large-tusked animal, he nearly bumped into the backside of another huge, feeding bull!

Before he could back away, the huge tusker sauntered by, so Paul shot it through the brain. The fright delivered to the feeding bull, with a shot going off right behind him, almost resulted in the great beast collapsing in fright, so Paul dived through the clump of bush beside him and emerged from the other end, lest the elephant land on him. One of the others thundered by immediately behind him, so he ploughed straight back into the bush he'd just left. It was comedy-movie stuff, and if it hadn't been so thoroughly dangerous, Paul might have had a chuckle. Bennet watched all of the pantomime from the safety of a huge fallen tree trunk. It was a successful day regardless: the big bull's tusks went over seventy pounds a side.

*　*　*

Game departments and game wardens began to appear in British Colonial Africa in the early 1900s, commencing with East Africa; but it wasn't until the 1950s when Southern Rhodesia followed suit. The first Game Officer was Archie Fraser, whose first Ranger was to be none other than Ian Nyschens, until then a notorious poacher. By 1957, he'd added Rupert Fothergill, Tommy Orford, Barry Ball and Paul's old friend, Danie Bredenkamp. Paul was still called on regularly to protect the locals; the District Commissioners had used and trusted him for years. One day, Paul got back to the house after a strenuous day in the tobacco fields, to be greeted by Marie with a message from Karoi's District Commissioner: someone in that area had been killed by an elephant, and Paul was to assist, but urgently. Over lunch, Paul ran through the farm's affairs which Marie would have to oversee in his absence, then taking Bennet, Paul arrived in Karoi in the late afternoon.

There they were met by one of the D.C.'s men, who directed them to the tribal grounds where the incident had occurred. A woman had been killed the previous afternoon by an elephant, but as yet no body had been found. Stopping at huts for information, another woman had stayed at the stream to wash clothing, and she had heard a terrified scream followed by a short, sharp elephant trumpet-blast. A group of five bulls had been in the area, but until now had caused no harm. No-one had since been for water – somewhat understandably – but when the village men tentatively investigated, the smashed water jug was found, no body however. The local guide led Paul and Bennet down the well-worn path, and just before they reached the small valley, they saw large numbers of vultures atop an acacia. This is often a sign for the hunter to approach with extreme caution, as it usually indicates the presence of a predator, and that it is still on the kill.

As the men quietly approached, the bulk of the carrion-eaters flitted to adjoining trees. There was plentiful elephant spoor and some dung balls; then Bennet looked up. Suspended some fifteen feet (5m) up in the tree was the woman's pitiful corpse, putrefying in the heat, foul fluids dripping down the twisted frame and torn clothes. It was suspended in a morass of tight thorn where the vultures couldn't reach it. The local covered his mouth in shock, which provides some idea of the sight; rural Africans that live tough lives in dangerous places aren't sensitive. Ever the perceptive and empathetic soul, Paul sent the man back to the village to bring people and a blanket while he and Bennet took turns setting to the tree with the axe; there was no other way to get the poor woman down. The huge hole tusked through the stomach was only the prelude to the crushed spine which ended the woman's life.

Paul back-tracked to the path and put the story together from the spoor; the bull had been on the other side of the path and took exception at the sight of the woman, her scent, or maybe the soft crooning song she was likely humming. She'd dropped the jug and dashed away, but only covered a short distance when she was caught and tusked. The bull then tossed her into the air, or purposefully into the tree. Either way, it was academic to the woman. There she'd been caught, and had hung, suspended, until they found her. When the villagers had retrieved the body, Paul and Bennet returned to fetch the Land Rover and camp down near the stream. They'd make an early start and track the guilty bull. Paul lay awake, staring at the stars in the small hours. His normal enjoyment of sleeping in the open in the African bush was somewhat diluted by the recent killing. In the distance, a branch snapped and a village cur yapped.

With the dawn, a figure appeared out of the gloom, squatting down a respectful distance away to await an audience, with news: the previous evening, a boy from his hamlet had seen the bulls while searching for honey, and had been directed to the hunters. Paul thanked the man; they all had tea, then set off. They reached the man's kraal as the sun rose, left the Rover there and headed on foot for where the boy had seen the bulls. The fresh spoor of large adult male elephants was indeed apparent. The wind was steady in the early hours and the going was good. Since they'd not been harassed in this area, the bulls travelled into the wind, allowing the men to track them. The hunters came upon them in a small valley, all five feeding off a *mfuti* tree they had knocked over. Paul shot the one furthest away first, then dropped the remaining four while they milled about in their confusion. Paul instructed Bennet to look for blood on tusks, and for snares or other wounds which might explain the elephant's lethal actions.

Sure enough, one tusk was streaked with dried blood, but no wound could be found to explain the bull's temper. Although they couldn't examine the bull's underside, there was no obvious explanation for the woman's death, and in an eerie co-incidence, an African girl suffered a similar fate just a few miles from the first instance, three years later. Although Paul accounted for the group of three bulls responsible, again no reason for the animal's attack could be found. There was possibly a connection; people in that vicinity may have been in the habit of venturing out at night to send spears and arrows into crop-raiders. We've seen before how well that facilitates the peaceful co-existence between people and pachyderms...meanwhile, there was to be no rest for Paul: he was immediately summoned to the Doma area, to help eradicate some cattle-killing lions.

Perhaps a quick word on the flora would be appropriate here, so the reader has full context. Read any topographical summary of what is now Zimbabwe (formerly Rhodesia, and before that, Southern Rhodesia), and you will learn that most of the country is elevated, between 1,000 and 1,600 metres above sea level, is mostly savannah and is known as the central plateau. The extreme east is mountainous, and is known (logically enough) as the Eastern Highlands. The tropical, evergreen and hardwood forests include fine teak, mahogany, fig, white stinkwood and others. Some 20% of the country is under 900 metres above sea level, and like South Africa's Mpumalanga Province (previously known as Eastern Transvaal), is termed *Lowveld* (pronounced low-felt). These lower areas feature the yellow fever trees; mopane, combretum and baobab trees abound. The fabled Victoria Falls lie in the extreme North-West, on the Zambian border. But what the encyclopedias don't tell you, is that in the riverine forests of the *Lowveld* areas grows a vegetable nightmare.

This is the *Combretum-Commiphora* scrub, its proper name being the jesse-bush bushwillow. Left unchecked over time, it is a veritable morass, an impassable maze which has caught and held many a hunter, poacher and wanderer; and if these were being pursued by something large, hairy, toothy or a combination of the above, has resulted in the demise of a staggering number of individuals. It runs through a huge stretch of Southern Africa, from Angola and Namibia in the west, through Botswana, Zambia and Zimbabwe, all the way into Mozambique in the east. It thrives at altitudes of 500-1,200 metres, and thus covers an immense piece of the continent. In the wet season, it holds men fast; in the dry season, silent stalking is impossible. The Zimbabwean hunters speak of "the jesse" in hallowed tones, and like the murderous thorn scrub which runs from Mozambique all the way up Africa's east coast, it assists aspiring hunters not at all.

It grows to six and more metres high (20 feet); in the jesse, the wind can be so fickle as to be totally unreliable, or there can be no wind at all, so close and claustrophobic is the scrub-growth. To provide some idea, you will recall such accomplished and brave men as Wally Johnson and Harry Manners – men who had many miles and years on the clock in a dangerous occupation – deciding against hunting in the scrub forests, where elephants remain silent and hidden, even though mere feet away from a hunter, until the time is right to explode out and flatten their tormentors. Even a fatal heart or lung shot from a heavy double rifle is not necessarily enough to prevent the hunter being ground decisively into the sand of Mother Africa, and even a .375 is largely rendered inadequate in the jesse.

The phenomenal hunter-scout, Major P.J. Pretorius – who among his "kills" counted nothing less than the German cruiser *Koenigsberg* during World War 1 – was sent to the coastal scrub of what is now South Africa's Eastern Cape Province, to deal with a murderous herd of elephants in what is now the Addo reserve. The conditions there were similar, and Pretorius – who was no mere mortal – declared the conditions too dangerous to hunt elephant there, although he did later relent, and effectively completed his task. What this all drills down to, is that even in the remarkably-esteemed company in this book, Paul Grobler (and the subject of the following chapter, the volatile but mercurially-gifted Ian Nyschens) had to operate often and for extended periods in terrain in which almost none of the other famous ivory hunters did, and in which many of them outright refused to even consider hunting, due to the level of risk. It is interesting to note that these two men couldn't be more different: Paul Grobler being the calm, unflappable constant, while Ian Nyschens harboured a fiery temper and often came across as rash. Paul and Ian were actually to meet a few times over their careers.

One time, Paul was accompanied by John Dryden, who with his brother ran the hunting agency National Safaris, out of Salisbury (now Harare). They were in the Copper Queen area, where elephants were wreaking havoc in the tribal croplands. A group of seven bulls were the culprits and both Dryden and Paul held a £1 open license. The region was in the fly belt, so killing as many of the seven as possible was preferable. When at last the men closed with the group, they moved about, deciding which to shoot and in which sequence. This is essential when intending on getting an entire group, as the confusion, noise, danger and dust which result once the firing starts, renders random shooting risky and animals often escape. But only six bulls were visible; circling a termite mound, the men got a fright when the seventh bull was prone, asleep, on the slope of the mound's far side.

Paul winked and motioned Dryden quietly forward. Both laid a hand on the great ridge of backbone! Paul had touched sleeping elephants before, but this was Dryden's first time, and he was understandably elated. Dryden was allowed the best tusker first, then Paul collected the remaining six, chasing the last for several hundred yards fast on foot.

*　*　*

Time passed; Paul and Marie's children were growing up, the tobacco farming continued and between the floods and droughts, Paul Grobler continued to hunt elephants. There were more game reserves and controlled areas around the country, so elephant numbers increased, spilling over into tribal land, which as the human population surged, moved to meet the wildlife too. The elephant herds moved onto farms and into the tsetse fly control areas as well. Isn't it ironic, that as humans intervene to preserve the species, their very interventions make culling inevitable, as the huge animals inevitably outgrow their enclosed areas? At length, the Department of National Parks and Wildlife Management could stand the destruction to the Wankie Reserve (now Hwange) no longer, and large-scale culling was instituted in 1966. One of the pioneers in this field was, naturally, one Paul Grobler.

Most of Paul's heaviest shooting had always been in the tsetse fly areas. The idea of stopping the reach of the disease-bearing flies by killing the game beyond a certain point held some water, but was agonisingly slow, and the wanton destruction on the game – where more effective fly eradication could be undertaken with minimal damage to wildlife – was tragic. On one such tsetse control hunt, Paul was as usual camped on the Hunyani River with Bennet. He'd just acquired a .416 Rigby to add to his .458 BSA (Birmingham Small Arms), and was looking forward to verifying the former rifle's vaunted performance. Bennet lugged the .458 while Paul cradled the Rigby. They trailed a herd of at least 30-40 animals, which was some hours ahead and moved in and out of valleys, munching bamboo here, acacias or *mfuti* there, taking water in between. At length, the pair closed with them, and in the oddest place; a constriction at the bottom of the gorge some five or six yards wide.

Bennet said the herd was returning, so the men scrambled up a ledge some 30 feet (9m) above the path. Already, Paul's hunter spirit was feeling uneasy; although adrenalin filled his system as usual when the hunt was imminent, the safe position he and Bennet enjoyed watered it down. The unfair advantage (which so many people erroneously believe hunters to have in the normal course of events) was at odds with Paul's hunting ethos. The men felt rather than heard the low vibration as the lead cow entered the gorge, suspiciously sniffing the man-scent on branches and pebbles; the others were pressing on behind her, and Paul opened fire. He methodically kept shooting, lethal and well-spaced head shots dropping elephant after elephant. He emptied the Rigby, then it's spare box of rounds; grabbing the .458 from Bennet, Paul kept firing. When it was all over, Paul reloaded the .458 with three fresh cartridges, careful not to touch the barrel.

A wave of sadness swept over this serene and gentle man, which I can well believe having met him. At least no animals had been hurt or lost; Fraser's brief to the men had been to kill as many as possible in the region between the Hunyani and Angwa rivers, and Paul had certainly done his job: below him and Bennet in the gorge were no fewer than 49 dead elephants. The men sat quietly eating their sandwiches. The tsetse officer for the region, Gordon Thompson, arranged for the meat to be recovered, the farms and tsetse camps benefitting from several tons. Paul was glad that the wastage was thus minimal. He was also quite content for Fraser's team to retrieve the ivory from the carnage. When Paul stripped and cleaned the Rigby, the barrel had been so hot that the stock immediately touching it had darkened, but at least the rifle had performed faultlessly. There was no hint of the nasty surprise the rifle had in store for Paul on the very next hunt…

Each European (read: white) tsetse field officer had a team of twenty *magotchas* (African hunters), each armed with an old .303 and with instructions to shoot kudu, warthogs, bushbuck and wild pigs in the fly corridors. These men traversed far and wide, and were the eyes and ears on the ground for the culling hunters, like Paul. They provided invaluable information on the whereabouts of the elephant herds. Not far west of Paul's camp, a herd of cow elephants were located by two *magotchas*, who were sent to alert Paul. The remaining men were told to evacuate the area until the herd had been investigated, and if necessary, eliminated. The tracking started at a small waterhole in a valley. The wind was fickle and as the men neared, the herd crashed away. The hunters closed with them again an hour later. The cows were wary, nervous, and clearly up for a fight, if flight wasn't immediately possible.

The herd chose fight; Paul knew that several were coming, and darted to the side so he could see the first cow through a gap in the foliage. She went down to his shot, but right away Paul knew something was very wrong; there was a dull metallic clink, the bolt shot forward unrestricted, and something landed on his foot. The sound was the magazine's floor-plate opening, and the bolt shot forward because there was no cartridge for it to pick up: three of these lay at Paul's feet! This is concerning, as it isn't the first time that I've read of exactly this, for this legendary model of hunting weapon. I have no doubt at all that whatever caused the problem will have been attended to long ago, and that modern Rigby rifles will be flawless, but this is a fatal fault which doubtless cost lives when facing dangerous game. I'm sure that even the calm Paul was closer to apoplectic than just merely concerned, with three angry cow elephants bearing down on him!

Although angry cow elephants are nowhere near as large (and thus technically as destructive) as angry bull elephants, these terms are all relative: they are both many times the size and weight of a human being, and the difference between what an angry bull elephant leaves after it has smashed a human, and what a cow leaves when she is done, is I assure you purely academic to the person thus caught. The value of a decent tracker / gunbearer cannot be overestimated, a point I've laboured several times already; Bennet merely handed Paul the .458, the black man standing by to hand him replacement cartridges while the white man fired like an automaton. The next four cows were shot, forming a wall which protected the men from the rest of the herd, which was now milling about a tad confused; Paul ran up onto one of the carcases and shot six more before the herd decamped. Although he had never before had the magazine plate fall out of any bolt-action rifle - having fired many thousands of rounds - Paul immediately stopped at Salisbury's gun shop to have both rifles' plates closed permanently.

*   *   *

The town of Marandellas harboured a real character in Piet Nilson, a huge, hale and humorous man with a giant moustache. He owned a sports goods store and would drop by the schools to repair cracked cricket bats, replace broken racquet strings or fix punctured rugby balls. He developed a sudden desire to go big game hunting. Sensibly, he selected Paul Grobler to guide and mentor him. All Piet needed was a rifle and a license; the latter he acquired for a cow elephant, but Paul wouldn't let him take the battered old .303 Piet owned, a relic literally from the Boer War, at the end of the previous century. Since he, Paul, was using heavier calibres at the time, he made a gift of his venerable .375 to Piet. Soon, Paul & Marie, Piet & his wife Mary and all their entourage of servants were headed to the Zambezi Valley.

It was well into the late afternoon, the day having proven fruitless so far, and the Land Rover bumped and scraped along the rough trail back to camp. Bennet tapped on the roof and Paul stopped; the elephant tracks in the road showed a recent appearance by a cow herd. The men left the vehicle and with the breeze favourable, closed with the herd within ten minutes. A small gully led into the bush where the herd fed; moving quickly, the animals were soon visible to the men. Beyond the gully was a stretch of 40-50 yards of open mopane woodland. A large cow with good ivory was facing them, and Paul whispered to Piet to wait until she turned, rather than risk a trickier frontal shot. When she turned, Piet dropped her with an excellent side brain shot, the herd beyond her instantly fleeing. Suddenly, the herd was returning, and fast!

"Run!" shouted Paul, and run they did! Paul turned to see a screaming cow elephant about to grab Piet. In full stride, Paul yanked his pith helmet off and heaved it into the animal's face, the move having the desired effect of allowing Piet to escape; it was however an unfortunate next few moments for the helmet. The enraged cow smashed it into a pulp. The men crouched, panting for breath, waiting for the adrenalin rush to come off as the herd moved away. They returned to where the helmet lay, right beside one of Piet's boot prints; it had been most thoroughly crumpled. "Buggered," Piet commented; and promptly undertook to replace it with a new one, which he did. When the men again united with the trackers, Pedro's observation was of a similar ilk: "*Eet ees buckud, Bwana!*" he quipped, in his broken English! And they were both spot-on.

During 1961 Paul fitted a new aperture site to his .416, and took it to a gunsmith to have a new front site fitted, which would align accordingly. Somehow, the rifle was returned with a visible bend in the barrel, an absurd thing to happen, and one which would likely have had fatal consequences. Paul rightly refused to accept the weapon in this state, and was offered a .460 Weatherby to replace it, suitably discounted of course. Introduced in 1958, it was at the time and for some time afterward the most powerful rifle in the world, featuring a phenomenal measure of 8,095 foot-pounds of muzzle energy. This exceeded even that for the .600 Nitro Express. It always pays, however, to carry a back-up weapon, especially when hunting elephant. For Paul, that would normally be the old BSA .458; he had however only recently sold that weapon to Richard Harland, his biographer for *African Epic*....

Paul was summoned almost immediately to the tsetse fly area of the Zambezi escarpment, and bearded an aggressive herd some forty-strong on a small, thickly wooded plateau in the foothills. The wind was shifty, which alerted the herd to the men's presence, and a large cow approached with her head raised, looking for trouble. Paul lined her up and pressed the trigger; in reply, he heard what Peter Capstick referred to as the most fatal sound in big game hunting: the dull, distinctive click of a misfire. The herd picked the sound up too, and to them it was the proverbial red rag to a bull. The bush came alive with the sounds of trumpeting elephants crashing through foliage, and not away from the men, either! By now, the murderous cow was bearing down alarmingly on Paul, who had reloaded, aimed and fired again. Again, there was a dull click, this one signalling that Paul had better make rapid tracks or suffer a most decisive demise.

Paul raced off, the cow now disturbingly close, the danger exacerbated by the fact that bushes which impede humans aren't even noticed by jumbos. His desperation escalated as his eyes searched for something, anything, to avoid his impending and singularly-unpleasant doom. Next thing he was tumbling down a small ravine some 3-5 metres deep (10-15 feet), then gratefully going up the other side on pure adrenalin. He stopped to breathe and reload the Weatherby, alarmed when another pachyderm appeared. The herd knew the area and had traversed the ravine a short way down. Again, Paul fired; again, that dull click, by now unsurprising but no less foreboding. Paul barrelled gratefully down an elephant path, which at least allowed him to sprint unimpeded, but after half a mile or so (some 800 metres) at full tilt, he paused to listen, dismayed to hear that the herd were still in pursuit.

In mounting desperation, Paul crested a rise, overjoyed to recognise his whereabouts; the Land Rover was not too far away. Wondering where the trackers were, but reasonably confident that they had commenced their flight before him, and would thus have gotten to safety, Paul benefitted from some good fortune in that the wind was in his favour. He made good time, the following herd having to sniff him out from ground scent rather than wind; this bought him crucial seconds and he reached the Rover a few hundred yards ahead of them. Overjoyed to see both trackers waiting there for him, they drove off, Paul breathless, shaken and mightily relieved. After 5 minutes' hurried drive, Paul stopped to have a long drink and recount the experience to the trackers. He examined the rifle but there was no obvious reason for the misfires.

Back in camp, Paul had time to examine the Weatherby more minutely; the cartridges showed a small mark in the primer, nowhere near enough to fire the cap. When the gunsmith dismantled the bolt, they found the firing pin adjustment had not been set and locked in the correct way to ensure that enough projected to prime the cartridges, a small but lethal mistake. Paul never again took an untried rifle on a hunt, a point which has been pressed home to many a hunter, both the lucky ones – like Paul – and the others. In later times, while on solo culls, Paul developed the method of using three BSA .458s on a rotational basis, Pedro and Bennet reloading the empty one while Paul used the next loaded one. I find this interesting, as the .458 has a reputation as having poor penetrative performance, and is most experienced pros' least favourite larger calibre rifle. Perhaps using three of them offset any shortcomings.

*   *   *

The concept of culling developed much over the 1960s, pioneered in Rhodesia and later adopted most successfully in South Africa. In today's terms - in the second decade of the 21st century - it is roundly condemned by salivating pacifist-preservationists, which is concerning and annoying, because the bare, unemotional facts prove them wrong. Nobody *likes* to kill thousands of animals, much less elephants, with their recognised intelligent social structures. Hunters and game control officers are not blood-lusting maniacs; it is similar to killing any animal for meat, and I won't go into how even that is a crime for some people. Suffice to say, dear vegetarian / vegan, that a balanced diet, including meat protein, has likewise been proven to be healthier than the alternative. But in the world of game management – and remember, with old migration routes forever shut off, animals subsist in reserves, which are closed off – actively managing the numbers of animals in a given area is unavoidable.

Even that is questioned; pacifists want elephants relocated; but what happens when *all* the reserves are full? Elephants multiply exponentially if not managed, Also, relocating has been found to be even worse: the prone animals can't regulate their temperature and often suffocate or die of overheating, a slow and agonising death. Most conservationists – as opposed to preservationists – know better; they have seen the results of not managing game numbers. Human population numbers exploding is what has created this situation; the animals, particularly large and dangerous ones, can only now survive in reserves. They therefore have to be managed. The anti-culling brigade have never seen the effects of an elephant herd on a stretch of woodland in an enclosed area; the destruction so wrought literally takes at least two human generations to recover. But it doesn't have that time in an enclosed space; what happens then is the slow starvation of all species in the reserve.

Richard Harland recalled witnessing the conditions in reserves which were overrun by elephants. The edible vegetation had been stripped, the gaunt cow elephant mothers and babies, dead and dying at the dry waterholes with insufficient energy to make it to the next water source. The antelope species – kudu, impala and others – were starving and weakened, killed off in the sudden and unseasonal September cold spells. He mentions it as not being a pretty sight; and it is the constant lot of wild animals in reserves - the only place they and people are safe from one another - if the game is not managed (read: if culling is not undertaken). The practice is as humanely undertaken as is possible. In the early days, young elephants were spared, a major mistake; their memories are indeed good and the animals were traumatised by witnessing their families' demise. They understandably were violent and killed people in later years, so entire family groups were then culled.

This was done by teams of expert rangers who were excellent shots, two or three at a time. They would eliminate groups of elephants numbering 20-50, in mere minutes using brain shots. It was cost-effective, quick and efficient. The products were marketed and assisted to conserve the entire area for the longer term. This is not hunting, the act of paying (often handsomely) to pursue a quarry for food, or for the challenge; it is instead the act of actively managing the entire habitat's flora and fauna. Sadly, the anti-culling movements have been successful, by fair means or foul, due to their huge influence and emotion-based argument. It remains however, misrepresented and misinformed. These same activists proclaimed that elephants would be extinct by 2000, which was why they were CITES-listed. The fact is, both Botswana and Zimbabwe now have as many as three times' each country's carrying capacities of these animals. Namibia and South Africa are both well over capacity. If the alarming message from the preservationist fringe about supposed extinction were true, and was based on excessive poaching in East Africa, why was Southern Africa targeted with this message of doom while drowning in pachyderms?

Culling is a huge job, which would normally be undertaken a few months after the rains, as it starts getting cooler then, in Southern Africa (May onward). When it was commencing in what was then known as Rhodesia (independent from Britain since 1965, as Nyasaland became Malawi and Northern Rhodesia became Zambia), the researchers informed Paul that the numbers would run into the thousands in coming years. A processing plant, drying racks and equipment had to be bought, built and implemented. Within a few years it was a huge mini-industry all of its own. One season's records show 1,000+ elephants and 500 buffalo in Wankie Reserve, then 1,100 elephants and 100+ hippo in

Gonarezhou Park (the "refuge of elephants", pronounced Gor-nah-reh-zhoh), 4,000 plains game on Liebigs ranch. At this time, Paul employed over 600 people, ran a fleet of some 60 vehicles and three aircraft. This, the preservationist would shout, is the problem; but remember, the people in Africa are there to stay, and will only increase in number. The culling allowed them to thrive, plus the reserves to be sustainable, long-term.

Paul had graduated away from farming, now fully occupied with game ranching. He acquired the hunting rights on the afore-mentioned Liebig's Ranch, and over an 11-year tenure of cropping the hoofed game, employed and mentored dozens of young game ranchers. Paul and Marie spent a few weeks in the world-renowned Kruger Park in South Africa, when that institution commenced its own culling operations; this was after the Kruger people had visited Paul to see how things were done. Around this time, Zambia's Luangwa Valley reserves commenced same. In the early 1970s, Paul and Marie upped pegs and set camp in Rokari, south of Lake Kariba. They ran a hunting concession, a kapenta fishing enterprise, then started crocodile ranching. Paul and Steve (his son, now grown, and whom I also met and chewed the fat with) developing concrete enclosures which were easy to clean, and from which the crocodiles could not dig their way out.

These enclosures were later used in South Africa and all over the world. At the time, they held the largest captive croc anywhere in the world, a massive bull called "Ume" (pronounced Oo-meh), after the river; Rokari is at the mouth where it drains into Lake Kariba. He measured sixteen feet eight inches long (around 5.5 metres).

*   *   *

Paul had many other brushes with death – during the bush war he rescued a group of military special ops personnel, for which he was decorated; he had several very real scares with lions; way too many to recount with buffalo, and particularly many with elephant. Worst of all though, both he and Marie were directly involved in a sickening attack by insurgent terrorists, which befell many in those dark years. I won't dwell on it, and I strongly urge the reader to buy Richard Harland's book *African Epic*, for more on this and other staggering tales of their lives, but Marie still has part of a bullet lodged in her skull, and has subsequently lost her sight as she aged. Not content with receiving various shards of shrapnel in the same attack, Paul next survived an accident with one of the Cessna planes. Eventually, they settled in Australia, where I was sufficiently lucky to meet the family. In his 90s, Paul was serene, mentally sharp, and simply wonderful. They bred them tough back then, and gentlemanly; people to be admired.

15. Ian Nyschens

Ian Nyschens (the surname of Danish origin, pronounced 'nations') is one of the more remarkable protagonists in this book, and not only because he was for extended periods a blatant poacher, operating beyond the law and committing numerous recorded and unrecorded crimes. Nor was it because of his occasionally-violent, anti-social behaviour; many if not most of the other ivory hunters poached too (particularly in latter times, when there were game departments, game laws and regulated hunting) and several were eccentric loners to boot. What marks Ian out as almost unique was the insane courage - plus the ability to sustain that courage, over many years - required to hunt in Southern Africa's murderously thick jesse bush. Like the phenomenal Paul Grobler, who operated over a similar time, Ian could go into the jesse and successfully account for groups of elephants, in an environment which was so downright terrifying and likely to end in death for the human, that many luminaries in this book flat refused to hunt even one pachyderm there.

To further enhance his reputation, Ian at least equalled the total of over a thousand elephant gathered by the benchmark in this genre, Walter Bell; but Ian did so over a time when elephants were conditioned to men hunting them, and this would make the jesse bush an even more perilous place. Elephants are intelligent and learn fast; like people, some will be peaceable characters, some lazy, some even vindictive and violently-inclined. When hunted, the calmer ones can understandably become vindictive, and the naturally hot-headed ones can be literally murderous; many hunters have experienced several different species – principally the Big 5 – clearly reversing the hunter / hunted role, and the elephant's smarts elevate it to a different level in such cases. I can almost hear the preservationist fringe shouting that hunters deserve to feel what it is like to be hunted, and there may indeed be something in that; but remember that hunters consider the danger to themselves to be fair, part of the hunt; and in days gone, gathering ivory was like mining: merely collecting a commodity.

Ian was an interesting individual, one who could never have survived in Europe; it is simply too cold for what his constitution was able to stand. In that way he is exactly like my mother, and I suppose many others. My mother never got too hot; when others would swelter and wilt in the humidity of cities such as Durban or Brisbane, my mother would thrive. Of note, both Ian (Danish) and my mother share Scandinavian ancestry, my maternal grandmother having been of Swedish descent. One would think them comfortable in Arctic climes, but it's the opposite. Born in 1923, Ian Reginald Nyschens was a weak and sickly child, stricken by rheumatism. When eventually it departed, it left behind a boy who had to learn to walk again, with a weak heart and poor eyesight to boot. His skin was covered in psoriasis and it was advised that Ian forever more avoid the sun. Medical knowledge in days gone was often shaky, and this was just another such case: when eventually exposed to sustained sunlight, Ian grew strong.

Ian was sent to a convent school where the harsh discipline of the nuns had the opposite effect of what was intended: the boy grew to detest authority and religion, at least together. The educational attitude of the time – and I recall it well, schooled toward the end of those disciplinarian times – was obey or be beaten; for sure, that instilled obedience and backbone in the majority, but an outsider would be rounded upon and crushed, until they towed the line. The modern psychological approach would have been far more effective with someone such as Ian, but these were not those times. Bullied constantly at school and misunderstood by adults, by the time he reached adulthood, Ian Nyschens was an extremely poor fit for society. Battling in the Highveld winter of 1947, Ian received a letter from an acquaintance, the hyper-energetic (some would say part-time madman) Fanie Jooste (more often recorded as Faanie Joosten). Having left sometime before for Southern Rhodesia (later Rhodesia and now Zimbabwe), Faanie invited Ian to join him in the warm climate; Ian didn't take long to decide.

*　*　*

It is with a mixture of nostalgia and discomfort that I read Ian's definitive work, *Months of the Sun* (Safari Press, 1997); I recognise many similarities between Ian and myself, more so than with any of the other famous ivory hunters. Ian clearly was an individual ripped between two worlds: one wherein he married, had two children, worked in several industries and even ran a stud for thoroughbred racehorses; the other being the Africa to which his soul was inexorably drawn, the world into which his anti-social character blended far more seamlessly. In contrast to Ian, I benefitted from a wonderful childhood, a supportive and loving family, and am nothing like as ill-adjusted, volatile and anti-social as what he was. But certain nagging similarities remain; I am also drawn to Africa's wild and removed places, but that's hardly common to only Ian and myself: many millions feel the same way and many more will in future. I did however read some of the occasions where Ian lost his temper with a cringe of recognition. These hot-headed flashes of murderous temper have never left me, although one learns to control them. Most of the time.

Before his death in December 2006 in Harare, Zimbabwe, Ian waxed melancholy as people so often do when approaching death's door; his observations were however noteworthy. His son Clive had died sometime before and Ian spoke sadly of him; he spoke too of the great bull elephants which had occupied so much of his time, creating stark and powerful memories of danger-filled times. No surprises there; but he also touched on some of the legendary magic and mystery of Africa, stating that nobody really understood the great, visceral continent. Most telling to me was that Ian Nyschens, who during his formative years understandably learned to hate religion in the harsh convent schooling system, felt that the remote African bush harboured the uncanny presence of the Divine. Most Africans – who are extremely spiritual, and mostly religious in one way or another – would easily concur. Perhaps there is more to the magic of Africa than is immediately obvious.

In this secular time, those who are too intelligent for religion, or any spiritual life at all, would do well to note Ian's comment. Perhaps, as I've so often mentioned to my family, the modern Westerner needs a healthy dose of mortal danger on a regular basis, so they can be reminded of their place in the scheme of things. Ian mentioned in his later years how overcoming one's fear is imperative when after any dangerous game; it merely adds to the bravery of those who are successful in hunting and culling circles. Knowing what one is headed into, particularly in the jesse, with the odds so stacked against one, is truly courageous. To do so repeatedly, and survive, gives some idea about nervous fortitude, capability and the ability to control one's primal emotions.

* * *

Ian's first taste of his future life came soon after joining Faanie on the mighty Zambezi River. Faanie was a physically-impressive specimen, with a disdain for danger that the hyper-fit and powerful sometimes have; allied to a careless, even crazy nature, his own tendency to emotional, often irrational, reactions did not bode well when hunting dangerous game. Such traits usually make for a short and stormy career, which is bad enough for the individual concerned; but become less acceptable when those tendencies endanger others. Tracking his very first herd of elephant, Ian froze when he almost walked slap-bang into them. He felt his weak heart pounding away in perfect working order, noting the odd feeling of extreme fear mixed with heightened senses. The rifle in his hands – a .303 – suddenly (and somewhat understandably!) felt woefully inadequate; Ian could scarcely believe the size of the nearest beast that slowly approached, trunk raised, sniffing for information. This reaction is common when people first encounter wild elephants on foot in the bush. The sudden realisation of their size - and your lack thereof - induce a clear, confronting sense of one's own mortality.

Ian knew a frontal shot would be a risky proposition with so light a rifle, but as the elephant continued to close the distance between them, he was rapidly running out of alternative options. Just then the elephant stopped, shook its great head and turned to re-join the herd. Relief flooded Ian as he started to back away, carefully keeping as many trees between himself and the herd as he could muster. Suddenly a gunshot sounded from the direction of the river, and the world became a mass of fleeing pachyderms. Rushing away, Ian was further relieved after some tense moments to see that the herd was headed inland, away from the shot, and had not spotted or scented him. Shaken, he got to the riverbank, splashed his face and had a drink. He wondered where Faanie was and was just roundly cursing him for shooting, when another .303 shot rang out.

Thinking that Faanie may be in trouble, Ian fired an answering shot. It wasn't long before a happy Faanie emerged radiant from the bushes as if nothing had happened. He'd shot a bushbuck, gutted it and hung it up in a tree, and suggested that Ian assist him in fetching it. Ian castigated him for firing, telling him that he had been right up with the elephant herd when the Afrikaner had fired his first shot. "What did they say?" was all the carefree Boer offered in response! Ian was livid, but in retrospect, how could Faanie have possibly known where Ian was when the shot presented itself on the buck? Frightening, no question; but this was merely a precursor to the relationship between the two. It would play out again, many times, and eventually end in hatred. Following this initial jaunt to the Zambezi, Faanie caught gold fever, which left Ian cold. Perhaps providence was keeping them apart!

Ian headed to Mozambique (then still Portuguese East Africa) in the company of two Greeks, one of whom's father owned a trading store in Umtali, on the border of Rhodesia and the Portuguese colony. It was here that providence would later indeed seem to play a hand, because Ian's desire to become an ivory hunter was to be fulfilled when he eventually would be schooled in the craft by the legendary John Taylor. Initially though, he would be angered and disillusioned by traditional colonial attitudes (as indeed was Taylor). Learning from his initial elephant encounter, Ian had acquired a 10,75mm rifle, far better-suited to the job. Trailing a herd of eland for a time, the men had just decided to give best – the huge antelope trotting in that easy gait which covers endless miles – when a large elephant appeared, feeding at the fringe of the forest.

Without warning, one of Ian's Greek companions grabbed the 10,75mm out of his hands and shot the huge animal, the dust cloud of bullet impact clearly visible on its head! In spooky silence the great bull charged down the *vlei* (a grassy plain that used to be a river), straight for the men! Realising in short order that their first hope of not being seen was dashed, Ian shouted at the Greeks to split up, but one was totally panicked, muttering and invoking the Madonna. Ian shoved him one way and dashed the other, when one of the black trackers came back from where the first Greek had disappeared, shouting and distracting the giant bull. The elephant paused, confused, which allowed the men to get away. Ian was infuriated, dismayed at the Europeans' reaction – or lack thereof. When he pointed out that the tracker (Forey by name) had saved their lives, the others could not understand his reasoning. Ian left them in disgust, returning to Rhodesia further north, via Nyamapanda.

Ian's next foray after elephants convinced him to get rid of the 10,75mm and obtain something more reliable, and of better quality. During the Second World War, rifles had to be surrendered to the government, but post that conflict, many rifles had become available on the market. These included surplus military .303s, which were battle-proven and of good quality. The penetration of the .303 is legendary, similar to that of the .375H&H, but perhaps a level or two down in the gauge of savagery of animals one can consider tackling with it. A good one converted for sporting use could do the job, even on elephants; ideally however, one wouldn't use so light a weapon on elephant, particularly in thick cover such as the jesse. In such close proximity, one sometimes needs the instant knock-down capability of a large calibre, or the charging pachyderm will reach the hunter. The results of that can be most impressive. Ian bought a converted army-surplus .303 from a furniture shop, strange though that sounds!

As he noted, the process of obtaining a license then differed somewhat to the current one: the weapon was bought and the license applied for afterward. Sometimes it would arrive, sometimes it never did! Nowadays, the process is (rightly) far more stringent. In a single paragraph, Ian captured the essence of what it meant to be a professional ivory hunter: *"The professional's lifestyle required a different stamp of man as I was to learn later. He had a code of honour that few city folk could live up to, and he had to develop exceptional mental, emotional, and physical stamina and nerve. It was nothing for him to follow the spoor of wandering elephant bulls for many days with only the barest essentials of life: water, fire, food, and rifle. Other hunters would favour stalking resident herds with bulls, but even there, many failed and wounding incidents were high."* This paints the picture; few could fit the mould. It sounds romantic, but the lifestyle crushed all but a very few.

Ian's very real, very human writing allows one to feel the fear, the doubt, the panic needing to be quelled, the courage taking control again. In Mozambique's Urema area he was tracking a lone bull that had chased some women from a waterhole. Around midday, the tribesmen serving as trackers led the party into a large bowl-shaped depression of thick scrub forest. In the tense still air, hot as a blast furnace, the trackers melted away, the bull very close. He may have heard or sensed the men as he'd clearly frozen in order to listen. Ian too froze, waiting for the giant to move off so he could place him, based on noise of movement. Acutely aware of the extreme danger, Ian fought back the urge to get the hell out of there in haste. Feeling the rifle's perfect balance in his hands, his brain slowly calmed his panic; he was no unarmed savage. Slowly, confidence returned and he edged forward, tense but alert, the best mental condition to hunt under.

It's when fear takes over and becomes irrational that the hunter is in the gravest danger. Bear in mind that the quarry – which the anti-hunting fraternity deems a helpless murder victim – is a lethally-dangerous animal, far faster than a human, far bigger, and with a range of senses which make man's civilisation-dulled equivalents seem as useful as a calculator to a horse, particularly when one is after a member of the Big 5. Consider too that these species have been hunted for millennia, and that often the very animal being pursued has been hunted before; the hunter is in serious danger to start with. This is just one reason why people hunt; the animal has a far greater chance than the pacifists imagine. When fear is in control, the hunter is onto a hiding to nothing; lion, buffalo and elephant in particular are then almost certain to destroy the puny human. Controlling that fear is imperative. When one feels that rising panic, and can't quell it, it is better to call off the hunt; or at least retreat until one can feel in control again. Otherwise, someone is bound to get hurt, or worse.

Ian moved slowly on, sensing the elephant ever more vividly; at a turn in the path, he wisely heeded his inner sense to go no farther. He scanned the green vegetation, the upper part of the great bull's head suddenly appearing wraith-like; as the man had sensed, the animal stood watching him, silently. Ian's pulse pounded in his temples, his heart threatening to beat out of his chest. The bull lurched forward, no real charge but a sudden reaching dash to get at the man. At the same time the gun roared, the shot having no visible effect. Aiming to get a quick temple shot in as he turned to run, Ian's helpless dismay can be imagined. He threw himself to one side as the bull thundered by, then again all was silent. Crouched in the green ferns, Ian listened intently as the bull tried to locate his tormentor. It was clear he'd been hunted before and was reversing the roles.

When he neared, Ian could see his great front footpads expand and contract as he shifted his weight, clearly turning his great head to listen and sniff. The man knew that the bull would kill him if it located him. It slowly approached, passed just by, then stopped. The ferns shielded Ian from view but a change in the wind – still no notable breeze – would mean the man was done for at that range. Ian was tired of waiting to be executed, and spotting a gap in the foliage, loosed off two rapid shots. The bull roared, Ian dashed off down the path, distance between them all that mattered now. He knew the bull would outrun him in a flash if it spotted him, but to his immense relief the elephant was smashing plants where Ian had shot him. Then the trackers sounded some yodelling calls to distract the animal. Ian's weak heart and the nervous tension overwhelmed him and he passed out against a tree, he knew not for how long.

When he came around, it was late afternoon and Ian headed for the village, some seven miles (eleven km) distant. Nearing it, he came across his trackers, who sheepishly offered him the life-giving water bag. The men admitted abandoning Ian as the bull had a reputation for killing people. When pressed as to why they'd not told him this somewhat vital information before, they merely shrugged, and said *'Meat, Bwana! We hoped you'd get him for us!'* The men hopefully enquired as to whether Ian thought the great animal would succumb to his head wounds, thus providing that glorious commodity of flesh; but Ian got his own dig in: *'Why don't you all go in after him and find out?'*, which was met with much laughter. Ian cringed thinking of the outcome when people would try chase that bull out of their croplands that season; his brush with certain death had matured him fast however, and Ian Nyschens was now a far more bush-savvy hunter than the version who had first ventured into the wilderness after ivory.

Now equipped with a .404 Jeffery magazine rifle, Ian was in the north of Mozambique and headed toward Northern Rhodesia (now Zambia), which he found interesting and exciting new country. He considered it beautiful and dangerous, as only wild Africa can be; but more primal than the areas he was accustomed to, with wild animals and primitive men in evidence. A few decades later, Peter Capstick would traverse these same haunts, and Zambia has remained largely so, nowhere near as commercialised as other African countries. It has a unique convergence of biomes, animals and people unlike any other country on the continent, and pursuing animals there is no picnic. The foliage can be dangerously thick, making the hunting of lethal species such as lion, buffalo and elephant a real lottery. Ian Nyschens was about to find this out in no uncertain terms.

Tempered by fire; proven in combat; there is no teacher like experience. Whichever expression one uses, this is an undeniable fact; and one of the reasons is that many of those who build up such experience have survived against the odds, often by the skin of their teeth. How many combat soldiers have turned to the man beside them, only to see that fellow's head cut cleanly off by shrapnel, or have them shot to ribbons, or simply blown out of existence while the other lives. Death can be so indiscriminate an enemy, often taking the large, powerful and capable while leaving behind someone seemingly less so; but that survivor has luck on their side, at least then, which is sufficient to thwart the Man with the Scythe. Ian's little party ventured from village to village, seeking news or information about bull elephants as is the custom throughout sub-Saharan Africa. At one small hamlet, an elderly tribesman told Ian that most of the bulls had been shot or had departed, leaving lethal female herds behind.

The old man told the trackers where the herds were likely to be found, and Ian's party set out the following morning. The spoor proved the old man right, indicating some ninety, perhaps a hundred animals. Although none was visible, Ian hoped the herd would harbour at least a bull or two. Ian was no fool, already well aware by reputation of the lethality of cow elephants; he was acutely aware that today might be his last if he wasn't very careful and alert. The going was deceptively easy, through open forest with the wind in the men's favour all the while. The party felt they'd close with the herd around midday, but as the temperature rose, the herd sought thicker bushland and denser cover. It didn't bode well and one by one, the bearers fell away. Eventually Ian was left with just his two trackers, and the remaining men's strain had risen in direct reverse-proportion to the diminishing staff complement.

The dung ahead was becoming progressively fresher, the wispy wind in the scrub the only sound; tensions escalated with each step. The trackers slowed their pace and became even more alert. The second tracker cracked first, whispering to Ian that he was terrified, seeing pachyderms where there were none. Ian tried to bolster the man, telling him the fear before action was worse than the action itself, but the phrase and nuance were lost in the gulf between cultures. A knocking sound was heard, likely tusks against wood; then Ian clearly smelt elephants, the wind still favouring the men. He was amazed that the trackers seemed not to notice. They stopped to roll their shag-tobacco and newspaper cigarettes, visibly shaking less after a few drags. Ian thought their ferocious part-cigarette, part bushfire smokes were laced with *m'bange* (hashish or marijuana), since they calmed the trackers markedly. The men obviously knew the danger they were walking into.

Ian felt a wave of warmth toward his trackers, as have so many hunters and game officers before them; these men knew the massive peril into which they were walking, unarmed, with nothing but their agility and the shooting ability of some (often inexperienced) white official between them and certain perdition. And human agility, adrenalin-fuelled or not, is woefully inadequate against the senses and power of the Big 5. The cover thinned very slightly and the lead tracker froze into an ebony statue; they had almost walked slap-bang into the rear-guard of the herd. With the wind still mercifully in the men's favour, they might have gotten away with it; but this time it was the lead tracker that faltered. He slid in behind Ian and softly whispered *"Ku heenya"*, which is a shorter, sharper way of saying that apprehension is causing me to soil myself!

The real problem was that two large cows noticed the slight movement, and advanced in that bowel-loosening way cow elephants have: ears spread, trunks reaching, heads raised menacingly, and all done in total, eerie silence. The entire herd noticed the approach, Ian sensing rather than seeing them all mobilising. The cows were now too near, and Ian's brain was just telling him that they could now reach him, when he heard the trackers flee. The flight was like a red rag to the elephants, and the nearest cow exploded into a charge. Aiming at her forehead, Ian dropped her, then the other; the entire herd went berserk, a lethal killing army looking for blood. Ian pushed right up against the stomach of the first dead cow, and started to fire like an automaton. Elephants dropped like flies to frontal brain shots, Ian chancing a side brain shot on one that turned side on. She staggered but stayed upright. Where was the brain from the side?

The herd moved still closer around the fallen pachyderm used by Ian as a fort, an old cow with a sunken head taking over leadership of the herd. She headed past the feet to get around and reach Ian and in so doing exposed her side angle; Ian fired and when she dropped like a stone, he knew where the side brain shot should be placed. The man knew he had to make every shot count as the half-circle of huge, screaming animals moved yet closer. Firing like a madman, Ian's ammunition was running low when the insane shrieking suddenly died away, then stopped completely. Ian loaded the scorching-hot rifle yet again, noticing that the survivors looked demoralised, heads hanging, small gurgling noises emanating from them. They looked utterly defeated. Too frightened to move off lest his movement spark another attack, the hunter watched and waited.

To Ian's consternation, foliage crashing and enraged trumpeting behind him signalled more elephants; he was fully aware that a further attack would likely do for him, but these animals raced past, the demoralised ones suddenly alert and joining them. The entire bunch fled, their shrill noise receding until a hanging silence was all that shared the clearing with the lone white man. Slowly, the blood crashing in Ian's ears eased and his shell-shocked feeling was replaced by a sad regret, then utter exhaustion. He collapsed against a tree, thirst suddenly assailing him with a vengeance. At this first major sortie of his career, Ian Nyschens was filled with the sudden conviction that, although the vastness of the forest had all but swallowed him in the wake of the action, just one man and a gun had brought about all this carnage. He knew then that man will destroy the wilds. Such is the destructive nature of man, and Ian was intensely aware that he was a man.

News spread of Ian's achievement, the herd having killed countless people at waterholes and at night in the crop fields, vindictively led by three nasty old cows. It was probably as well that he had not known, as he would've been unlikely to beard the herd. Ian soon learned that the deadliest charge was the silent meaningful one, trunk flattened against the chest, ears swept back against the head, not the spread-eared posturing with trunk reaching for scent; yet the shadow charge was always impressive, terrifying, and would remain so for Ian. All the meat went to the locals while the ivory was Ian's. He headed for the Zambezi, managing to gather nine bulls in twos and threes. They were well-tusked, a decent yield for the hunter. Compared to the cow herd, the bulls were a soft touch; Ian Nyschens was learning fast, and adjusting to his dangerous life.

*   *   *

In *Months of the Sun*, Ian echoed the severe physical, mental and emotional toll on the foot-slogging elephant hunter which Wally Johnson and others conveyed. Finding the spoor of bulls around sunrise, the hunters need to follow for twenty to thirty miles (32-48km) or even more that day; water, rifles and ammunition have to be lugged along. Elephants easily lope along at a rate of one stride for every three a man takes and when the heat becomes intense, the hunters can close the gap as the giant beasts head for the thickest cover available, so to while away the hottest hours. One can drink, but can't rest. The heat becomes crippling, the insects unbearable; tsetses drain your blood, mopane flies seek the moisture around your eyes. You have to remain vigilant, because you may happen upon the bulls in thick cover while they rest. Eventually only stamina, willpower and the promise of white gold keep you going as the crushing heat drains you, rest rapidly becoming imperative but remaining impossible. The wind can change at any time and the quarry bolt off, wasting the entire day up until then.

Wounded or aggressive dangerous animals can circle back in the changing wind and set upon the puny human like a nightmare. Buffalo are renowned for this, but elephants often do so collectively. It was one of the reasons Ian preferred thick cover, as some of the herd may pass one by. Ian disputed the common misbelief that elephants don't have good eyesight, having established that they can see people at 150 yards, positively identify a person at 80, and at 50 yards are liable to become angry. He referred to elephants that had been hunted before. In close proximity their physical presence is frightening, large ones topping 4 metres at the shoulder and big bulls exceeding 6, sometimes even 7 tons. Your sense of inadequate puniness is horribly appropriate and you know you are surrounded by the mightiest animals on earth.

Knowing where each herd animal is will keep you alive when the firing starts; some elephants can be so close that they may even fall on you, provided you can drop them before they reach and decimate your laughable little self. In the close bush, it's a deadly game, speed and accuracy imperative now to your survival. Their panic and fear can save you as they flee, and when eventually the remnants of the herd stampede off, the noise following them, you collapse to the ground, physically and mentally spent, your nervous system jangling.

*   *   *

Ian headed north toward the Ruvuma, the border between Mozambique and Tanganyika (now Tanzania), hoping to find even more ivory there. The party crossed and Ian had a look around. Returning to their camp, they heard that a lion had attacked a woman gathering water in a village, then returned that night to pull a man, woman and child from a hut. This was Ian's introduction to Africa's man-eating problem. His co-hunter, Chirenge, told him about his own attack by a hyena, wherein Chirenge was lucky to retain his face. Many in Africa have disfigured faces, limbs or groins where hyenas have taken a bite and made off. Chirenge's wife assisted him and between them they drove the blood-aroused beast away. Crossing the Ruvuma back into Mozambique, the party spotted a massive crocodile, some 16 feet long (exceeding 5 metres), and of huge girth. Ian knew at a glance that if one were to be seized by such a creature, that would be that.

Before reaching their camp, they were told that one of their carriers had been taken by lions. The men had slept around two fires, the carrier not initially missed as the others supposed he'd merely gone to relieve himself. But the drag marks and lion spoor changed their ideas, and they tracked as far as the place where the cats had fought over the body; all that remained were some blood-stained clothes. The men returned closer to the Ruvuma, but more news of man-eating some 20 miles south soon arrived, and Ian decided to move much further south, far away. He considered the experience of man-eaters to be the worst one can have in Africa; the all-pervading terror creeps into the people's souls as the sun sets, Ian chillingly proclaiming the night to belong to the man-eaters. The measly human remains that are left after a lion attack are pitiful to behold, and a lion's fearful power is all too evident. Unless heavily armed, a human is powerless against the great cats.

Ian then made for the fabled Senna Sugar Estates, hunting buffalo (as had Harry Manners) with the legendary Swiss, Gustave Guex. Ian considered a large buffalo herd to be most intimidating, but with a distinct advantage for hunters over hunting elephant: the great black cattle tended to run away from the gunfire... Ian left Marromeu and returned to Salisbury, where he invested in an unsuccessful business venture. The lure of wildlife coupled with his entrepreneurial failure however drew him back; it was time to hunt elephant again.

* * *

When he reached Salisbury, Ian was no sooner there than Faanie arrived, only a season late! Over a shared bottle of whiskey at a restaurant they chewed the fat. Ian had to admit to being pleased to see the big Afrikaner, and they relaxed together. When he told Faanie about the 27 elephants and their ivory waiting to be collected, Ian proposed splitting the proceeds if Faanie would help him retrieve the ivory; then they could hunt around the Zambezi and Niassa, before crossing the Ruvuma into Tanganyika. Faanie consented to this, but proposed putting outboard motors onto the dugouts; Ian happily agreed.

The ivory-gathering trip happened without incident, although it was a hard slog in the rains. The pair's next jaunt, however, was anything but straightforward. Faanie still suffered from exuberance and a lack of caution, born of a confidence which supreme physical ability can give one. Ian saw that the man was a natural at hunting dangerous game; but Ian had learned the hard way to respect elephant herds. Faanie would merely ridicule him, ignore warnings and refuse to give in to fear. These tendencies can result in one ending up under the ground prematurely or mashed into it. In an attempt to tone him down, Ian suggested hunting a cow herd. Faanie agreed. Bearding a herd, Faanie set off too quickly, Ian reining him in. The Afrikaner objected and Ian let him go. As Ian was listening intently – an essential tactic with elephant in thick bush – Faanie opened fire.

In short order, two cows were down; Ian signalled Faanie not to move, as the herd were trying to place the men. It is imperative at this point to freeze and make no sound. Heavy bodies crashed through the bush, trumpeting in rage. To the left, Ian spotted some of the pachyderms. Then to his amazement, Faanie was racing alongside them, the panic-stricken tracker fleeing down the elephant path. Faanie was out of sight now but firing methodically. Ian had to back him up and raced in pursuit, discerning a human scream above the herd sounds. Then he saw the crazed Afrikaner; he was spectacular. With his great physical co-ordination, he was hurtling alongside, brain-shooting elephants at a few paces. Despite his disbelief and rage, Ian had to admire the sheer magnitude of the achievement. Ian's presence seemed to provide Faanie with even more confidence and he fired like an automaton. As Ian reached his partner, a cow elephant crashed through the bush just behind Faanie and Ian felled it.

At the shot, Faanie seemed to jolt out of his savage reverie, and he stood staring at Ian. Everything he'd been told had gone in one ear and out the other. Survival was the point; Faanie seemed not to care. "I think they got the tracker" Ian said; "I heard a scream." They changed position to get the wind in their favour, approaching the herd from a different angle. The herd's fury was unnerving at such close quarters; all that could be seen was destroyed foliage, elephants and dust. To beard the herd now would mean a fight to the death, as the entire herd would now attack *en masse*. For the first time, Ian saw Faanie hesitate. The herd's fury had had an effect, but he was still game to push on. Sensibility prevailed and they backed away. Faanie had shot seven elephant. When Ian questioned him as to why he'd thrown caution to the wind and ignored all of Ian's advice, he claimed to have been carried away. Ian blasted him; the herd had smashed the tracker into small heaps of crushed humanity and soil.

The next day the villagers had excitedly descended on the meat, and the two white men approached where the tracker had been. All that remained of him were his sandals, some cloth mixed with blood and sand, a few minor bones and part of his skull. The rest had been trampled into the earth. "The work of many great, angry feet", said Ian.

*   *   *

The old story of increasing human populations and game populations shrinking in direct proportion raised its head as Ian heard of the Nyasaland (now Malawi) District Commissioner coming to assist the Portuguese side with a serious outbreak of man-eating lions. By now it will be no secret that the entire phenomenon fascinates me, and Ian concluded this little piece of his story with a real lesson for people in civilised and protected areas, particularly those with a bent toward lecturing or looking down upon hunters. Ian wounded, tracked and killed a large lion which was likely a man-eater, with the entire process somewhat understandably ensuring that he'd not suffer from constipation for the few days following. He had the men collect the skin and skull...the lesson was that, were it not for the hunters, the terror of the people would've remained while the lions continued with impunity to feed upon human beings.

The following day saw Ian arrive at a small hamlet, typical of the area with its rudimentary methods of agriculture, several undernourished children and the odour of stale millet beer, poorly-cured biltong and human urine. The headman showed him where the District Commissioner was encamped. That man was on the spoor of some man-eaters that had killed and eaten a woman and child from a neighbouring village. As Ian mentioned, the sense of terror pervading the place was palpable, and even if the man were exaggerating, it would be a dreadful place to live. I won't go into detail – this being a book on ivory-gathering exploits; the details are in *Months of the Sun* – but will cut to the chase in that nearby, a hunter who specialised in hunting man-eaters was also in the area. Ian met and teamed up with this individual, whom the natives had named Katasoro (which meant the man who shoots more than one animal with a single bullet).

This Katasoro was an ex-military man from India, and his quaint British outfit and strange accent amused Ian. What was unquestioned, however, was the man's knowledge, skill and above all, immense bravery. The party followed a pride and Ian was impressed with the caution on the stalk and with Katasoro's lethal shooting at the climax. Predicting the next attack, Ian was placed under the thatched-roof overhang in a village, with Katasoro's one tracker armed with a shotgun. The moonlight was strong and the approaching lions were clearly visible as they sauntered carelessly into the village. Others such as John Taylor have written similarly about the brazen confidence of man-eating lions from that area and particularly how they behave at night. With no pause for thought, the lead lion effortlessly leapt upon a thatched hut roof, the cat's great weight breaking through the flimsy structure.

As the screams from the people within commenced, Ian started firing upon the remainder, lions dropping like flies. At length, the rear-guard of the pride deigned to jog off, a blast from the tracker's shotgun urging the last cat on its unhurried way. During the fusillade, the screams from the hut had ceased but the sounds of a growling, feeding lion were clearly audible. Ian and the tracker approached, the sounds ceased – the lion had heard or scented them – and with a disturbing purr, the cat shot up through the hole in the roof, with a large piece of human remains in its jaws. It landed beside the men and both instantly shot it. At length, after much enticing, some villagers emerged with spears. When they saw the dead cats, joy exploded and the villagers all poured out. Ian had difficulty in preventing the people from spearing the dead cats to bits. Then they remembered the attacked hut; Ian had no stomach for what he knew must be inside, the tracker going in and confirming what they all knew anyway: all the hut occupants were dead.

The villagers pulled out the bodies: a man, woman and four children. With the lion beside them, they made a "ghastly but moving sight". The family had been killed by heavy paw strokes, with much meat missing from the man and one child. Thinking of the fear of the children in their final moments, Ian felt violent hatred rising up in him – as have many before in his situation – and derided himself for hunting for gain. This killing of man-eaters seemed so much more honourable, more worthy. He immediately however chided himself for his emotional reaction, reverting to control and cold reason, which would far better serve him when after elephant. Large fires were built and people stood around until Ian reminded them about any possibly-lingering man-eaters. The villagers stole away to barricade themselves into their huts again.

Looking past the gleaming black skins of the few remaining tribesmen at the dead lion, Ian thought of the self-righteous, opinionated and over-civilised people who consider hunters to be mad, unfeeling, indifferent; he felt they should see sights such as this one.

*   *   *

Out on a remote hunt in the jesse one day, Ian sat contemplating the situation he was in. Across the fire from him sat a master tracker, Zaratina, and the brave water carrier, Jacoba. These small, insignificant-looking men were both far superior hunters to the vast majority of their fellow Korekore tribesmen, and streets ahead of almost any white men. The jesse featured a frightening sameness, in Ian's words. In time, twisting and turning in the maze of paths, dust swirling and elephant fleeing or charging, screaming, appearing and disappearing, with vision dangerously limited, Ian actually started to learn his way. Eventually, the only time he would lose direction was when closing in on bull elephants, a most hair-raising time to do so; but always, Zaratina and Jacoba were there, with uncanny directional sense and instincts, keeping them all alive and in one piece. Given these conditions and the number of wounded animals holed up there, this time in the jesse was Ian's most difficult, nerve-destroying and downright dangerous.

One day, they heard that a highly skilled Tsetse Fly Department hunter had been killed following a wounded buffalo into the jesse; Zaratina found the remains of both. It wasn't pretty. Others too joined the choir invisible; several times Ian himself nearly joined their ranks, knowing that if he mastered his fear and his thirst, his skill would have to complete the job. He continued, successfully, but the cost to his nervous system was considerable. The elephant knew where they could not be seen, often standing dead still mere yards away, only to lash out with their trunks and crush men's skulls like grapes. The counter was to aim a snapshot at the head, then instantly move to find the next target. Like people, each elephant has different levels of temper and self-control; some would lie doggo, others dash out in an all-out charge. To miss then meant death to the hunter.

One morning they followed two large bulls. Their spoor was near-invisible over the paths trampled by countless elephants before them; around midday they entered some of the thickest jesse the men had ever seen, the thickets springing back behind the great beasts, leaving no trail to follow. Ian was gob-smacked, the bulls invisible at two paces. Neither party could do anything until the other moved, so there they all stood, men and elephants not two metres apart, frozen in the jesse maze. The men eventually retreated and left, by Ian's recollection only the third time he'd been totally stumped by the great, grey pachyderms. But this was to be the first of many such occasions at that place, so dense was the jesse there. So Ian, marvelling at the phenomenon of so massive a beast being literally invisible in its dark grey coat, decided to make himself more visible and invoke charges. This was deadly dangerous, but if one shot straight...and had no misfires or hangfires...

Ian's theory was to wear visible hats, so secured three such straw examples, dolloping each in glossy white paint. This proved successful, most elephants either charging or exposing themselves while trying for a better look. And so, the trio continued, the strain eventually telling on Jacoba first. Brave as he was, the poor man would shiver whenever they neared elephant, so they stopped for a time and resumed again later. Then the "bush tap" started to affect the stalwart Zaratina, so Ian called time on their long stint in the jesse. The men lounged around the huge hollow baobab they used as a base, now stocked nearly full of ivory. Then they made their way to comparative civilisation: Ian to Salisbury, and his two companions to their villages.

*　*　*

Faanie had come to hunt with Ian, and panic momentarily rose within Nyschens. Faanie was unfortunately a convincing conversationalist. We've all had friends like this; wild, humorous, adventurous. And they are fun to be with; it's ranger-boys-in-the-woods stuff, and Ian felt himself consenting, even as he cursed himself for his stupidity. Faanie wanted to hunt crocodiles again, to which Ian was willing to consent, provided he could get away later to beard the big bull elephants in the jesse. Faanie announced they would go together, and Ian drew the line: Faanie in the jesse hunting bull elephants would spell likely disaster for anyone foolish or unfortunate enough to accompany him there. Ian said they would start on the crocs, but that he would desert Faanie immediately at the first sign of stupid, irresponsible behaviour.

Faanie had assembled some excellent boats and equipment, and his ordnance was top-notch: besides a sawn-off shotgun, he had a .600 double rifle and a .416 Rigby rifle on the Mauser action. Before the croc-hunting commenced, Ian had to hunt cow elephant for Chief Mudzeemo, in the Nyamaque jesse. This wasn't as dense as the Naukaranga, but it was bad enough. As the men followed the cow herd into the vegetable morass, Faanie got to see the tracking and manoeuvring of Zaratina first-hand. He was mightily impressed, likening him to the best trackers from Mozambique. At a V in the path, Zaratina went one way and Faanie made to go the other, but Ian stopped him with a hand action, motioning that the Afrikaner follow the black man. Faanie wisely complied, and crucially, did so silently. Suddenly, Zaratina froze, the remainder of the party following suit. He indicated that the unseen pachyderms were facing the men in the dense thickets. It was D-Day!

Nothing could be seen but the men could absolutely sense the great beasts in close proximity, a primal awareness between age-old creatures and their age-old tormentors. At the height of the tension, incredibly, almost inconceivably, Faanie put his left hand to his mouth, raised his rifle and yodelled! The reaction was immediate: trumpeting morphed into roars and the bush opened above the men, elephant foreheads replacing the animated foliage. Zaratina dropped to the side as the white men commenced firing. Some way ahead the herd went crazy, the crashing bush indicating that some were fleeing while others raced to crush the humans. The men's experience told in their standing stock-still, allowing their ears to inform them as to what they could not see. Ian could see from the look on Faanie's face that this was a whole new type of hunting. Sensing his uncertainty, Ian motioned with his hands that the men remain on paths only, taking time in the bedlam to place a reassuring hand on Jacoba's neck: as usual, the poor little water-carrier was shivering in terror.

There was only one way out: to head into the herd and shoot a way out. To flee would be fatal, and within seconds. To head into a murder-crazed elephant herd when your entire existence is screaming at your body to run, takes some nerve. To do so at the vanguard while unarmed – as Zaratina was doing – takes perhaps a person in a million. The men neared the main body of the screaming, heaving, raging Zambezi Ladies. "Well, Faanie," thought Ian, "you are a man of war; you're about to get your wish!" With elephant smashing all around, the men opened fire, controlled, rapid and deadly shooting dropping lethal cow-elephants in their tracks. The thickets gave way as if they were tissue paper, irrelevant in the path of the huge grey bodies. Then the men realised that they were almost clear; there were no more elephants in front of them and they kept going.

After half a mile the men collapsed, Ian pouring some water for himself and Jacoba into cupped hands. Faanie looked calmly about; "Strange place," he mused. "Nerve-wracking and definitely easier with the elephants coming on to you." He had reached the same deduction that Nyschens and his men had reached when deciding upon the white-painted hats. Ian was pleased when Faanie noted that the men owed their lives to the manner of hunting; he commended Zaratina's remarkable bravery for moving into the herd while unarmed. But the biggest compliment was reserved for Jacoba, the little water-carrier. Ian asked whether Faanie could see himself bearding herds again and again, knowing that each time he would be so terror-stricken and struck by shivers.

With no sarcasm, joking or wordplay, Faanie answered in the negative, and called Jacoba a plucky little bastard. No-one argued.

The men rested, restoring their nervous systems. Ian nodded off and awoke to Faanie and Zaratina speaking in low tones. Faanie even had a compliment for Ian; he had been telling Zaratina how much Ian had grown as a hunter and as a healthy, physical specimen, since the men had first canoed the mighty Zambezi. The men returned to Chief Mudzeemo; a meat-cutting orgy would ensue.

* * *

Ian Nyschens and Faanie Joosten crossed to the west bank of the Zambezi and headed upstream, hiring skinners. The west-bank tribes were unreliable and Ian wasn't overjoyed at the prospect of making use of them. Inevitably, Faanie drove Ian's blood pressure to murderous levels; Faanie raced the boat too fast into a pod of hippo, cutting one's back with the propeller as they went over it. He never even slowed down and ignored Ian's shouts, until the latter stalked the length of the boat and knocked the powerful Afrikaner into the river. Ian gained the controls and swung around to pick Faanie up; their blood was up and Faanie promised that Africa would swallow Ian when he, Faanie, decreed it. This set Ian off yet further and when he grabbed the shotgun, threatening to perforate Faanie, he meant it. He knew he needed the gun though: Faanie was a bit heavier than Ian but at least twice as strong. It took them both a long time to cool off. Reaching camp near Mudzeemo's kraal, there was bad news: one of Zaratina's children had been taken by a crocodile.

Becoming pensive and reflective, Ian thought of all the dangers humans lived through in the Zambezi Valley, malaria clearly the greatest; he knew that the advancement of human medical technology would result in unchecked overpopulation and has been proven correct. Habitat loss is the greatest threat to Africa's wildlife, and the exploding human population has meant that irreversible habitat loss is a sad reality. Ian gloomily predicted that future African generations won't even be able to visualize primitive Africa; it will be another world. Again, tragically, he is already on the way to being proven correct. In the late afternoon Ian bathed in the river, emerging to see Zaratina and Jacoba approaching. The men discussed the child's death, the croc rushing across some shallow water, a mere few inches deep, to grab the child and drown it in deeper water. Ian pained for Zaratina, who must have been boiling with vengeance, but showed nothing.

It was that strange time of dusk when the world is at a momentary peace; the tides are still, the surface calm, even the animals silent, before the night shift ramps the noise up. In the final moments of dusk, Zaratina looked into the waters and vowed to the croc that he would hunt it down with the bwanas. For days the men hunted into the Kariba Gorge, Zaratina vengefully driving his spear into crocs' brains, which seemed to relieve his sorrow, albeit momentarily.

A few days later, the boat hit a rock shelf and sank instantly, everything gone except the .404 rifle in Ian's hand with three shells. Losing his prized .450 was what pained him most, but Faanie's losses were far greater: not only were all their equipment and food lost, but the .600 double rifle nestled on the bottom of the Zambezi with the .416 Rigby and the shotgun for company. It was a catastrophe. A dugout on the west bank hove into view; its owner had seen their plight and conveyed the white men to the bank, one by one. After much walking, bargaining and arranging, the men made it back to civilisation before returning to salvage their equipment. It was a superhuman feat by Faanie to raise the craft, jammed by weight and water pressure between the rocks; but then, Faanie was superhuman. Near Nemana Pools (now the world-famous Mana Pools), Ian saw a sight now made popular by the elephants there: a large bull stood on its back legs and reached pods far higher up in the tree as a result. So much for climbing a tree to escape a bull elephant, thought Ian…

A short time later, an unusual thing happened, about which I have often wondered; my father used to comment on the possibility whenever he'd see footage or a movie, wherein people fired into the air: those bullets have to come down somewhere. Ian and Faanie travelled on past Kanyemba Island near the Zambezi's junction with the Kafue, then on to Chiawa's village. They were told that a large crocodile was about and had already taken many people from that stretch of river. At that place, due to the two rivers converging, the flow accelerated and the canoe sped with the current. Daydreaming in the warm sun, Ian suddenly realised he was looking at a large crocodile on the shore, making for the water. He quickly shot it in the shoulder, which immobilised the giant reptile, the bullet whining off somewhere into the distance. The men approached the furious beast and Faanie shot the croc in the brain, the variety of bangles and ornaments taken from its stomach seemingly evidence sufficient that this was the culprit.

As the party landed at the village, several armed villagers grabbed Faanie, who was unarmed; but the powerful Afrikaner threw them off, sending several into the current. Ian was starkly reminded of the trouble he would have if his on-again, off-again fight with Faanie were ever to reach a point of no return. Ian stepped between the warring factions – the villagers on one side and a single Afrikaner on the other – and enquired as to what was wrong. One angry man shouted that Faanie had shot and killed a villager, a young woman who had come to marry. It turned out that Ian's bullet, which had whined off after disabling the large croc, zoomed off in the direction of the village, where it killed a young woman at the door of a hut. The chief restrained his people from avenging the woman, but Ian had to report the death to the officials. This he did, but remember that Ian was a wanted poacher in the Zambezi Valley, whom had never before been seen in the flesh by the authorities. He would eventually be cleared of culpability, some months later at a hearing.

The elephants were becoming wiser, faster and more savage in the jesse. For the first time, and despite Zaratina's uncanny ability, Ian started to question the superiority of man in the hunt. They left the area, giving best. Ian left Zaratina and Jacoba back at Chief Mudzeemo's; he needed them to recover and rest. The Months of the Sun were coming and Ian needed these men in the Naukaranga jesse. In the mopane forests, Ian continued to hunt bulls. He enjoyed some good fortune when he met D.C. Lilford, the Chairman of the Rhodesia Game Association. He had Ian and John Connor over for a meal, which was wonderfully luxurious compared to the food Ian was accustomed to. But the best part was when Lilford offered Ian the use of a fabulous .450 Rigby double rifle, Ian's most beloved calibre; his own rifle you will recall lay rusting in the Zambezi.

Ian remembered this kind gesture forever more; it meant that he could hunt the bull elephants in the jesse again and Ian believed the rifle kept him alive for many years longer than would have been the case with his previous, lesser weapon. As a tragic aside, many years later, Lilford – like so many other white Rhodesians – was lured from his farmhouse at night, attacked and murdered with his own sidearm. At this juncture, Ian was cleared of the death of the unfortunate woman in the village; then he and Faanie met up again, replenishing their stores, which for Ian was to gloriously include four hundred rounds of .450 ammunition.

Ian had much time over his career to study elephant body language and behaviour, which served him invaluably when after them in the thick bush. He noted how young male elephants eventually leave the herd – as do young male humans – and form bull herds away from the noisy young and females. He remembered sometimes finding old emaciated bulls. A wide-eyed and fierce staring, often with trunk raised, was the surest sign of an imminent charge. Ian described what he'd seen elephants do to hunters they caught up with: a blow from the trunk would smash a man to the ground where he'd then be trampled, or torn apart with trunk and feet. Sometimes the giant would kneel to gore the man, but most often would press him into mush with the wide trunk and forehead. It was rare that a man was picked up on the run, but when he was, he'd be impaled on a tusk or flung aside, which was usually followed by a trampling.

Jeffrey, a man of mixed-race who often hunted with Ian and Faanie, was once snatched up by an enraged pachyderm, which doubtless intended to impale him on its tusk; but the ice-cool hunter had the presence of mind while in that position to a) fire his rifle at the beast, and b) actually hit it in the brain. He was flung to the side among some branches (quite lucky in itself, I thought; the animal could've fallen onto him), and his leg was damaged for life. He forevermore dragged the injured limb behind him.

* * *

Zaratina was still hunting crocodiles, although Ian sensed that some of the sorrow of losing his child had eased; he was more like his old self. Jacoba's nervous system had recovered and Ian had the .450 rifle; it was time to go back into the jesse. The heat was intense, crippling; but the men had stocked the hollow baobab with water. The trio plodded the elephant paths of the jesse, overwhelmed again by the stillness of air, the closeness of vegetation and the sheer immensity of the featureless grey mass. Standing in the shade of massive baobab trees, probably hundreds of years old, Ian thought it regrettable that most of the venerable trees would one day be cleared for farmland. The bush was so dense that the men slept the first night at a convergence of elephant paths. They immediately struck elephant spoor the next day, but the heat drove them to break off contact and seek out their hollow baobab, with its life-giving water supply. They reached it luckily around sunset, enjoying the rest, food and water of camp.

The next morning the elephant were easy to find: they noisily entered the jesse after a night in the swamps. As the men neared, the pachyderms fell silent, sensing them. Even though Ian had his white hat on, nothing happened. The bush was likely too thick; so, borrowing a leaf from Faanie's book, Ian yodelled. As it had the previous time, it worked, but almost too quickly. Firing fast, Ian dropped three bulls. The rest of the herd fled, reaching the safety of a path and racing off in silence up it. Ian knew a hip shot would be possible on the rear-guard animal if they hurried, and at a twist in the path thought he'd get his chance. But fortune was even more generous: coming toward them was a huge lone bull, ambling pleasingly along as giant bulls do. Ian disabled the monster with two shots at the hip joints, the massive hindquarters collapsing dramatically. This allowed the hunter a raking shot at the brain through the nape, which Ian took. The huge elephant fell instantly.

Zaratina declared the bull a *garonga*, a giant elephant of tribal myth. The men left all the dead 'phunts where they lay, knowing that no-one would enter the jesse. The heat – 120 degrees Fahrenheit (49 degrees centigrade) at ten a.m. – would ensure that the tusks could be prised loose in a matter of days. After seven weeks of this hunting, the men started seeing imaginary elephants, the conditions damaging to the nerves. All three were by now having nightmares. It was time for a break. The men started to gather the ivory, moving it by night to avoid the phenomenal heat, which gave their nervous systems a chance to recover. As bulls were still entering the jesse, Ian decided to hunt a few more. They were closing on a group of elephants when they came across two human skeletons in the path. The two black men were affected, seeing this as an omen, and for the first time Ian saw them falter on a spoor. Ian felt shaken too, so they left the hunt.

* * *

Zaratina recalled hearing large bull elephants taking water at night at the Ruwee Pools, and this was the part that really made Ian's ears prick up. They all considered that the Ruwee Pools should still harbour such large bulls. Although Zaratina voiced his downright fear at the thirst awaiting them should they make such a journey – a fear which easily exceeded his apprehension for lions, which proliferated there and were notorious for eating people – Ian's mind was made up: they would make for the Pools. Travelling light as possible, the men stocked up on water. The going was rough underfoot and the terrain an inferno of sun-baked hills, gullies and slopes. Their thirst was crushing, worse than ever before. The men made it until the afternoon before taking their first drink, a towering achievement in itself.

The men undertook to travel by night, but by dawn were that far off course, they reverted to daylight travel. On the third day they finished the water. Jacoba was now in a bad way, the others leaving him to try find game, which could at least yield stomach water, blood, even bodily fluids. They tracked a rhino but as they closed with it, barking baboons alerted the huge beast and it ran off. Then Zaratina saw a cleft in the hills down which a bushbuck disappeared, and instinct led them to water. Laughing like madmen, the pair slaked their thirst with care: large quantities of water can be fatal at a time like that. Ian had Zaratina take water to Jacoba, falling into an exhausted slumber.

He awoke to the two trackers cooking a meal in their small pot, on a cheerful fire. The men relaxed, reprieved at least temporarily. The men stayed at the spring for a few days and Ian shot a rhino, recovering slowly all the while; when he had sufficient strength, Zaratina started exploring, each day moving further afield, always back by sundown. On the fifth night he reported back that he had found the Ruwee Pools a day's walk away. Although he'd not seen the spoor of any large bulls, there were signs that elephant were numerous. The next morning the party set off, arriving at the Pools by sunset. The terrain had changed much; hills were widespread, valleys of tall grass were interspersed with thickets. The water was clean and sweet; after drinking and restocking, the men moved off to camp some four hundred yards from the water, to limit disruption to the game. Sunset brought the sounds of lions roaring, the darkness hours punctuated by the sounds of elephants bathing and drinking.

Rhinos were audible and there was other animal disturbance too; Ian contemplated approaching the water to watch the activity, but decided against it when the sounds of lions pulling down a zebra reached their ears. The men determined to move still farther from the water. Dawn brought optimism at the many spoor by the water; the spoor of a large elephant herd was found and followed. Eventually the animals wandered apart, which was ideal for finding bulls. Three were identified and spoored; the men knew the bulls would leave the herd and join other bulls, and this is what happened. Oddly though, these bulls didn't stop to rest out the worst of the day's heat. Just as the temperature was at its staggering worst, the bulls veered off into some of the thickest jesse they'd ever seen. The going became slow and dangerous in the isolated, swirling wind. Still no rest for the bulls; did they sense the men? Then they found a place where the bulls had indeed stopped for a time and had been joined by two other large bulls.

The bush was dense, leafless and the same grey as elephant hide; Zaratina's body-language indicated more care, so Ian knew the quarry was nearby. Adrenalin coursed through the trio, the first audible evidence of the pachyderms reaching their ears. The men quickly closed the distance but were too hasty: a great head appeared above the scrub, ears spread. Ian snapshot the animal, then two more, all with brain shots. None so much as moved. Ian saw that none of these three were large, the men sensing other elephant nearby. He thought of running up onto one of the slain beasts, but decided against it for being too noisy. He studied Zaratina's face, reading the master-tracker's strange abilities as he looked in a particular direction, just *sensing* that something was there, fully alert. And so it proved; a snapping of vegetation and rushing of something large toward them had Ian's concentration in top gear. They could do nothing until the elephants burst through the cover of foliage.

The noise of exploding vegetation increased and the head of a large bull appeared; Ian brained it and was almost crushed as it slammed down; another appeared and was also snapshot, but this shot wasn't fatal; the animal staggered, revealing tremendous ivory, then veered off and though the scrub. It stood listening, deadly-dangerous now with a wound; but Ian's nerve had returned, his blood was up and he bellowed at the great beast: "I'll hunt you in hell now!" On queue the huge animal ploughed through the foliage, crashing bush accompanied by the screams, roars and trumpeting of an enraged bull elephant. Ian had only a split second when the bull's head filled his rifle sights, and the great creature fell dead a few paces from the men. After a few moments of stunned silence – such as always accompanies such moments of extreme danger – Zaratina climbed up the elephant's back leg and started a slow, triumphant dance. He stopped and sagely stated: "We truly understand the value of living after moments like these." Wise and true words.

The men rested in the shade provided by one of the bulls, waking late in the day. They then headed back to camp, *en route* accounting for two more bulls without incident. It started to rain heavily, the men knowing they could now return to the Zambezi at their leisure: water was no longer a problem, for now. It was odd to walk among the rivulets and pools where just days before they had nearly perished of thirst. They were chilled and sodden, but by the time they emerged on the Zambezi Valley floor again, it was hot and parched once more, water bags keeping death at bay as so often before. Tsetse were voracious and in plague numbers. At the river several large crocs submerged at their approach, and Zaratina vowed to the reptiles that he would kill them one day. Mudzeemo told them that Faanie had returned from Tanganyika (now Tanzania) and was waiting at Kam Cha Cha's.

Nemana Pools had proved a happy hunting ground to Faanie's crew of croc-hunters; the men dynamited the pools and when the crocs rushed to adjacent pools, the men would disable them with shoulder shots, returning to brain them with choppers. On one such occasion, Faanie had ventured too close to a croc and had been grabbed by the arm, but the powerful Afrikaner spiked the huge reptile in the brain with his free hand. He recounted to Ian how strong crocs were, even a medium-sized one capable of throwing a man by merely flicking its neck. Ian laughed at Faanie's scars, reminding him that he'd always underestimated danger. Still - a giant croc would've killed Faanie, so this one was likely a 'mere' 2-metre specimen - having the presence of mind and sheer power to brain one while it's clamping your arm, and then retaining your arm, unbroken, provides some idea of what sort of individual Faanie Joosten was...

Then Ian told Faanie his plans of becoming a game ranger; Faanie was unimpressed and even angry. But a ranger, Ian was to be: he left the ivory-hunting life behind and became the Southern Rhodesian Game Department's first appointed ranger. It was 1954.

*   *   *

On one occasion Ian had to visit a man named John Posselt, who had lodged complaints about elephant. John had many wild animals roaming uncaged on his property, among which a herd of eland, the largest antelope. In a brick-walled enclosure he kept many venomous snakes, mostly puff adders, which he would 'milk', sending the venom to South African laboratories, where antivenin was made. Bearding the problem elephant herd, Ian shot one, then his game issue Westley Richards .425 repeater jammed with a second cow elephant bearing down on him like a nightmare. Ian Nyschens was about to shuck his mortal coil; but John Posselt saved him by shooting the animal through the brain. She smashed down right in front of the men.

*   *   *

The tribes were being removed from the Zambezi Valley to make way for the rising waters which resulted from damming up the river; the massive lake would be known as Lake Kariba, the world's largest man-made reservoir. It was filled between 1958 and 1963 when the Kariba Dam at its north-eastern end was completed. The enormous mass of water – 180 petagrams or 200 billion tons' worth – has directly worsened the area's seismic activity, contributing to more than 20 earthquakes that exceeded 5 on the Richter scale. Although it's an impressive ecosystem all of its own, the disruption it caused to the Amatonga people who had lived there for millennia was complete; Ian had other business elsewhere in the country and left Jacoba and Zaratina to their removal. They were to be settled in the Hurungwe area and were convinced Ian would not be able to locate them upon his return, but he assured the pair he would find them. Ian had to attend to problem elephant all over the country, and found the solo going very tough indeed.

He persevered and one of the places he had to visit brought him into contact with an age-old Africanism: a manipulative and vindictive witchdoctor. Nyschens was enraged by these witchdoctors, the type who preyed upon the simple folk with their naïve and believing ways. It was especially easy in communities rife with superstition. This particular piece of work went by the moniker *Mhondoro*, or lion. Ian would gladly have treated him as they used to treat such witchdoctors in Mozambique: a quick and decisive rifle-butt blow to the throat, but was warned off from doing so by the area's native commissioner. The government was trying to build a criminal case against the man and didn't need their process derailed by hot-headedness. The crop-predations by elephant were bad here. Ignoring the local advice to consult and seek permission from Mhondoro, Ian soon found the villagers becoming obstructive, even lying to him.

A couple of days' hard slog for no return ensued; then the witchdoctor summoned Ian. The ranger found the emaciated old man at his fire with some elders. Fighting the urge to plunge his rifle butt into the creature's throat, Ian noted the man's aura of evil menace as he leered out from under the lion cape adorning his head. He demanded to know why he'd been summoned and the old witchdoctor told him to pay homage, failing which Ian would not locate any pachyderms in the area. He cheerfully added that if he did, they would surely kill the white man. Ian refused to honour the old fool and left, finding elephant spoor the next morning, but bent on relying on his trackers for results. Where the elephants were about to enter the forest, leaving the baking grasslands, Ian scaled a 12-foot tree, leaving his rifle at the exposed root system. He espied a large elephant some 30 yards away, two others partly-obscured beyond it.

Without warning, the closest bull looked directly at Ian and sped silently through the grass, murderous intent written all over it. The grass-obscured men below were none the wiser as the silent killer rapidly closed the gap, Ian leaping down to retrieve his rifle. He was just in time: as the bull's massive, silent head broke cover, the ranger fired, dropping the animal within trunk-reach. A second elephant raced for the men, the swishing grass betraying his intent; he too was sent to elephant paradise while the third decamped. The first elephant had a huge sinus infection, the nasal-bone formation full of thick mucus. This explained its violent demeanour, its discomfort clearly considerable. The hunt had been unusual, but the successful outcome had broken the authority of the evil witchdoctor: the people started co-operating. As an interesting aside, the state's case against Mhondoro was eventually pressed and the unpleasant old sot died in confinement.

The power of the witchdoctor over tribespeople throughout Africa is incredible to the modern, educated First-World person; to illustrate my point, Ian once entered a village with his friend (a doctor) and their party. At the entrance to the village sat a man with emaciated legs. Ian thought his doctor-friend would find the situation interesting, asking the sawbones why he thought the man's limbs were so withered. Paralysis, ventured the doctor; but Ian knew better. The curse of a witchdoctor had caused the condition, the man absolutely convinced he would die if he put weight on his feet ever again. To prove his point, Ian had his men raise the man, who put up such a terrified wailing that they lowered him again. Ian let the doctor examine him, who was gobsmacked and nonplussed, but had to admit the man was not paralysed. He questioned how this could be so, that the man would forever more crawl about, despite fully functioning legs; but the workings of Africa make no sense to Europeans.

I once worked with a remarkable indigenous man in the second year of my career; it was back in Apartheid South Africa and he was an immensely intelligent, sage old soul, who had worked in the same firm when my father was there, a full generation before, in the self-same role: producing the reports at the copiers, which were hugely expensive machines and the most phenomenal I've ever seen. My father told me to befriend him and keep him close, as urgent business might be allowed to jump the queue for favoured people, whereas the nasty, cruel or racist might be made to wait...wise advice from my paternal parental unit, from which I duly benefitted! That said, the old man was far, far superior to the role which the supremacist system had deemed he could not progress beyond, able to discuss a broad spread of topics from politics to sports and hold his own on all of them, with anyone. Like many older people, he was a great calming influence to me in times of bedlam. Although what followed never diminished my respect for him, it does provide some idea of the tribal beliefs in Africa.

My elderly friend once told me – with the utmost conviction – that a fabled medicine man had recently come into the city, often utilising his ability to become invisible at will. He was fully convinced that this happened, and would've become incredulous had I scoffed. Another indigenous man I worked with, years later and of the younger, more enlightened, educated and opportune generation, one day surprised me too when he was utterly convinced of one old Zimbabwean tradition (he came from there). I have always had great enthusiasm for African snakes and we were repeating some of the many stories about the legendary black mamba (*Dendroaspis Polylepis*) to our fellow employees. The skittish, lethal and highly-strung mamba needs little introduction. As with many deadly animals, the stories surrounding it often exceed reality, but disturbingly-many of the legends surrounding it are true. Large, irate specimens have killed many people and animals. It is not a serpent to be trifled with.

My work colleague ventured, again with the utmost belief and conviction, that the snake – which does spend some time spookily raising itself to the height of a man when incensed – raises itself up in order to strike at a man on the head, but not with the intent to inject venom; rather to pluck some hair, in order to line its nest! Utter poppycock of course, but it shows how deeply the tribal beliefs run in Africa. There are so many crazy and often downright frightening stories of African black magic, which I have been told, read about or experienced myself, that I hope to one day write of them. It is a subject which has interested many. Not everything in Africa can be easily explained.

*   *   *

Ian Nyschens's life seems to be inexorably linked to the elephant; his next sortie was to procure elephant meat for the workforce employed to build the dam against which Ian had campaigned: that of Kariba. The locals were dead-against the project and refused to work for the white engineers overseeing it, so labour had to be brought in from neighbouring Nyasaland (now Malawi). Ian knew his job would be perilous in the dense thickets and summoned Zaratina and Jacoba. They duly arrived and Ian knew he could function to his full capability with these men supporting him. He received a pleasant and unexpected surprise, however; the crooked-limbed medicine-man Juda arrived too, and he brought several other reliable tribespeople with him. Among them was another fine tracker, Chakadama. This individual was pure gold under trying and exhausting conditions; his energy was unmatched and his sense of humour often kept the party in high spirits.

In the pre-dawn one morning, an elephant herd trumpeted, the men up and on the spoor as soon as light permitted. The herd was restless and entered dense cover early. The spoor showed a large cow backing up the herd and facing the men in a protective manner. Ian got onto a fallen tree trunk for a better view and from this elevated position, he fired at a cow near the back of the herd. She fell, followed by total silence; a single cow raced toward the party in a full-out charge, still in total silence. Ian let her close the distance since she was alone; but not long before she would reach the men, the cow roared and trumpeted, which caused several other cows to swing into line after her. Suddenly, the men had several problems, all of which were bearing down upon them at a rapid rate! As usual, Zaratina had been correct: he'd identified the lead cow as a Zambezi Lady, prone to charge immediately at the sound of a rifle shot. Ian duly shot the irate elephant.

Nyschens usually made use of a glove to protect his left hand from the burning .450 double-rifle barrel, but that day he'd not yet donned it; it would cost him a badly-burned left paw, but that beat the alternative by far: being well and truly crushed into the earth. The men fired like automatons as the cows bore down on them in earnest. Zaratina assisted Ian, ably wielding the .416 with which he was a poor shot at distance, but effective at short range. At length the remaining cows retreated, much to the relief of the men; it had been a frightening experience and as so often under those circumstances, might have ended very differently had just one crucial shot not found its target, just one round of ammunition not performed optimally. The odds in hunting elephant herds are ever-changing and often very long indeed. As the adrenalin came down, Ian's hand started to hurt like the dickens. The large blisters rendered the hand useless for a time.

Even amid the carnage, interesting evidence of the game ranger on elephant control's ultimate goal of conservation shines through: when clearing an area of elephant for human settlement, it is vital to reduce their numbers quickly, regardless how dangerous the terrain. The key is that the herd find no sanctuary in the area which people will inhabit. If this is done, elephants vacate the area, taking perhaps three-quarters of the herd when they leave. If, however, they are half-heartedly pursued over an extended time, they learn to adapt and accept the occasional loss to their numbers. If the hunter is afraid to enter the really thick cover into which they invariably retreat – and that is understandable for most people bearding elephant – the pachyderms will over time lose perhaps three-quarters of their number, sometimes the entire herd, thus saving nothing. This tendency actually applies to most wild animal species.

Of course, this theory assumes that there is an eventual sanctuary into which the herd can go; this was no problem in Rhodesia at that time. Many troublesome herds were driven into the Sebungwe district, at the time a vast wilderness area the size of England.

* * *

As did many of the great ivory hunters, Ian felt remorse at several junctures during his career. One of the starkest periods of regret descended upon him when he was based at his Umzingwane camp (pronounced Oom-zing-wah-neh). His two assistants were Manwere (Mahn-weh-reh) and Kadigedige, who had to monitor the movements of the elephant herds when Ian had to be off elsewhere. A troop of bulls had crossed the main road between Beit Bridge and Bulawayo – this latter the country's second-largest city – and kept on the move, stopping to water at a borehole on a cattle ranch. The ranch manager told Ian the bulls had passed through his cattle to reach the water, crushing and tusking several in the process. Ian masked his scent by waiting inside the kraal, surrounded by cattle. He hoped the bulls would arrive in the light, but of course they appeared when the darkness had already descended. Initially Ian could see them as they passed close by the kraal, firing a left and a right barrel into the shoulders of the last two elephant; these two ran off.

Almost immediately, however, the darkness became like a blanket and the cattle panicked, stampeding at the shots. Ian was now in danger from the very safe haven he'd chosen. He dashed to the kraal barrier, easily vaulting the five feet up on his adrenalin. The remaining elephant had not dashed off and Ian sensed them nearby, watching him in the darkness. It was a discomforting thought and the stampeding cattle crashing into the barrier did nothing to relieve his sense of unease; firing could knock the man into the kraal, so Ian decided to take his chance with the bulls. He jumped down outside the enclosure. Slowly Ian approached the metre-high water trough (a mere three feet), checking that he'd reloaded the rifle after his initial altercation; on the other side of the trough, he discerned two massive forms, which moved as he approached. Two huge bulls! Ian's eyes could make out the giant bulks and great heads. He realised that if the two chose to charge, each choosing a side around the trough, at least one was likely to get to him; shooting both would be highly improbable in the pitch darkness.

All Ian's senses were tingling on high alert; he knew he was in real danger, the elephants' eyesight superior to his. For a second Ian Nyschens questioned his own sanity; walking into danger of one's own creation, however, is one thing. Turning your back on that danger and exposing that back in the pitch dark is quite another, particularly given the tendency of dangerous game to charge. One bull swung away and as it did so, Ian fired into what he discerned was the chest of the other. The shot elephant lurched forward, smashing the trough in the process. Ian knew he could settle its hash with a headshot, provided he could see the head; the animal was some 25 yards off but he had to let it come closer in order to see. The trumpet it emitted was so loud, Ian was momentarily frozen; then the bull luckily crashed to its knees and rolled over. His shot – over the top of the heart – had been a winner. Had the shot taken the lower heart, the elephant would have reached him.

Ian Nyschens sat down in the coal-black darkness, staring at the hulk of the huge bull; he had survived yet another close call with violent death. He wondered why he was killing these great creatures to make way for people. Most of the elephants Ian had shot never knew what hit them; he instantly knew that if he hadn't done this, others would, and probably not as cleanly. That would mean even more death, for people especially. But it seemed like such a waste of life; his, and certainly theirs. Ian no longer needed ivory to survive and suddenly resented the killing; there in the pitch dark, surrounded by the sounds of the milling cattle, Ian realised that no single hunter could drive off the massive herds. His nervous tension came out in hysterical laughter; Ian was clearly showing the signs of years of exposure to extreme danger. When, a short time later, he nearly lost his life due to the incompetence of another ranger, Ian made for Messina to see the doctor there.

Tick-bite fever had beset Ian, but the doctor was more concerned with Ian's frayed nerves. He spent a week recovering before mentoring a new ranger who'd been a policeman. Ian was growing immensely disillusioned with the Game Department, and went so far as to state in *Months of the Sun* that the reader should not see this as a result of personality clashes; rather as the Department failing to take advantage of the excellent men available in Rhodesia to be turned into game rangers. He felt had they done, the Department would've been Africa's best, no small claim but for all that, at that time, a not unreasonable one. Ian had no time to dwell on this short-sightedness; looming up was the building of the massive Kariba Dam on the Zambezi. Here, too, ineptitude raised its head: the Amatongas had been instructed not to grow food, since they were to be moved to the Lubu, Umbelele and Kariangwe areas (all beautiful unspoiled valleys). The result was starving people and in their increasing desperation, doing anything for even unsuitable food – such as grinding grass seeds – resulted in rampant dysentery.

A doctor was to be parachuted into the area, and in tow were Ian Nyschens with the two trackers Manwere and Kadigedige; Ian was to provide the people with meat by shooting a few elephant. Ian reported back after this expedition that the game would have to be chased from the Zambezi Valley, or be drowned in their thousands. In the rising waters, the team saw herds swimming desperately, eventually slipping exhausted beneath the waves, never to rise again. Ian and his men eventually closed with some large bulls in the *sinanga* thickets, a dense patch of jesse. The guide – Nilos – then demonstrated an extraordinary feat of bravery, which most would call insanity.

The group of bulls were perhaps an hour ahead of the men and thankfully heading for some hills, leaving the impassable jesse, when a leopard was spotted atop a branch with a freshly-killed impala ram. It was in plain view and stood in defiance of the men, not moving off as Ian thought it would. Nilos gripped his spear, locked eyes with the hissing package of gold, anthracite and razor-blades, and advanced slowly but determinedly. The leopard snarled ever louder, eventually rasping and spitting in fury fit to freeze the men's blood. When the two were so close that Ian could no longer assist the spearman, the big cat broke and melted away. Nilos claimed the meat as the tension came down, the others flabbergasted. Nilos himself wasn't overly impressed, intoning that he'd done similarly many times, even to solitary lions!

This sounds like even greater madness, and on balance probably is; but experienced hunters know, the speed and savagery of the leopard render it so likely to unzip a man, even if it has to run off, that it's a very brave man who makes a habit of robbing one of its kill. That said, although a lone lion is more likely to run off, when it decides to fight for its kill, your affairs, old son, had better be in order! It won't dissect your flesh quite like a leopard can, but one solid body-bite from a lion and your next task will be playing a harp on a cloud; of that I can assure you! The men continued on the elephant spoor, an hour passing before it suddenly freshened. This prompted the depositing of the impala meat high into a shady tree-fork as the men concentrated on the dangerous matter at hand.

The party moved up the nearest slope to utilise the vantage point; the backs and waving ears of the herd were clearly visible and the hunters relaxed, momentarily out of immediate peril. In the peace of the scene Ian started to daydream, recalling his hunting excursions with Faanie, Jeffrey, Katasoro and the wonderful trackers. He was growing melancholy, wondering if any of his old companions had died. Ian realised just how much he missed his old friends since joining the Game Department. He grew angry and dismayed thinking about how civilisation would result in the herd below them becoming hemmed in to the ever-shrinking Sebungwe, the great wilderness area. Even the calves among them would grow and attack men, as they would be almost constantly harassed. Ian rose and started to take a heavy toll of the herd, cool, regular shots felling the giants one after another. Nilos walked this way and that, ignoring the danger, picking up the white man's spent cartridge shells in fascination.

Nilos seemed that unaffected by proximity to Big 5 game animals, that Ian later tried to recruit him into the Game Department, but he refused. He did avail himself to Ian whenever the ranger was in the area, but the formal uniformed life was not for this man; it was a metaphor for Ian as well…this last shoot affected him badly. He sat surveying the destruction, all traces thereof removed within a mere few days as the Amatongas descended upon the carcases. For Ian, one of the final straws was coming across a group of men beside a rhino carcase. The horns had been removed – with Game Department sanction – and one must bear in mind that 60 years ago, rhino were nowhere near as endangered as they are in 2018; but the man in charge was an entomologist, and the rhino had been shot to collect its ticks for study in England. It is legitimate, but seems such a disproportionate waste that it's difficult to fathom. Ian certainly couldn't reconcile it in his mind.

In Ian Nyschens's twilight years, he was heartened to still see large areas reserved for wildlife; it is the most vital cog which many great hunters, conservationists and adventurers have espoused. Preserving virgin habitat is the only way to prolong the existence of the truly wild ecosystems and the megafauna species they support. Ian was dead-set against culling, but he could offer no legitimate alternative, admitting as much; the reality is the exploding human population in Africa, and the resulting proximity means many human and elephant deaths if the great pachyderms' numbers are not managed. In this regard, he was ahead of his time, the modern aversion to culling vocal and widespread; but as I mentioned, the longer time goes on, the more people populate Africa. In Ian's defence, he did mention the increase in people as the final nail, a situation from which Africa is unlikely ever to bounce back. He believed that foreign currency would forever have to bolster weak African economies as a result.

Ian Nyschens knew an Africa that is now gone; he was one of the last great hunter-adventurers and their lives were lived out frustratingly-recently for those of us that still harbour adventurous spirits within our chests: Ian died in Zimbabwe aged 83, late in 2006. Luckily there are still untamed areas, many and wild, within Africa. There is no question that Colonial times decisively wrestled the Dark Continent away from the great wildlife species, forever placing man at the top of the pile; but social media, a ridiculously well-meaning but uninformed social movement in developed countries and a nonsensical refusal to harm anything have only accelerated the demise of Africa's huge wild places, just when technology is that far advanced, that we may have rescued – indeed, restored – much of the phenomenal, visceral, maddening and wonderful continent to at least a semblance of its former majesty.

16. Select Bibliography

Wikipedia – http://www.en.wikipedia.org/neumann

Wikipedia – http://www.en.wikipedia.org/stigand

Wikipedia – http://www.en.wikipedia.org/sutherland

Great Tuskers of Africa – Johan Marais and David Hadaway (2006)

The Recollections of William Finaughty: Elephant Hunter 1864-1875 – William Finaughty (1913)

A Hunter's Wanderings in Africa – Frederick Courtney Selous (1881)

Elephant Hunting in East Equatorial Africa – Arthur H. Neumann (1898)

Hunting the Elephant in Africa and Other Recollections of Thirteen Years' Wanderings – Captain C.H. Stigand (1913)

The African Elephant and Its Hunters – Denis D. Lyell (1924)

Elephant Hunters, Men of Legend – Tony Sánchez-Ariño (2005)

Pete Pearson Elephant Hunter and Game Ranger – Reprinted from "Ararat Advertiser" – National Library of Australia (1934)

Wikipedia – http://www.en.wikipedia.org/P. C. "Pete" Pearson

Wikipedia – http://www.en.wikipedia.org/W. D. M. Bell

The Wanderings of an Elephant Hunter – W. D. M. Bell (1923)

Karamojo Safari – W. D. M. Bell (1949)

Death in the Silent Places - Peter Hathaway Capstick (1981)

The Adventures of an Elephant Hunter – James Sutherland (1912)

The Hunter is Death – T. V. Bulpin (1962)

No More the Tusker – George Rushby (1965)

The Last Ivory Hunter – Peter Hathaway Capstick (1988)

Kambaku! – Harry Manners (1986)

African Epic – Richard Harland (2003)

Months of the Sun – Ian Nyschens (1997)